REGIONAL RURAL BANKS
Performance and Perspectives

REGIONAL RURAL BANKS

Performance and Perspectives

K. Santha Kumari

GRP

GLOBAL RESEARCH PUBLICATIONS

NEW DELHI (INDIA)

First Published – 2011

ISBN: 978-81-89630-22-5

Published by

GLOBAL RESEARCH PUBLICATIONS
4830/24, 1st Floor, Ansari Road
Darya Ganj, New Delhi-110002 (India)
Phone : 23245225. Fax : 91-11-23272135
E-mail: globalresearchpublications@gmail.com, grpindia@vsnl.net

In Memory of My Beloved Parents

K. Venkataswamy & K.V. Subbamma

Contents

Contents

Preface

Regional Rural Banks (RRBs) have been in existence for around three decades in the Indian Financial scene. They have been seen as an unique experiment as well as experience in increasing the efficacy of rural credit delivery mechanism in India with joint share holding by Central Government, the concerned State Government and the sponsoring bank, an effort was made to integrate commercial banking within the broad policy thrust towards social banking keeping in view the social banking peculiarities. The genesis of RRBs can be traced to the needs for a stronger institutional arrangement for providing rural credit. The Narasimham Committee conceptualized the creation of RRBs in 1975 as a new set of regionally oriented rural banks, which would combine the local feel and familiarity of rural problems characteristics of cooperatives with the professionalism and large source of commercial banks. Subsequently the RRBs were set up through the promulgamation of RRB Act of 1976.

Over the years the RRBs, have taken deep roots and have become an inseparable part of the rural credit structure. They have played a key role in rural institutional financing in terms of geographical coverage clientele outreach and business volume as also contribution to development of the rural economy. The mandate or promoting banking with a rural focus, however, would be an ending phenomenon only when the financial health of the RRBs is sound.

The present work is the out come of my doctoral thesis. Keeping in view the importance of the problem and my own interest in this field I thought it pertinent to take up this study.

The study contributes to the literature of RRBs in two ways. First, it enquires such matters that influence the performance of the RRBs in terms of their branch expansion, deposit mobilization and advances given in India during the period 1975-85 subsequently, the study focuses on Rayalaseema Region of Andhra Pradesh covering the progress and performance of banks viz., Rayalaseema Grameena Bank, Sree Anantha Grameena Bank and Shri Venkateswara Grameena Bank.

It provides a comparative picture of the three RRBs with broad based results and robust growth. It also highlights the behaviour of the three RRBs for the profit and loss making ones, so that it helps in policy formulation.

In this connection, I am extremely grateful to Professor D.L. Narayana, former Principal, S.V. University College of Arts & Sciences for his valuable guidance in the conception and execution of this work. As a guide and supervisor, he not only gave me an opportunity to undertake this task, but also inspired me throughout the study.

I am very much beholden to Sri Ashok Sharma, Development Officer, NABARD, Bombay, for furnishing me relevant data on the subject.

I am particularly thankful to Sri A.Mallanna, Chairman of Rayalaseema Grameena Bank, Cuddapah, Sri K.Jaya Gopal, Chairman of Sree Anantha Grameena Bank, Anantapur and Sri N.Chandrasekhara Rao, Chairman of Shri Venkateswara Grameena Bank, Chittoor for granting me permission to use the official reports and records available in their respective offices.

I would like to place on record my profound sense of gratitude to Sri B.N. Nageswara Rao, S.V. Grameena Bank, Chittoor, who has provided me a fund of information that is incorporated in this thesis.

I am deeply indebted to my friend Dr. D.B.Krishna Kumari for the excellent cooperation she had given to me in extracting information from various sources related to research work. Also, I am grateful to Smt. G. Sudarshana (Kurnool) and Smt. K.Renuka (Anantapur) for their help in collecting the data.

I sincerely thank Dr. P.Balasiddamuni, Lecturer in Statistics, S.V. University for his valuable suggestions and help in the statistical analysis of the data.

I fail in my duty, if I do not express my sense of gratitude to Dr. V. Kodandarami Reddy, Professor, S.V.University, for his timely help in the process of statistical calculations and computer programming.

I extend my thanks to Sri P.Lakshmipathi for actively assisting me in the tabulation of data.

I owe my gratitude to Sri V.Shanmugam, Library Assistant, S.V. University for preparing the maps.

My special thanks are due to my husband Dr. V.Pradeep Kumar for his cooperation and encouragement and to my daughter V. Sirivennela for giving me moral support.

Last but not least, I express my sense of gratitude to M/s Global Research Publications, New Delhi for bringing out this book beautifully in a short time.

K. SANTHA KUMARI

Abbreviations

The following abbreviations are used in the thesis:

ARDC	–	Agriculture Refinance and Development Corporation
BIRD	–	Bankers Institute for Rural Development
CGC	–	Credit Guarantee Claim
CRR	–	Cash Reserve Ratio
DA	–	Dearness Allowance
DCCB	–	District Central Cooperative Bank
DCPS	–	District Credit Plans
DICGC	–	Deposit Insurance and Credit Guarantee Corporation
DPAP	–	Drought Prone Area Programme
DRDA	–	District Rural Development Agency
DRI	–	Differential Rate of Interest
FSSS	–	Farmers Service Societies
HO	–	Head Office
IDBI	–	Industrial Development Bank of India
IRDP	–	Integrated Rural Development Programme
NABARD	–	National Bank for Agriculture and Rural Development
NAC (LTO) FUND	–	National Agricultural Credit (Long-Term Operation) Fund
PAC	–	Primary Agricultural Credit Society
RRB	–	Regional Rural Bank

RGB	– Rayalaseema Grameena Bank
RBI	– Reserve Bank of India
SAGB	– Sree Anantha Grameena Bank
SBI	– State Bank of India
SSI	– Small scale Industry
SVGB	– Shri Venkateswara Grameena Bank
Twenty Point EP	– Twenty Point Economic Programme

1

The Scope of Research Study

"The Indian money market is a jerry-built institution, its parts are loose, independent and uncoordinated and un-organised. How to build and co-ordinate the ill-fitted, disjointed structures into a firm, well-knit and yet flexible whole, will demand a good deal of economic thinking"

Radhakamal Mukherjee[1]

Introduction

As the establishment of Regional Rural Banks (RRBs) is of recent origin and its true orientation towards the rural population has been accelerated only from the last five years, very few studies have been made in this area. Charan D. Wadhva's "Rural Banks for Rural Development, An Analysis of the Working of Regional Rural Banks in India with Two Case Studies" (1980) constitutes the first important study. The scope of this book encompasses the progress of Regional Rural Banks upto 31 December, 1977. Though it was very useful in providing the background and the basis of rural banks establishment, the book was unable to give a definite and comparable or comprehensive appraisal of Regional Rural Banks, since even the oldest five such banks did not complete three years of existence when the investigation was undertaken. The author himself was aware of this limitation in his book.[2]

The Rural Planning and Credit Cell of Reserve Bank of India made another significant study in 1981[3] on the financial viability of fifteen selected Regional Rural Banks which had completed three years of existence or which had a loan business of Rs. 3 crores by December 31, 1978. This study is very important from the point of view of scientific evaluation of the working of Regional Rural Banks. Nevertheless, a three year period is inadequate for a credit institution to achieve viability, particularly for a rural sector institution and more so for the Regional Rural Banks which have been operating with some constraints.[4]

Further, the publication of the Agricultural Finance Corporation on Regional Rural Banks (1981)[5] provided information on the functioning of the Regional Rural Banks and their progress up to the year 1980. It evaluated the performance of some selected RRBs. Since the problem of rural financing is a burning issue in India on which the welfare of the poorest of the poor depends and which in turn determines the country's prosperity, there is a great need for an up-to-date and a comprehensive evaluation of the working of the Regional Rural Banks in the country.

Objectives of the Study

The present research work aims to evaluate the performance of Regional Rural Banks in India from 1975 to 1985. It makes a special case of the working of the Regional Rural Banks in Rayalaseema, which has three Regional Rural Banks, namely, the Rayalaseema Grameena Bank (1976-85), the Sree Anantha Grameena Bank (1979-85) and the Shri Venkateswara Grameena Bank (1981-85). All these three banks are located in the districts of Cuddapah, Kurnool, Anantapur, Chittoor and some parts of Prakasam Districts of the Rayalaseema Region of Andhra Pradesh State. The Rayalaseema Region is a backward and a chronically drought affected area located in an arid zone. For the development of this region and for protecting it against the incidence of adverse droughts, adequate credit facility is a sine quo non.

A study of Regional Rural Banks in the Rayalaseema region throws light on the working of RRBs in drought–ridden region. Evaluation of the performance of Regional Rural Banks has a special significance as it constitutes a study of mass banking.

If the RRBs are performing in the right direction, it means poorer sections are benefiting more and the country is well set on the development path. On the other hand, if the performance is below the expectations, it may not break the vicious circle of poverty. So, a study of Regional Rural Banks is very important as well as noteworthy.

The following are the specific objectives of the research effort.

- To study the progress of Regional Rural Banks and their performance in India on the basis of branch expansion, deposit mobilization, advances, staffing pattern and profitability.
- The evaluate the overall performance of the RRBs in Rayalaseema since their establishment on a comparable criteria such as branch expansion, deposit mobilization, advances, staffing pattern and the study of profit and loss of the selected three banks.
- To appraise the functioning of RRBs, particularly to identify the factors responsible for losses, and
- To suggest measures for improving the performance of the RRBs and their branches.

Nature of the Study

The study covers the performance appraisal of RRBs both at macro and micro level. In a vast country like India with peculiarities in different regions, it is difficult to derive any worthwhile lesson from macro analysis alone. The Estimates Committee of Parliament in its Report on Nationalised Banks has laid stress[6] on the need for field reports to make an objective assessment of the benefits derived by bank credit. But the regional analysis, with one district or several districts of a region as the unit has not been attempted so far. In the present study, at the macro level, the investigation is confined to the origin, growth and overall progress and performance of Regional Rural Banks in India over a period of a decade. At the micro level. The study covers three Regional Rural Banks with different age groups covering a backward region of a backward state.

Detailed case studies are necessary to under stand the functioning of RRBs at their specific locations and economic background. Another important aspect of this kind of study is the comparative analysis. By taking three separate RRBs in three separate districts of a single region of one single state and comparing their performance among themselves, the study provides an objective evaluation of the existing position which may suggest scope for better management of the banks for achieving their objectives.

The Period of Study

The study covers a decade of working of Regional Rural Banks from 1975 to 1985, while a period of about 9 years in the case of coverage of the Rayalaseema Grameena Bank, 6 years for the Sree Anantha Grameena Bank, and about 5 years for the Shri Venkateswara Grameena Bank according to their establishment dates. This is a crucial period in the growth of RRBs as it is the first decade of their existence in the country. In view of fast changing banking scene in India where new developments are taking place, it is very important to scrutinize the performance of RRBs during this period.

Methodology

The data required for the study has been drawn mainly from the secondary sources. For the macro study, reliance was largely placed on various publications of Reserve Bank of India, its annual, monthly and several ad hoc occasional papers. Statistical data have been collected from several financial institutions like NABARD, Agricultural Finance Corporation, etc. and also from Government agencies. Articles published by individual researchers connected with different segments of the study in several weekly, fortnightly and monthly journals and magazines provided the necessary material which has been appropriately utilized.

For micro study, the Annual Reports of the respective selected RRBs are the main sources along with information collected from some branches.

Data Analysis

The data collected from various secondary sources were tabulated. The statistical tools such as ratios, percentage, liner and compound growth rates, etc. were used in analysing the data.

Plan of the Thesis

The thesis is divided into seven chapters. The first chapter indicates the scope, objectives, nature, methodology and data analysis of the study.

In chapter two, the role of finance in promoting rural development has been discussed on a theoretical basis. It also provides a historical perspective of existing financial institutions in the Indian rural credit scene.

Chapter three deals with the rationale of Regional Rural Banks. The weaknesses of cooperative banks and the limitations of commercial banks in supplying cheap and timely credit to weaker sections have been thoroughly examined. The institutional credit gaps which ultimately led to the arrival of RRBs were indicated.

The progress and performance of Regional Rural Bank's working in India is furnished in the fourth chapter. There has been a tremendous growth of Regional Rural Banks in India. By 1983, 188 banks were established covering 333 districts. As the evaluation of the working of the RRBs is at national level on the basis of selected criteria, the chapter has emerged as the biggest one.

Chapter five presents a study of the working performance and overall progress of three Regional Rural Banks namely the Rayalaseema Grameena Bank, the Sree Anantha Grameena Bank and the Shri Venkateswara Grameena Bank of the Rayalaseema Region, which is a well-known famine spot of India.

Chapter six presents a comparative picture of three selected RRBs in Rayalaseema. It contains a number of suggestions for improving the working of Regional Rural Banks.

Chapter seven sums up the main conclusions.

Footnotes

1. Quoted in : Raghavendra Rao, B: "The ABC of Banking (A Treatise on the Fundamental Principles of Money and Banking, as Applied to India & England)", Gemini Printers, Eluru (West Godavari Dt.), 1953, p.226.
2. Wadhva, Charan. D., "Rural Banks for Rural Development An Analysis of the Working of Regional Rural Banks in India with two case studies", The Macmillan Company of India Ltd. Delhi, 1980, p. 59.
3. Reserve Bank of India Bulletin: "Viability of Regional Rural Banks: A Study", Vol. XXXV, No. 3, March, 1981, pp.200-14.
4. They had to (i) lend only to the weaker sections, (ii) charge lower rates of interest, (iii) open branches in remote areas and (iv) keep up low-cost profile.
5. Agriculture Finance Corporation: "A Study of Regional Rural Banks", Bombay, 1981.
6. 62nd Report of the Estimates Committee (Fifth Lok Sabha, 1973-74), "Extension of Credit Facilities to Weaker Sections of Society and for Development of Backward Areas", New Delhi, April 1974.

2

The Role of Banking in Rural Development

"The power which stands in the way of India's economic development is the power of evil finance-the want of banking system for the people"

Sir Daniel Hamilton[1]

Introduction

The main objective of this chapter is to analyse the role of banking in facilitating rural development whose main objective in a welfare state is to provide minimum standard of living for the people in villages. India is a vast country of villages which were steeped in centuries-old stagnation. With Independence and the initiation of planned economic development the winds of change are blowing over the villages with differential impact in different states and regions. Any developing economy has to build up appropriate organisational set up to monitor the programmes of rural and urban development. Without suitable institutional set up, acceleration of economic development becomes impossible.

Banks, which are financial institutions have a crucial role to play in economic development even if they are not directly concerned with the initiation, implementation and evaluation of development programmes. Banking institutions constitute a powerful tool in implementing development programmes. Their importance becomes more obvious when the experience of the poor and under developed countries is considered by way of contrast with their role in the developed countries.

Organised banking is a pre-requisite for achieving steady and rapid economic development in underdeveloped countries, which were handicapped for a long time because of their failure to build up necessary banking structure. It is necessary to be clear about the definition and scope of banking, before analysis its role in economic development with reference to India and its rural development.

According to M.L. Tannan,[2] "Much time, ink and paper have been consumed in an effort to define what exactly constitutes banking. Even the best authorities have found it rather a hard nut to crack...." In view of the various functions which the banks discharge, definition of the banking business has become a complicated one. According to the Indian Banking Regulation Act of 1949 Section 5(b), "Banking" means the accepting, for the purpose of lending or investment, of deposits of money from the public, repayable on demand or otherwise, withdrawable by cheque, draft, order or otherwise". Accordingly the term banking implies the business of borrowing and lending of money. In general, a bank or banker deals mostly with other people's money. The bank or banker borrows at relatively lower rate of interest and lends at a higher rate, the difference between the two rates constitutes the major source of income. This is the quintessence of banking which is broadly confirmed by the definitions followed in other countries.

The Japanese Bank Act of 1927 defined banks as "institutions which carry on operations of giving as well as receiving credit".[3] The Banking Legislation in U.S.A. defined "by banking" we mean the business of dealing in credits and by a "bank" we include every person, firm, a company having a place of business where credits are opened by the deposit or collection of money or currency, subject to be paid or remitted on draft, cheque or order or money is advanced or loaned on stocks, bonds"[4] while the Japanese definition is specific and precise, the American definition illustrates the process of banking.

Depending on the nature and scope of operations banks are divided into different types, such as cooperative banks, commercial banks, industrial banks, investment banks, exchange banks and agricultural banks. The various types of banks differ in their methods of borrowing or lending or both, depending on their basic type of function, the core function being borrowing and lending for the purposes for which the different types of banks are constituted. Cooperative credit banks, land development banks, commercial banks, regional rural banks, and government finance through the taccavi loans are directly relevant to the financing of rural development in India. In an age of planning the State Planning and the plan programme of Central Government may have direct bearing on rural development in multifarious ways. But the direct financing of the different activities of farmers, agricultural labourers, artisans and such rural group of people matter much to improve the welfare of rural masses.

Function of Banking in Economic Development

The Power of Evil Finance

Banks as financial institutions have a significant role to play in economic development. According to Ali Issa Abdi[5] the direct contributions of financial institutions to economic growth is minute. It has been estimated that financial structure contributes only 0.5 to 1.0 per cent of gross national product in the mature market economies. In the case of developing economies, where the services offered by financial institutions are often fewer and far less sophisticated, the contribution of financial institutions is estimated to be less than 0.1 per cent. Therefore, the meaningful role of financial institutions in economic development is intrinsically indirect.

Long ago, Sir Daniel Hamilton postulate the case for development of organized banking to curb the evils of professional moneylenders in India and to promote economic development. For, the wide prevalence of evil finance stands in the way of India's economic development. The vision of Sir Daniel Hamilton is a truism today than even before in the light of empirical evidence, advancements in theoretical knowledge and the trends of banking development in developing countries like India as the following critical review reveals.

Indian history bristles with ample evidence about the role of usurious moneylenders in the absence of a banking system. It is a well-known proverb that the Indian farmer is born in debt, lives in debt, dies in debt and bequeaths debt. Indebtedness is the only companion of the farmer from cradle to grave. The Royal Commission on Agriculture in India noted the grim fact and observed that, "the most powerful obstacle in the path of rural development and the most crushing burden on the people is indebtedness".[6] To alleviates the suffering of agriculturists, Government has introduced several legislative measures and adopted different remedies to improve their material condition. In the words of Maclegan Committee, 1915, "A system of State loans was introduced, post office savings banks were opened, the civil law relating to debt was frequently and extensively amended, special legislation was initiated at various times in different areas for dealing with tenant right, the alienation of land, the general settlement of debt and the curbing of usury. But although much has been done by some, at any rate of these measures to help the peasant community, the general effect of the action taken can only be described as partial and incomplete".[7] Hence the case for developing a well-organised banking system lies in the need to evolve a suitable credit structure to meet the felt needs of farmers and villagers in order to undermine the evils of professional moneylenders or bankers. Market forces by themselves may not facilitate the evolution of a suitable banking system and credit structure in a situation of vicious circle of poverty and subsistence agriculture with low productivity as is prevailing in backward countries. The failure of market is an initiation to the initiative of the State to fill up the gap.

Two Systems of Bank Finance

Historical experience of the industrially developed countries reveals the operation of two systems of bank finance, demand-following and supply-leading systems as represented by the British and German banking systems respectively. As the economy moves from traditional subsistence production, it gets monetized and commericalised and grows more complex, certain demands are generated for the services of financial institutions. The growing needs of firms for external finance create demand for the funds of financial institutions which are expected to respond to the demand. If the existing or new financial institutions respond to such demand, it becomes a case of demand creating its own supply - demand following type of financial development that was associated with the English banking system of the late eighteenth and early nineteenth centuries. The demand-following banking system is characterized by bank operations that are traditional short-term, commercial loan specialization of the English banks. The demand – following financial development tends to be passive and slow in the tempo of growth as compared to the supply leading financial system, which acts as a leading sector as in the case of Germany since 1830 and Japan since 1870.

The supply-leading finance system, which is an exact opposite of demand-following finance system, has not only contributed to industrial expansion and economic development in the few historical instances, but also rests on sound theoretical justifications of more efficient allocation of resources and promotion of entrepreneurship. Supply-leading finance transfers resources from the traditional non-growth producing sectors to the modern sectors of an economy with higher growth potential either by collecting the savings of the traditional sectors or through forced savings by way of new bank credits. Both transfers enhance the growth of the economy as they are towards the more efficient and more productive sectors. This growth inducing tendency is compared to the Schumpeterian concept of "innovation finance" where innovative producers gain control of the factor resources through bank intermediation.

Another important growth inducing function of supply-leading finance is the promotion of entrepreneurship. Bank finance can stimulate entrepreneurship by inducing the operations of the small farmers, merchants and traders in the developing economies. In the worlds of Hugh Patrick, "The new access to such supply-leading funds may in itself have substantial, favourable expectation and psychological effects on entrepreneurs. It opens new horizons as to the possible alternative enabling the entrepreneur to "think big". This may be the most significant effect of all, particularly in countries where entrepreneurship is a major constraint on development"[8]

A third important growth inducing function of supply-leading finance is the direct promotion of entrepreneurial impulse through the participation of banks in industrial enterprises as the German development illustrates. The German mixed banking system provided short-term, medium-term and long-term operating funds and also non-financial assistance. The bank managers participated in the major financial decisions as well as the daily operations of industry. Indeed the banks in essence were the prime source of capital and entrepreneurship in Germany. Alexander Gerschnekron emphasized, "A German bank, as the saying went, accompanied an industrial enterprise from cradle to grave, from establishment to liquidation throughout all the vicissitudes of its existence. Through the device of formality is short-term but in reality long-term current account credits... the banks acquired a formidable degree of ascendancy over industrial enterprises, which extended far beyond the sphere of financial control into that of entrepreneurial and managerial decision".[9]

The Controversy over the Role of Banks in Economic Development

Sharp controversy prevails as regards the role of financial institutions in economic development. It raises over a wide range from postulating that of financial development as a pre-requisite of economic development to that of holding the view that is neither a necessary nor a sufficient condition of economic growth. The positive school of thought led by Schumpeter finds supports from Irma Adelman, Morris, Cameron et al., Gerschenkron, Goldsmith, Mckinnon, Minsky, Patrick and Shaw representing the advocates of financial and real development.

According to Schumpeter's theory of capitalist economic development, the two requisites are entrepreneurship to initiate the process of economic development and the provision of innovative finance by banks, financial institutions or new credit creation. Economic development is a spontaneous, discontinuous and internally generated change arising out of the new combinations of factors of production inducing a different employment of existing resources of labour and land by withdrawing them from previous employment. For initiating and carrying the new combinations in enterprises, a new class of entrepreneurs is wanted, in carrying out new combinations, "financing as a special act is fundamentally necessary in practice and theory".

The recent studies[10] on the role of banks and financial institutions in economic development relevant to the contemporary developing countries support the positive school of thought of Schumpeter. They are mainly concerned with the effectiveness of financial institutions in terms of increasing savings through the banking system and the volume of lending by banks to agriculture and industry.

The studies by Irma Adelman and Cynthia Morris are based on a quantitative model that focuses on the measurable determinants of a country's potential for economic development. The data used in their studies relate 74 developing countries for the years 1950-63. They have evaluated the relative impact of 39 socio-economic and political variables on the capacity of these nations to develop. Out of 14 pure economic variables explored, it was found that the level of financial institutions development to be the best indicator of a country's development potential. Moreover, the only economic variables with a high impact on increasing development potential are improvement of financial institutions, increase in physical overhead capital, more rapid expansion of industry and technical modernization of agriculture.

As compared to the effective positive role of banks in economic development, J. Gurley postulated inherent weakness of finance as a vehicle of economic development, with some references to the experiences of developing countries, concludes that the development of financial institutions is not necessary for growth. Further he states that "recent experiences strongly suggest that banking system as intermediaries are not highly essential to the growth process".[11] While he does not question the efficiency of the development of financial institutions per se, but insists on the existence of alternative techniques that may be utilized in a country's comprehensive planning approval. The close substitutes to financial development according to Gurley are central planning, the fiscal or tax-subside technique and the transfer of foreign savings. The actual choice among these techniques depends upon the social costs and benefits of each and it varies depending on the stage of development, the country concerned and the extent of centralization and decentralization contemplated. The technique of development of financial institutions flourishers, "when there is a decentralization of decision making, specialization of savings and investment, and heavy emphasis on external rather than internal financing of investment".[12] Thus, Gurley also accepts the role of financial development in economic development with due allowance as one of the alternative techniques.

The Central issue of the controversy over the role of financial institutions in economic development is whether the development of financial institutions has to proceed to accelerate economic development or it adjusts to the growth of the economic development, whether the financial development is a cause of real development. While the causal relationship is not conclusively established the interdependence of the two phenomena are beyond doubt and dispute as recognized by economists since Adam Smith.[13] The recent monumental study of Goldsmith also demonstrated the interdependence of financial structure and the real infrastructure on the basis of the study of 35 countries, developed as well as developing. Goldsmith concludes that with the exception of centrally planned economies, there is one path of financial development with economic growth: "The evidence now available is more in favour of the hypothesis that there exists only one path marked by certain regularities in the course of financial interrelations ratio, in the share of financial institutions in the total financial assets, and in the position of the banking system .... a path from which (countries) have deviated only to a minor extent".[14] Goldsmith did not resolve the causality controversy and he excluded the centrally planned economies in demonstrating the interdependence. The pertinent issue is whether countries have to emphasize the financial development in order to achieve rapid economic development?

The central problem of economic development in the under developed countries is one of raising the rate of capital accumulation, saving-investment ratio of National funds from 4 or 5 per cent to 12 or 15 per cent [15] or 20 to 25 per cent so that the rate of growth can be enhanced in the long-run to meet the needs of rapidly growing population in the developing countries. The mobilization and utilization of savings by banks for economic development through promotion of banking habit and nomination of investment gave rise to two important hypotheses: the financial repression hypothesis and the structuralist hypothesis.

The Financial Repression Hypothesis

Cameron, McKinnon and Shaw are strong advocates of the effectiveness of financial development in contribution significantly to the growth of developing economies. According to their recent studies, they contend that the banking system is invariably growth-inducing and that only when it is repressed, which in their view is often the case, would it fail to make a positive contribution and act as an obstacle to real growth. Shah emphasized that "financial sector of an economy does matter in economic development and destroy impulses to development".[16] According to them, banks will have largest impact on developing economies, if the free market system operates without deviations and distortions due to unwise policies and regulations by Government.

According to the financial repression theory, the lack of organized bank penetration of the "economic hinterland" is partly attributed to the interventions in market operations, which account for the extreme interest rate differentials on loans issued by the organized banks and unorganized moneylenders respectively. The rates of interest in the unorganized market are often anywhere from two to ten times higher than the bank lending rates. The mere existence of the organized and unorganized markets simultaneously in the same economy implies financial repression. An extension of bank lending to new enterprises is essential to eliminate the money-market dualism. The financial repression hypothesis advocates the virtues of reliance on market forces. If the banking system is allowed to operate under free market direction, it is most conducive to economic growth. The repression hypothesis accounts for the "poor" performance of the lagging economies in terms of internal policy induced distortions. Banking system will be less responsive to economic development, the more pervasive the government's intervention in terms of deposit and loan rates.

If the banking policies are evolved with interest differentials in harmony with productivity differentials in the different sectors of the economy, it may go a long way to promote banking habit and financial development instead of allowing the free-market forces to determine the interest rates under oligopolistic conditions.

The Strucutralist Hypothesis

The structuralist hypothesis, better known as the Gerschenkron hypothesis is derived from historical interpretation of the role of banks in the process of capital formation of early European industrialization. According to him it is the relative backwardness or the stage of industrialization that determines the contribution of institutions such as the State and banks to development. Although it is difficult to distinguish clearly the different stages of backwardness, Gerschenkron's analysis suggests that in "extremely backward economies" the contribution of banking system to capital formation is negligible. Only in the "moderately backward" economies, where the level of business trust increases and banks risk aversion decreases, the banks will have an impact. Gerschenkron's analysis postulates that at the different stages of backwardness, different sources of capital finances play an effective role, the State in extremely backward economies, the banks in moderately backward economies and the factories in advanced economies.

It means that banks are either unnecessary or ineffectual in the initial and advanced stages of development, they could be utilized as a source of capital only in intermediate stages. Accordingly, the effectiveness of bank finance depends on the stage of development. In the initial stage of development of underdeveloped countries, the State has to play the main role in financial development to monitor economic development. But, Gerschenkron's analysis cannot claim universal applicability. The role of banking in economic development is dynamic[17] and not passive. The effectiveness of its dynamic role depends on the pattern of evaluation of the banking structure and the banking policies pursued and the degree of their effective administration. Banking development, which was a concomitant of economic development in the industrialized countries is no longer true of the developing economies. Nor they are simply performing the traditional role as a depositor of the savings[18] of the country. Banks are now expected to shape their policies and programmes in India in the light of social objectives and national priorities envisaged in the Five Year Plans. They have also to conduct oversees operations having regard to public interest.

In the planned economic development of India, banks have a wider responsibility to support industrialization on one hand and transform the subsistence agriculture into commercialized modern agriculture through the provision of finance, on the other. They are also expected to involve in comprehensive planning and financing in different activities in villages to promote the development of rural areas. Banking as a tool for development[19] has to break the chain of vicious circle of poverty and under-development.

Nurkese's tautology 'a country is poor because it is poor' highlights the vicious circle of poverty, which perpetuates the chain of low income, low saving, low capital formation and low productivity and low real income completing the circle. Lack of adequate employment opportunities, overcrowding in agriculture, frequent recurrence of droughts and floods reinforce the vicious circle. Hence, capital has a crucial role to play in lifting the economy out of the vicious circle, banks as suppliers of capital have to break the chain of vicious circle.

Banks as Agents of Development

The financial institutions can influence the capital stock for development purposes in three ways.[20] Firstly they can encourage a more efficient allocation of a given total amount of tangible wealth or capital by bringing about changes in its ownership and composition through intermediation among different types of asset holders. Secondly, by intermediation between savers and entrepreneurial investors, the financial institutions can encourage a more efficient allocation of new investment additions to capital stock - from relatively less to relatively more productive uses. Thirdly, they can induce an increase in the rate of accumulation of capital by providing increased incentives to save and invest.

In developing countries this banking function i.e. creating, accumulating and efficient allocation of capital assumes great importance. The way in which banks function will determine the degrees of success of development effort. Financial intermediaries can advance rural development by means of (a) savings promotion, (b) investment effort and (c) sectoral and regional distribution of investment.[21]

If any scarce factor associated with under development of rural sector is singled out, it would be capital. The supply of funds in rural areas is small and limited because of low rate of savings, prevalence of barter system, lack of financial assets and lack of proper storage facilities. Increasing supply of funds is more important then simply the reduction of funds enables the promising entrepreneur to assume a greater debt that he could otherwise have and consequently provides him the wider horizons of conceivable opportunities of productive investments.

Regional and sectoral distribution of investment is more relevant for rural development. Investment funds should be evenly distributed regionally and funds should be deployed in those sectors which have linkages with rural economy. To this end, banks can modestly help by maintaining a balance between credit advanced in different regions and to different sectors. To achieve this, they have to abandon the role of market-followers and assume the responsibility of market-setters. If this can be achieved, credit to agriculture and small scale and cottage industries would increase, thereby giving a fillip to rural development.

A review of the trends of banking development in India reveals the evolution of innovative banking to facilitate the achievement of economic and social objectives of planned development. The saving promotion function of banks not only helps the cause of capital formation but contains impending inflationary dangers, since money when not saved is spent as wasteful expenditure, particularly by the poor people. The yeomen service of banks in spreading the banking habits now encompasses not only the cities or urban areas, but also the rural, semi-urban, backward and un-banked areas. By financing the farmers, village industries and a bulk of self-employed who are otherwise dependents on moneylenders, the banks serve the welfare of rural masses. They are financing smiths, cobblers, taxi-drivers, carpenters, goldsmiths, vegetable sellers, fisher-women and a host of other people with small means. No security is insisted on as the banks consider the welfare of the people is of paramount importance and faith in the integrity of the people has to be respected.

Banks are now undertaking useful social service activities.[22] They help to start and run schools, award scholarships to poor but brilliant young people to prosecute their studies; to start hospitals or health centres in rural areas; to provide medical relief to the poor at a cheaper rate to construct houses both for rural and semi-urban poor at a reasonably low rates of interest and easy instalments of repayments to give financial support to install drainage system and drinking water facilities in slum-areas and villages. Indeed, banks have widened and deepened their activities promoting mass banking to serve people.

Thus, banks have assumed catalytic role in the promotion of social welfare and the advancement of economic development. They have now accepted the precept that development should follow banks rather than banks follow development, and the bankers are to be considered not only 'dealers in money' but 'leaders in development'. They are today playing a development inducing and development sustaining role in the process of economic development of not only in India but in many developing countries of the world and acting as an instrument for establishment of an egalitarian society.

A Historical Perspective of Rural Banking in India

India possessed, since Vedic times[23] a system of banking which admirably fulfilled her needs and proved very beneficial to her, although its methods were different from those of modern banking. The literature of Buddhist period supplies ample evidence of the experience of "Arhties" (moneylenders) in all important trade centres and of their widespread influence on the life of the community. During the Moghul period[24] the indigenous bankers were prominently connected with financing of trade and affording credit and use of certain banking instruments.

However, the genesis of organized banking in India can be attributed to the beginning of trade relations of East India Company of European merchants with India. No doubt, the English agency houses in Calcutta and Bombay established the Hindustan Bank in 1770 in Calcutta but they served as bankers only to the company, whereas the rest of the community was deprived of this facility and was left to the mercy of moneylenders. "The Bengal Bank" and the "General Bank of India" established in 1785 were also chartered by the East India Company when the Britishers took possession of a greater part of India, they felt the need for having more banking institutions and as a sequel they opened more banks in the country.

After the depression of early thirties, banking legislation came to be directed to the wider objective of aligning banks' policies with the Government economic plans and policies. The imperial bank of India came into existence in 1920 and the Reserve Bank of India in 1935. However, the Banks role in financing rural development and agriculture was meager in this period. The Government assigned the sole responsibility in this field to the Co-operative Credit Societies (1904) only. The commercial banks, on the other hand, were mainly located in urban centres. They worked simply on the profit maximization principle and followed faithfully a security oriented approach. Rural interiors of the country and important sectors like agriculture and small scale industry were neglected.[25] Particularly, the inherent risks in farm operations, over-dependence on weather-God, cyclical uncertainty of agricultural production with primitive techniques and lack of organizational base for need based purchases and profitable sales at appropriate times were some of the reasons why agriculturists were treated as "untouchables" by banks.

At the same time, there was continued predominance of private agencies particularly the village moneylenders in providing credit to the capital-starved rural sector. Though the money lending system was proved to be very useful in the very past with relatively simple procedures and timely credit assistance, the system as a whole led to the growth of unproductive indebtedness which made the rural areas centres of poverty and low standard of living. The notorious and blood sucking activities of moneylenders and their exorbitant interest rates forced the poor villagers into vicious circle of indebtedness. Under the peculiar land acts of British Government during the second half of the nineteenth century, the passing of agricultural lands from the hands of the peasants to those of the moneylenders became a common phenomenon. The system still prevails in the country in spite of the declining trend of the influence of moneylender in rural areas with the increasing supply of institutional credit.

It is only with the adoption of economic planning as a means of national development the problem of rural indebtedness and rural underdevelopment received attention and concerted effort. Although planned approach to development started in India in early fifties, the initial plan document did not assign any specific responsibility to the banks. More recent plan reports, however, emphasized credit planning. The aim of Sixth Plan is to secure high rate of rural credit expansion to serve the productive needs of all with priority being given to the credit needs of various economic groups among the poor".[26] It was realized thus that the real growth of the prosperity of the country as a whole could never be possible, so long as the countrymen depend whether directly or indirectly on agricultural industry could not be lifted from the abyss[27] of financial misery. Especially in the context of the substantially increased requirements of agricultural finance consequent upon the "Green Revolution", it was thought that the cooperatives alone may not be in a position to meet the entire credit demand that may arise for modernizing the Indian agriculture. It was precisely from this stand-point that the concept of multi-agency approach was adopted. The timely realization in social context of under-development and inadequate infrastructure as an agent for growth has given a social purpose to commercial banking in our country.

Involvement of banks in the area of rural development dates back to the fifties following the recommendations of the historic Rural Credit Survey Committee. Accordingly the imperial bank of India was nationalized in 1955 and its branch expansion has been reoriented in favour of rural areas. However, it was the introduction of social controls in 1968 and subsequent nationalization in 1969 which marked the turning points in India banking history and also transformed the entire banking scenario.[28] The commercial banks received a special directive to give more emphasis to the hitherto neglected and economically weaker sections. They were also asked to move away from their security-oriented lending to purposive, productive and increment income oriented lending and to finance small and potentially viable farmers. In brief, they are advised to take greater cognizance of the viability of a project rather than creditworthiness of the borrower. With a deliberate slant in their licensing policies, the commercial banks have launched the programme of massive branch expansion favouring a thrust on rural areas. The banking infrastructure has grown rapidly spreading the banking facilities to the rural areas in a greater measure than ever before. The banking growth witnessed a substantial increase in the number of rural customers and volume of rural transactions. The implementation of lead bank scheme in consonance with area planning approach and formulation of district credit plans and annual action plans have gone a long way to facilitate a tremendous increase in the lending of commercial banks to agriculture and other productive sectors of rural economy. The enunciation of concept of priority sectors and stipulation of certain targets and sub-targets, 15 per cent of the total credit was expected to channelise by way of direct agricultural finance by March 1985 and 16 per cent by March 1987. In order to enhance the utilisaton of more resources in rural areas, it was stipulated that commercial banks should deploy at least 60 per cent of the deposits mobilized in the total areas. Moreover the commercial banks have to endeavor to enlarge the flow of credit to the rural sector with a sense of urgency, commitment and involvement giving boost to the priority sector like agriculture.

Table-1 reveals the phenomenal expansion of commercial banks.

Since the nationalization of commercial banks, banking in India has experienced unprecedented and out-standing growth during 1969-1985 within a period of 16 years. The number of branch banks has gone up by about 6.4 times, deposits rose by about 18.4 times and aggregate credit shot up by 15.6 times. Direct advances to agriculturists increased from 1.3 per cent in 1969 to 15.20 per cent in 1985; while the share of rural credit has gone up from 1.5 per cent in 1969 to 13.6 per cent in 1985. The share of rural deposits has increased from 3.11 per cent in 1969 to 13.82 per cent in 1985. Rural credit deposit ratio has gone up from 37.24 per cent in 1969 to 64.36 in 1985. Direct agricultural advances have gone up by about 12 times. These indicators clearly reveal that banking business shows some shift towards rural population, that class banking, while it is growing, is giving place to mass banking even on the par of commercial banks. The trends are conducive for rural development, even if the goals of integrated rural development are not achieved in full measure.

The three-tier cooperative structure (consisting of the State cooperative Banks (SCBs), District Central Cooperative Banks (DCCBs), and Primary Agricultural Credit Societies (PACSs) made a similar contribution towards the supply of credit to the rural community. For a long time, they were considered to

Table 1
Growth of Indian Banking during 1969-1985

Banking Indicators	*June 1969*	*December 1985*	*Index of Col.(4) over Col. (3)*
Number of branches	8,262	52,721	638
Share of rural branches in total branches (percentage)	22.20	55.61	250
Aggregate deposits	4,665	85,868	1,841
Share of rural deposits in total deposits (percentage)	3.11	13.82	444
Total credit (in crores)	3,609	56,326	1,561
Share of rural credit in total credit (percentage)	1.5	13.6	907
Credit-Deposit Ratio	77.36	65.60	85
Rural Credit Deposit Ratio	37.24	64.36	173
Direct Agricultural Advances as percentages of total advances	1.30	15.20	1,169

Source : Bank of Baroda Weekly Review, Vol. 24, No. 37, 12 September 1986, p.2.

be ideal single largest agency which possessed the necessary infrastructure to reach to the millions of small and marginal farmers spread through out the length and breadth of this vast country.[29] The very character of cooperative organisation, the voluntary nature of the membership, the principle of one-man one-vote and self-imposed curbs on profit have eminently qualified them to be an instrument of rural finance combining the advantages of private ownership and public good.

Almost all the Indian villages are covered by the Primary Agricultural Credit Societies at the grass-root level. The share of cooperatives in the borrowings of rural households has risen from 3 per cent in 1951 to about 30 to 35 per cent in 1981. As on June 1984, there were as many as 93,706 cooperative banks in the country as against 1,54,386 in 1974. Total outstanding advances of these banks were of the order of Rs. 14,516 crores as against Rs. 3,838 crores in 1974, the details of which are furnished in Table-2.

During the decade 1973-74 to 1983-84, the loan outstanding of State Cooperative Banks and Central Cooperative Banks Have gone up by about four times while that of Land Development Banks and Primary Agricultural Credit Societies increased by about 2.4 times.

Despite all this progress, both cooperative and commercial banks have had certain limitations in supplying credit to rural areas. Co-operatives, in spite of their long existence have failed to meet the credit requirements of the rural population. At many places, they are suffering from mounting over dues, shortage of resources, poor deposit mobilization etc. On the other hand, the commercial banks suffered from the organizational gaps and personal deficiencies. Their urban-oriented methods and high cost of operations could not be changed to the desired extent so as to suit the objectives of rural credit.

Thus, the failure of existing agencies in providing rural credit created wide gaps and the need for sponsoring more institutions in the area of rural development was realized. The National Commission on Agriculture (1971), recommended[30] commercial banks and cooperatives for sponsoring Farmers Service Societies. Provision of the package of inputs including

Table 2
Cooperative Credit

Type of Institution	*1973-74*		*1983-84*		
	Number	*Loan Outstanding (in Rs. Crores)*	*Number*	*Loan Outstanding (in Rs. Crores)*	*Index of Col. (6) over Col. (4)*
State Cooperative banks	26	706	28	2,916	413
Central Co-operative Banks	341	1,163	349	4,707	405
State/Central Land Development Banks	19	914	19	2,236	245
Primary Agricultural Credit Societies	1,54,000	1,055	92,000	2,554	242
Primary Co-operative Banks	NA	NA	1,310	2,103	NA

Source : RBI: Annual Report on Trend and Progress of Banking in India, 1973-74 and 1984-85 issues
Note : NA Not available

credit to marginal and small farmers was the objective behind constituting such societies.

It was, however, the establishment of Regional Rural Banks in 1975 as a third pillar of the multi-agency credit system which opened a new era in the country's banking system. They were State owned, regionally based and rural oriented organizations. The main objectives of these banks are to develop the rural economy by providing industry and other productive activities in the villages, credit and other facilities particularly to the small and marginal farmers, agricultural labourers, artisans and small entrepreneurs. They are devised to provide finance through direct loans and also undertake indirect finance via PACs/FSSS to the villagers.

By the introduction of these banks the focus of Indian banking has considerably shifted from class banking to mass banking and social banking to rural banking. The superiority of these banks lies in their lower cost structure, local staff and the use of local conditions and local languages. Within a few years after establishment of a number of Regional Rural Banks, the Dantwala Committee (1977) which assessed their performance, recommended for continuation and further expansion of these banks. Since then, there has been tremendous increase in their number. As a 'small man's bank' the Regional Rural Bans are now playing a more meaningful role in growth-oriented activities in rural areas. Despite facing various types of problems, they have so far achieved, to an extent, the main objective of helping the weaker sections by purveying the credit. In future, they are expected to make the village economy more viable and help in the regeneration of poorer sections. On 2nd October 1985, the Regional Banks completed their first decade of existence and their position by the end of the year in comparison to 1975 is given in the following table.

With in a period of ten years, India has developed a big network of 188 Regional Banks with 12,606 branches covering 333 districts out of 433 districts. The outstanding advances of the Regional Rural Banks are Rs. 1,40,767. It is significant that credit deposit ratio increased from 50 in 1975 to 109 in 1985 indicating that there is more ash inflow into the villages as against the deposits.

Table 3
Position of Regional Rural Banks

	1975	*1985*
Number of Regional Rural Banks	6	188
Districts covered	11	333
Number of branches	17	12,606
Deposits (in Rs. Lakhs)	20	1,28,582
Outstanding Advances (in Rs. lakhs)	10	1,40,767
Average Deposit per RRB (in Rs. lakhs)	3.33	683.95
Average Advances per RRB (in Rs. lakhs)	1.67	748.76
Average Deposit per Branch (in Rs. lakhs)	1.18	10.20
Average Advances per Branch (in Rs. lakhs)	0.59	11.17
Credit – deposit Ratio (in per cent)	50	109

Source :
1. RBI: Statistical Tables Relating to Banks in India, 1976
2. NABARD: Statistics on Regional Rural Banks, Institutional Development (RRBs Division), December 1985.

During the Sixth Plan period, the share of term loans to the Rural Sector of commercial banks was 49 per cent, Regional Rural Banks was 33 per cent and cooperatives was 18 per cent in a total of Rs. 3,102 crores.

Recently, the National Bank for Agricultural and Rural Development (NABARD) commenced its functioning from 1982.[31] It took over the functions of erstwhile Agricultural Credit Department, Rural Planning and Credit cell of Reserve Bank of India and Agricultural Refinance and Development Corporation. It provides investment for promoting various development activities for rural development indirectly through cooperatives, commercial banks and Farmers Service Societies.

During the past few years, several steps were taken by the banks in India, at the instance of Government of India and the Reserve Bank to facilitate the flow of credit to weaker sections. These measures include[32] (i) easier terms of repayment of loans, (ii) grant of medium term loans for subsidiary occupations like dairy and poultry upto a limit without the security of land, (iii) lower down repayment for availment of investment credit for agricultural development, (iv) no margin requirements for loans up to certain limits, and (v) simplification of application forms.

Apart from these measures, banks in India are continually striving for introducing innovative credit schemes suitably designed to benefit agriculture and its allied sectors. They have also a multi-pronged drive for intensive rural financing through innovative strategies like adoption of villages, scheme of differential interest rates, rural service centres, Gram Vikas Kendras and organisation of credit camps. The banks involvement in rural development programmes has been further enhanced with the implementation of various national poverty alleviation programmes like Twenty-Point Economic Programmes, Integrated Rural Development programmes and enunciation of special welfare measures to weaker sections.

Incidence of Poverty in Rural India

The pace of economic development of India depends upon the speedy development of rural areas, for about seventy five per cent of the population of the country is rural. According to 1981 census, nearly every four out of five Indians live in rural areas and within the rural areas every five out of six are dependent on agriculture.[33] Agriculture along with its allied activities contributes[34] as much as forty one per cent of national income and accounts for nearly forty either per cent of foreign exchange earnings. It also provides raw materials to agro based industries such as cotton textiles, jute, sugar and edible oils. Thus, agriculture is the backbone of the Indian economy. Therefore, in any development effort, failure to recognize this central fact would mean neglecting the heart of India.

History tells us that India was once looked upon as a "Golden Orient" by the rest of the world, both in the ancient and medieval epochs of her history.[35] Indeed it was her lure of fabulous wealth which was primarily responsible for waves of invasions across her borders. At that time Indian economy was predominantly a rural economy with people engaged in agriculture and traditional crafts and whose needs were mostly met within the village itself. Village communities enjoyed self-sufficiency and they were self-reliant.

Rural India under the British rule lost its self-sufficiency and people became poorer due to colonial exploitation.[36] On the eve of Independence in 1947, India inherited a crippled economy with a stagnant agriculture, underdeveloped industries and peasantry steeped in poverty and most of the Indian villages were left with[37] a look of despair, dismay, factionalism, misery, religious sentiments, customary practices and untouchability.

Independent India ambitiously and enthusiastically launched several five year plans[38] gigantic in scale in a bid to transform the socio-economic picture of India into a better and prosperous one. Extending benefits to India's 5,75,000 villages and improving the living standards of rural people particularly to those living below the poverty line have been avowed goals of India's planning. The alleviation of rural poverty was the prime objective of the Sixth Five Year Plan. The Seventh Plan envisages an expanded coverage under the various anti-poverty programmes at a faster rate than before. Despite massive doses of investment during the 36 years of planning, it is still a long way to go in achieving the prime goals. The objective of achieving welfare state assuming a minimum standard of living to the teaming millions of rural people appears to be still a distant goal.

Today India presents a paradoxical situation of tremendous development[39] on one side and persistent poverty on the other. The achievement of self-reliance in food grains production (when it touched to an all-time peak of 152.4 million tons in 1983-84 as against 126.4 million tons in 1977-78) is the most outstanding feature of free India. It is a source of economic security and a tower of strength for accelerating the rate of economic growth in India today. The other major achievements on the economic front are note-worthy.[40] (a) the area under high-yielding varieties of food grains increased from 35.2 million hectares in 1979-80 to 8.4 million tons in 1984-85, (b) chemical fertilizer consumption rose from 5.3 million tons in 1979-80 to about 56.0 million hectares 8.4 million tons in 1984-85, (c) sixty four per cent of villages were electrified by the end of Sixth plan and consumption of electrified by the end of Sixth Plan and consumption of electricity rose in agriculture by 8.9 per cent per annum, (d) the number of tractors in use at present is of the order of 500 thousand which, in terms of draught power is roughly equivalent to 3.5 million animals (e) irrigation potential went up from 22 million hectares in 1951-52 to 68 million hectares in 1984-85, (f) living conditions of the poor in rural areas improved through the provision of assured water supply to 192,000 out of 231,000 villages facing the drinking water problem and house-sites are provided to 5.4 million rural families, (g) the primary school system now covers about 95 per cent of the rural population and (h) the average life-span registered dramatic rise from 32 years in 1950-51 to 52 years in 1980-81.

Although India achieved self-sufficiency in food grains, it is still steeped in poverty of a vast dimension. 269 million people are below poverty line accounting for 37.4 per cent of population. The problem of poverty is persisting; a large number of rural families are living in misery without having access to the basic necessities of life, food, clothing and shelter. Out of the 269 million living below poverty line, three fourths are in rural areas. Thus poverty in India is predominantly rural as a national phenomenon. It may be further noted that while 40.4 per cent of the rural population are below poverty line, it is 28 per cent in the case of urban population according to the Seventh Five Year Plan estimates as the following table reveals.

Table 4
Trends in Percentage of People Below Poverty Line

Percentage of Population below the Poverty Line	*1977-78*	*1983-84 (Provisional Data)*
Rural	51.2	40.4
Urban	38.2	28.1
Total	48.3	37.4

Source : Government of India, Planning Commission, Seventh Five Year Plan 1985-90, Vol. 1, p.4.

The rural census report of 1971[41] highlights the regional distribution of the poor among the different states are having a sizeable population of rural poor with income less than Rs.100 per month. Their number state-wise is as follows, Bihar – 3 crores Uttar Pradesh – 3.8 crores ; Andhra Pradesh– 1.5 crores Jammu and Kashmir – 1.1 crores; Madhya Pradesh – 2.1 crores ; Maharashtra – 1.0 crores; Orissa – 1.4 crores and West Bengal – 2.0 crores. These figures have gone up further during the 1981 census. The report also reveals different aspects of poverty. Seventy per cent of the rural families own less than 2 hectares of land each and thirty per cent of rural population have no assets whatsoever. The per cent of rural house holds have no durable assets i.e. all their earthly possessions consist of a few earthen pots and cooking pans. Sixteen per cent of a few earthen pots and cooking pans. Sixteen per cent of the rural poor have no houses of their own and forty five per cent of households have no implements and machinery and the army of marginal farmers had increased from 24 million to 36 million and the multitude of landless labourers had increased from 27 millions to 48 millions. Among the rural poor special mention should be made of Harijans and Tribes who are largely landless.

Thus, in rural areas poverty assumes a sinister proportion. It is a matter of grim concern posing a challenge to the entire economic structure itself.[42] With the majority of population dependent on uncertain agriculture, they have no steady source of employment or income. This lack of adequate employment manifestating[43] quantitatively and qualitatively in terms of low income, low purchasing power, inadequate housing, poor health, limited or no nutrition, higher infant mortality, low life and work expectancy and in most cases a general despondency and despair. This phenomenon of vicious circle of poverty further intensified by recurrent drought and famines which are the normal attendants of village life, have brought into sharper focus the need to solve the problem. The World Bank in its Sector Policy Paper[44] on rural development reflected its increasing concern for the rural masses. According to this paper about 85 per cent of all absolute poverty is in rural areas (i.e. annual income equivalent to $50 or less). That is about 550 million people are suffering from absolute poverty in rural areas of the developing world in the mid-1970's. Worse still, about four-fifths of this total is in the developing countries of Asia, with almost two-thirds of the number found in only four countries - India, Indonesia, Bangladesh and Pakistan. Presently, there are about 700 million people living below poverty line of the developing world.

Hence, there is a need for a total and integrated approach for removing poverty and raising the level of productivity and employment. Increasing employment and productivity will automatically reduce poverty and inequality and at the same time instilling hope and sense of security in the minds of poor people. In a predominantly agrarian economy such as ours, the solution to these basic problems lies in the integrated development of rural areas with emphasis on agricultural production.

The Strategy of Rural Development

Rural development is designed to improve the economic and social life of people in villages. Unless the lot of the rural poor is alleviated, Achievement of welfare state will be a distant goal. It calls for the extension of the benefits of development to the poorest among those who seek a livelihood in the rural areas–the small and marginal farmers, tenants and the landless. It also involves "optimum utilization of the natural and human resources of a given area for the enrichment of the quality of life of its population".[45] Rural development constitutes a basic strategy[46] for faster economic development and also a matter of growing urgency for considerations of social justice, national integration and over-all uplift of people in India. Rural development is an imperative of national development in India.

The concept of rural development encompasses[47] wider spectrum today than over before. It is a process of modernization and monetization of rural societies and its transition from traditional isolation to integration with national economy for faster economic development and welfare of common masses. Viewed thus, the objectives of rural development encloses (a) improved productivity, increased employment and higher incomes for weaker sections[48] as well as the minimum acceptable levels of food, shelter, education, health etc. (b) a decreasing inequality in the distribution of rural income and in urban–rural imbalances in incomes and economic opportunities and (c) the capacity of rural sector to sustain and accelerate the pace of improvements overtime.

Thus, the main aim of rural development is to break the vicious circle of poverty through economically better and improved production, reasonable distribution and better living standards and balanced development among the regions as well as the various sections of rural population. It is not to be defined merely in terms of economic outputs, or indicators like increase in agricultural income as social indicators of development cannot be ignored. Real rural development[49] should always reflect improvement in the standards of living of the poor.

Indian experience and experimentation of rural development reveals the utilization of a number of changing strategies. Realising the utmost need for extension and development services in rural areas, in the post-Independence period, the Government of India has initiated a number of programmes so as to solve the chronic problems plaguing the villages. Guy Hunter has rightly remarked[50] that there may not be other developing country in the world which over the past 33 years has invented and put into practice various measures in the field of rural development as India has done. A plethora of rural development plans were spread over different fields like agriculture, industry, trade, commerce, education both general and technical, social welfare, transport, communications, etc. The basic objective behind all programmes implemented by the Government of India was an integrated development of the farmers, the agricultural labourers and the rural artisans and to improve their standard of living by means of reducing poverty, raising productivity and increasing employment opportunities.

Starting from the First Plan period, a number of experiments have come to be made in this direction at the All India level. Early in 1952, the Community Development Programme was launched with the object of bringing about social and economic transformation of village life by creating an awareness in the rural communities of the potential and means of development.[51] The primary plank of this programme was self-help and people's participation. The scheme failed to enthuse people at all levels and its impact was not perceptible.

The Land Reforms which were also introduced in early fifties were expected to contribute much in the process of rural development by abolition of Zamindari and intermediary tenures. Tenancy reforms, protection of share-croppers, land ceilings and land consolidation measures were introduced later. The main objective behind these reforms was to redistribute the property infavour of landless and small cultivators and transfer of assets like land and livestock to those who had no asset base at all. However, till today the reforms have neither been completed nor strictly implemented in many parts of the country.

Consequently a new setup was introduced in 1959 as the Panchayat Raj system[52] where people were empowered to choose their representatives with whom the Government could interact in a real manner in the task of nation building.[53] This scheme again did not achieve the expected results.

Intensive Agricultural District Programme and Intensive Agricultural Area Programme of the sixties were production-oriented programmes specially tailored for the most promising areas i.e., areas which had adequate rainfall or irrigation or basic infrastructure facilities. Instructive though the lessons of their successful experience, they were not easily replaceable elsewhere. There was greater concentration of efforts on the well-to-do.

The new agricultural technology comprising of HYV-cum-Fertilizer-cum-Irrigation introduced in sixties in respect of few crops and in a few irrigated areas, brought a technological break-through in Indian agriculture and resulted in the so called Green Revolution. The main aim of the new technology is that application of knowledge, techniques and disciplines of various fields of engineering to the solution of problems arising in the field of agriculture and rural living with the object of improving production work, raising the standards of living of the farmer and their overall earnings.

Empirical studies, however, have brought to light that the Green Revolution benefited only a few large and progressive farmers. The marginal and small farmers have not been able to take advantage of the new technology due to several reasons such as wide communication gaps. Lack of credit facilities, risks and uncertainties involved and hesitancy on the part of the tradition bound farmers. This led to an unequal distribution of the benefits of the increased production giving rise to the danger of class conflicts between the have and have-nots.

Keeping in view the need to ensure that the benefits of development were realized by the truly deserving poorer sections of the rural society, a series of programmes were launched in the early seventies. The Small Farmers Development Agencies (SFDA) and the Marginal Farmers Development Agencies (MFAL) were launched[54] aiming at the specific target groups of small and marginal farmers. The problem of arid areas was sought to be solved through Drought

Prone Area Programme (DPAP)[55] and a special programme was evolved for the desert areas with a view to remove regional disparities particularly in less endowed or disadvantaged areas like the Hill and Tribal areas and special sub-plans of development were introduced.

A "Food for Work Programme (FFWP)" was launched in 1977 for rural unemployed in slack seasons and a 'Minimum Needs Programme' was designed to secure certain basic amenities.

It was soon realized that many of these programmes meant for the upliftment of the poor did not form parties of a united effort to tackle the different endowments in any given area. A systematic, scientific and integrated use of local resources needed to be made. Accordingly the concept of 'Integrated Rural Development Programme (IRDP), was launched[56] in 1976-77 intending to assist the rural poor to derive economic benefits from the local resource potential of each area. It was mainly designed to alleviate rural poverty claimed to be a unique effort by the Government of India to operate in all the blocks of the country replacing the ongoing SFDA, IADP and SLPP programmes.

Increasing production and productivity in agriculture and other sectors in rural areas, creating substantial additional employment opportunities and making rural families viable and self-sufficient are the main objectives of the Integrated Rural Development Programme. The programme seeks in particular to improve the lot of the poorest of the poor - small and marginal farmers, share-croppers, agricultural labourers, rural artisans, scheduled castes/tribes and other weaker sections. After identifying in each block "the bottom deciles of the rural population below the poverty line (BPL)", the IRDP envisages to cover them in a phased manner - 600 families per year (at least 30 per cent of the families under this programme should be from Scheduled Castes/Tribes). The selected families[57] would be given easy credit facilities to purchase productive assets in subsidized costs. They will also be supported with social services like health, education, and housing. All the grass-root beneficiaries are expected to work as a team towards integrating various elements of the scheme. It is also hoped that the IRDP would initiate active involvement of the people for whom the programme is envisaged.

The essence of the programme lies in its approach based on decentralized micro-level planning at the block level. The comprehensive block planning based on the procedures of (a) compilation of basic data and resource inventory, (b) household survey and (c) man-power budgeting and involve the inclusion of all the projects of IRDP and sectoral projects. The primary aim of the block plan is to raise the living standards of the poor by eliminating poverty and inequality in rural India. It also proposes to bring about integration in the area approach and the beneficiary approach of the various developmental schemes currently in operation to achieve the objective of rural development in terms of production and full employment.

The IRDP launched for implementation in 1978, covered, 2,300 blocks in the first year and 2,600 in the second year. With effect from 2nd October 1978, all the 5,011 blocks in the country were covered under the same programme. The total outlay on IRDP constitutes Rs.5,364 crores in the Sixth Plan (or 5.5 per cent of total plan outlay). Under the same plan period, the programme is supported by a provision of subsidy of Rs. 1,500 crores to make the scheme viable and the banking system has been called upon to provide an amount of Rs. 3,000 crores to the beneficiaries. The following table shows the progress of IRDP.

Table 5

Progress of Integrated Rural Development Programme

	1980-81	*1981-82*	*1982-83*
Subsidy expenditure (Rupees in crores)	156.2	262.4	320.6
Total term credit mobilized (Rupees in crores)	236.6	484.6	660.1
Number of families assisted (million)	1.78	2.83	3.26
Subsidy per family (in rupees)	561	928	983
Credit mobilized per family (in rupees)	850	1713	2025
Investment per family (in rupees)	1411	2641	3008

Source: Government of India, Planning Commission, Seventh Five Year Plan, 1985-90.

The progress of IRDP in quantitative terms between 1980-81 and 1982-83 as shown in the above table reveals that the total number of families assisted increased from 2.78 million in 1980-81 to 3.26 million in 1982-83. Subsidy per family as well as credit mobilized per family showed a marked improvement while investment per family has more than doubled. By the end of Sixth Plan, against a target of 15 million families, 16.5 families were assisted for improving their economic conditions so that they may rise above the poverty line.

However, there appear quite a few impediments in the way of effective implementation of IRDP. For instance, in spite of directives issued by the Central Bank, not to insist on formalities, officials at the branch level still insist on a security cover and guarantors for loans to IRDP beneficiaries who are mainly illiterates and ignorant. Other difficulties have been encountered at the administrative organisation at the block level and uneven spread of infrastructure.

The national scheme of Training of Youth for Self-Employment (TRYSEM) is being operated as a part of IRDP which was initiated in 1979 with the principal objectives of alleviating unemployment among the rural youth. The main thrust of the scheme is equipping the rural youth with necessary skills and technologies to enable them to take to vocations of self-employment. The National Rural Employment Programme (NREP)[58] and the Rural Landless Employment Guarantee Programme (RLEGP)[59] are also in the field to provide employment opportunities.

There are several such other programmes like National Grid of Rural Godowns Council for Advancement of Rural Technology, Development of Women and Children in Rural Areas (DWCRA), etc. At the commencement of the Sixth Plan, different development agencies engaged in the task of rural development were merged, at the district level to form District Rural Development Agency (DRDA). The Seventh Plan strategy for rural development is to integrate the various rural development programmes for the effective implementation and avoidance of duplication.

The upshot of above analysis reveals that the Government has done so much and still working for the cause of rural development. As a result of all these programmes, there has been considerable growth in infrastructure for rural areas. The process of socio-economic evolution took different forms attempting to transfer of assets like land and livestock to those who had no assets at all. There has been marked increase in agricultural production particularly in food grains, increased consumption of fertilizers, and increased technological facilities.

Rural development programmes bristle with several criticisms. While success is limited in different sectors, the programmes have not been able to make much impact. The benefits of development did not percolate to weaker sections. The beneficiaries of all these programmes are mostly the rural rich. It is well known that roads, electrification and others have benefited more the land owners and cultivators. They have installed electric pumps and lighted their streets and homes. They have been able to grow more food and transport their produce more easily and quickly to the market. These measures then provide the infrastructure for those who have the capacity to use them for their benefits. It is also true that streets and surroundings of the upper castes and classes in the villages are cleaner than the streets and surroundings of the Scheduled Castes and agricultural labourers.

The reasons for the limited success of rural development programmes[60] are:

(i) The programmes are piece-meal in nature rather than integrated and comprehensive.

(ii) Bureaucracy and red-tape concentrate more on achieving paper targets while often widen the gap between the rich and the poor. Government often resorts to launch alternative schemes to cover up the deficiencies of earlier programmes without comprehensive approach to tackle the chronic problems.

(iii) Development implies sociological as well as psychological approach and this has never been taken into consideration.

(iv) Most of the programmes continued to concentrate on institutions at the national or sectoral level (macro level) but did not pay enough attention to the local levels (micro level).

(v) There was also shortage of trained local manpower and lack of adequate marketing arrangements for output.

(vi) The fundamental conflict in the structure of economic relations in the village-society[61] is also responsible for the failure of rural development programmes in India. The existing power structure in the village society vitiates the aim of distributive justice by siphoning off the benefits intended for the rural poor. Gains are concentrated in the vested classes arresting percolation to the lower levels.

(vii) The role of banks and their efficiency in accelerating rural development schemes and reducing regional disparities through the instrumentality of credit is another governing factor determining the success of rural development effort.

Conclusion

The mutual interdependence of financial development and economic development is axiomatic in the long-run. The current theoretical formulations and empirical studies support this long-run inter-relationship. The demand following English banking system and the German supply leading system converge in the long-run postulating the inter-relationship of financial development and economic development. This long-term mutual interdependence is tautological as it fails to throw light whether financial development is the cause of economic development or vice versa. Accordingly, it has very little significance either for shaping the development of financial institutions or guiding the programmes of planned development in under developed countries which are aspiring to achieve a higher problem of the development of under developed countries to mobilize savings to the maximum extent possible and enhance the role of investment of National Income to a higher level over the norm of about five per cent. The increasing pressure of population warrants them to save even to 20 to 25 per cent of National Income for increasing their productive investment. In such a situation financial development becomes a pre-requisite for economic development in planning for rapid economic growth.

Schumpeter is the pioneer of positive theory of banking in economic development. Alexander Gerschenkron's structuralistic hypothesis supports the active role of the State in the initial stage of development in under developed countries, while banking institutions accelerate their contribution to economic development during the intermediate stage. Therefore the hypothesis supports the need to shape financial development during those two stages to monitor economic development. The financial repression hypothesis postulates integration of the dual money markets in the underdeveloped countries. The evil finance of the autonomous professional moneylenders necessitates the development of institutional finance to discipline them and to promote rural development. When the State policy is for welfare state and rapid economic growth, it has to utilize financial development as a vehicle of economic development. Therefore banking has a crucial role to play in economic development in mobilising savings, allocation of resources to more productive sectors, stimulation of entrepreneurship by bank financing. The German mixed banking system and the Japanese banking system are outstanding models that have fostered economic development. In the underdeveloped countries innovative banking has a wider role to play in fulfilling the objectives of State policy. Hence, the pressing need to evolve various techniques of banking, nay mass banking to facilitate rural development and economic development is quite obvious. It is no wonder that banks cease to be mere repositories of financial resources. They have to play a catalytic role in spreading industrialization, advancing rural development and to development of social services germane to a 'welfare state'. Banking thus becomes a tool of economic development and social development. India today is rich in the banking techniques and developments. A person who has to run cannot do so without necessary mental preparation and perspiration.

Rural development has come to be recognized as an important approach in India for minimizing object poverty, gross inequalities in income and distribution of wealth, chronic unemployment, ignorance and miserable living conditions in rural areas. It also aims at the development of the rural communities by generating a process of self-reliant and self-sustained growth.

A number of experiments have been made through earlier Five Year Plans and later for strengthening the rural economy at improving the conditions of the rural people. These schemes were viewed with a lot of hope and expectations.

Along with various schemes, different types of development financing agencies were also instituted. Particularly the banking industry has traversed a long way specially during the last decade as one of the accredited agencies of rural development. The multi-agency system comprising the three pillars of cooperative, commercial and regional rural banks for financing the agricultural and rural development sector has emerged as a significant institutional setup. Despite the operation of several institutions, there is still a big credit gap to meet the requirements of rural communities which postulates the need for enlarging the rural banking further.

Footnotes

1. Quoted in : Wofl, Henry: "Cooperation in India", 2nd Edition, W. Thaker and Company. London, 1927, p.8.
2. Tannan, M.L. : "Banking Law and Practice in India", 17th Edition, Thaker and Co. Ltd. Bombay, 1979, p.124.
3. Quoted, *Ibid.*, p. 125.
4. Quoted, *Ibid.*, p.124.
5. Abdi, Ali Issa: "Commercial Banks and Economic Development: The Experience of Eastern Africa,", Praegar Publishers, New Delhi, 1977, p.21.
6. Government of India: "Report of the Royal Commission on Agriculture in India", 1925, p.445.
7. Government of India : "Report of the Committee on Cooperation in India 1915", pp. 1-2.

8. Patrik, Hugh: "Financial Development and Economic Growth in Underdeveloped Countries", Economic Development and Cultural Change, Vol. 14, No. 2, January 1966, p. 176.
9. Gerschenkron, A: "Economic Backwardness in Historical Perspective : A Book of Essays" (Cambridge, Mass: Harvard University Press, 1962), p.14, quoted from Ali Issa Abdi, *Op.cit.*, p.33.
10. Abdi, Ali Issa : *Op.cit.*, p.12.,
11. Gurley, J: "Banking in the Early Stages of Industrialization", Ed. Rondo Cameron, American Economic Review, Vol.57, No. 4, September 1967, pp. 1450-53.
12. Abdi, Ali Issa : *Op.cit.*,p.13.
13. Smith. Adam: "Wealth of Nations", Modern Library, New York, 1937, p. 281.
14. Goldsmith, R.W.: "Financial Structure and Development", Yale University Press, New Haven, 1969, p.390.
15. Lewis, Arthur : "The Theory of Economic Growth", Harper and Row, New York, 1970, p.226.
16. Shah, Edward : "Financial Depending in Economic Development", Oxford University Press, London, 1973, p.3.
17. Narasimhan, M: "Some Reflections on the Indian Banking Scene", Pigmy Economy Review, Vol. 29, No. 7, February 1984, p.2.
18. Roy, T.S. : "Banking as Tool for Development", SBI Monthly Review, Vol. XVIII, No. 10, October 1978, pp.367-73.
19. Shetty. V, Vasudeva: "Bank Finance and Rural Development", paper presented at the National Seminar on Bank Finance and Rural Development at S.V. University, Tirupati, 7-8 April, 1984.
20. Sharma, K.S. : "The Role of Financial Intermediation in Mobilisation and allocation of Resources for Rural Development" The Indian Economic Journal, Vol. 26, No. 2, October-December 1978, p.84.
21. Datar, M.K. : "Banking and Rural Development", The Indian Economic Journal, Vol. 26, No. 2, October-December, 1978, pp.51-60.
22. Shetty K. Shanker :"Welfare Stae and Bank Nationalisation in India", Macmillan Company India Ltd., Delhi, 1982, p. 51.
23. Bagga, Autar Singh: "Role of Banking in National Economic Development", The Banker, Vol. XXIV, No. 3, May 1977, pp. 17-21.
24. "Changing Scenario of Rural Credit" Agricultural Banker, Vol 9, No. 1, January-March, 1986, pp.14-18.
25. Sankaraiah, A and Madhusudana Rao, K. : "Uneven Spread of Banking in India–A Post-Natinalisation Assessment", The Banker, Vol. XXX, No. 11, January 1984, p.33.
26. Government of India, Planning Commission, Sixth Five Year Plan, 1980-85, p.17.
27. Pal, D.N.: "Agricultural Finance, Commercial Banks and Cooperatives", Economic Affairs, Vol. 21, No. 6, June 1976, pp.219.27.
28. Joshi, P.N. : "Banking as a Lever for Rural Development", Pigmy Economic Review, Vol. 29, No. 6, January 1984, pp.3-6.

29. Vyas, M. Mahendra : "Financing Agriculture-Multi-Agency Approach", The Banker, Vol. XXVI, No. 9, November 1979, pp. 21-24.
30. National Commission on Agriculture : "Interim Report on Credit Service to Small and Marginal Farmers and Agricultural Labourers", New Delhi, 1971.
31. Agarwal, A.K. : "Entry of NABARD on Rural Credit Scene", Southern Economist, Vol. 21, No. 23, 1st April 1983, pp. 31-33.
32. Ghosh, B.K. : "some Reflections on Rural Banking and Agricultural Financing by Commercial Banks", Agricultural Banker, January-March 1986, Vol. a, No. 1, pp.3-9.
33. Joshi, P.N. "Banking as a Lever for Rural Development Pigmy Economic Review, Vol.29, No. 6, January 1984, p.3.
34. Desai, Vasant: "A study of Rural Economics: A Systems Approach", Himalaya Publishing House, Bombay, 1983, p.1.
35. Chatterjee, Rabindranath: "Indian Economics", H. Chatterjee and Co.Ltd., Calcutta, 1951, p.36.
36. One of the serious consequences of the British rule in India was the gradual decline of traditional crafts and craftsmen in village society through unequal economic competition. The goods turned out of factories in England swamped the economy whereas those produced with the local skills suffered for want of adequate markets. With the decline of the villages crafts, gradually agriculture remained the only main occupation, thus increasing pressure on agriculture.
37. Sankaran, S: "Agricultural Economy of India" Progressive Corporation Pvt. Ltd., Madras, 1980, p.19.
38. The country has passed through six five year plans since 1950-51 to 1984-85 and three Annual Plans from 1966-67 to 1968-69. The Seventh Plan has commenced recently. Besides the Government of India has already introduced two sets of Twenty Point Programmes in order to bring forth the socio-economic development in the country.
39. Government of India: Planning Commission, Seventh Five Year Plan, 1985-90, Vol. 1, p.2.
40. *Ibid.*
41. Pande, P.N. : "Reaching Benefits of Rural Development to All", Kurukshetra, Vol. XXX, No. 9, 1 February 1981, pp.4-7.
42. Ghodke, Manju: "Poverty and Alleviation Programmes", The Economic Times, Vol. 1, No. 264, 26 June 1986, p.3.
43. Joseph, S.C.: "A Strategy to Eradicate Poverty", Yojana, Vol. XXX, No. 19, 1978, pp.20-27.
44. World Bank :Rural Development : Sector Policy Paper, 1975.
45. Rao, V.K.R.V. : "Integrated Rural Development", Eastern Economist, Vol. 69, No. 16, October 14, 1977, p.742.
46. Copp. H. James: "Rural Sociology and Rural Development", Rural Sociology, Vol.37, No. 4, December 1972, p.519.
47. Lal, G.M.M. : "Commercial Banks and Goat Development Programmes", Himalaya Publishing House, Bombay, 1982, p.5.

48. The weaker sections in priority sector is defined as that which comprise (i) small and margial farmers with landholdings of 5 acres and less, landless labourers, tenant-farmers and share croppers, (ii) artisans, village and cottage industries and artisans as defined by Tamble Group includes small industrial activities, manufacturing, processing, preservation, serving in villages and small towns, etc., (iii) IRDP beneficiaries (iv) Scheduled Castes and Scheduled Tribes and (v) DRI beneficiaries.
49. Bajpai, Brijesh: "Rural Development : Some Constraints", Kurukshetra, Vol. XXX, No. 23, 1 September 1982, pp.9-12.
50. Hunter, Guy: In his Forward on "Integrated Rural Development Approach–Strategies and Perspectives", by S.K. Sharma and S.H. Malhotra, Abhinav Publications, New Delhi, 1977, p.7.
51. "Rural Development : Problems and Tasks", Bank of Baroda Weekly Review, Vol. 19, No.1, 18 December 1981, p.1.
52. These institutions were intended to better appreciation of local needs and capabilities of eliciting local participation in the formulation of the plans. As on March 31, 1980, there were 2,25,832 Gram Panchayats, covering 5,94,837 villages and a population of 445 millions, 4,451 Panchayat Samithis and 274 Zilla Parishads in India.
53. Gupta, B.N. : "The Changing Scene of Rural Development", Rural India, Vol. 41, No. 3, March 1978, pp.63-67.
54. Mohanan, N: "Development Finance for Small Farmers", Rainbow Publications, Coimbatore, 1981, p.3.
55. The DPAP was launched during the Fifth Plan period agricultural sector, It aims at optimum utilization of land, water and livestock, resources and restoration of ecological balances, stabilization of the income of the people, particularly the weaker sections of the society. The DPAP covered 554 blocks in 763 districts of 13 States in 1980-81. Central allocations of various State Governments under this scheme amounted to Rs. 42.22 crores.
56. Sundaram, I.S.: "Anti-Poverty Rural Development in India", D.K. Publications, New Delhi, 1984, p.39.
57. "Poor families" broadly cover families owning less than five acres of land and other families with a total annual income of less than Rs. 3,500. The Government of India gives a subsidy, ranging from 25 per cent to 50 per cent of capital investment depending upon the category of the beneficiary.
58. NREP: The NREP was launched in October 1980 replacing the earlier food for work programme. It is being implemented on 50:50 sharing basis between the Central and the States. The objective of this programme is to generate additional employment opportunities for the unemployed in the rural areas simultaneously creating productive community assets for strengthening rural economy. This programme is implemented through the District Development Agency. During the Sixth Plan, as against a target of generation of 1500-2000 million man-days a total of 1775 million man-days a total of 1775 million man-days were generated.

59. RLEGP: The RLEGP was launched during 1983-84 to have a more direct attack on the unemployment status of the landless. The basic objective of the programme is to improve and expand employment opportunities for the rural landless, so that the employment is provided for atleast 1 member of every landless labour up to 100 days in a year, and creation of favourable assets for strengthening the rural infrastructure. The programme is fully funded by the Central Government. During the Sixth Plan its allocation was Rs. 500 crores while the outlay for the Seventh Plan is fixed at Rs. 1744 crores.
60. Desai, Vasant : *Op.cit.*,p.692.
61. Mishra, S.N and Sharma, Kushal : "Evolution of Rural Development Strategies". Kurukshetra. 16 June 1983, pp.8-11.

3

The Rationale of Regional Rural Banks

"The lesson of universal agrarian history... is that an essential input of agriculture is credit. Neither the condition of the country nor the nature of land tenures, nor the position of agriculture, affects the one great fact that agriculturists must borrow"

Frederick Nicholson[1]

Introduction

An attempt is made in this chapter to analyse the rationale of the emergence of Regional Rural Banks in 1975 in the historical perspective of the existing institutional framework of rural credit in India.

From a long time, rural credit has been one of the most important economic problems of India which calls for immediate attention and solution, on account of the appalling poverty and extremely low standard of living of rural population. As credit facilitates the successful implementation of all agricultural and rural development operations, its non-availability often posed a serious obstacle to the welfare of rural masses. Particularly, with the onset of Green Revolution, which was investment oriented, the importance of credit in farm operations has intensified. In this context, credit is more needed by small and marginal farmers, agricultural labourers and rural artisans with professional terms than others. And providing required finance to agro-based industries, cottage and small scale sector, distribution services, small trading and other self-employment schemes is vital for the uplift of around 327 million unemployed and underemployed rural poor[2], specially those belonged to weaker sections. Obtaining capital resources for setting up of subsidiary occupations like animal husbandry, forestry, fishing, etc., will be impossible if needed funds are not available. Thus, the whole rural development programmes resolve themselves into finding better and better means of financing a complex industry of agricultural sector. Yet, the persistent low production in many parts of the country can be attributed to the inadequate and none-too-timely supply of rural credit.

The main objective of rural credit policy in India since 1951 has been to enlarge the geographical and functional coverage of institutional credit agencies and the dependence on non-institutional credit agencies particularly the village moneylenders gets reduced. The All India Rural Credit Survey, in its historic report in 1950-51, revealed that the institutional agencies comprising the Government, cooperative and commercial banks supplied an insignificant portion of 7 per cent of total rural credit, while the corresponding share of private moneylenders constituted as high as 69 per cent[3]. Later on, the All India Debt and Investment Survey conducted in 1971-72 revealed[4] the disheartening fact that even in the relatively scanty flow of credit to rural sector, a disproportionately larger share of organized credit was cornered by rich farmers. It clearly showed that the group with assets upto Rs.2,500 received 11.7 per cent of total rural credit from all agencies, whereas groups with assets up to Rs,20,000 received 44.3 per cent. Government agencies supplied only 4.7 per cent of their credit to the poorer sections compared with 53.1 per cent of wealthier sections. The commercial banks, on the other hand, contributed only 2.2 per cent of the total rural credit needs in 1971-72.

The above two surveys revealed two important facts. Firstly, the organized credit system in India neglected the financing of rural areas in favour of urban ones and of the meager resources flown to rural areas the rich farmers with larger holdings got benefited than the poorer sections. Secondly and most distressingly the private agencies especially the village moneylenders predominated the rural credit structure.

In the pre-British times, and in the absence of proper growth of institutional agencies like commercial banks or credit cooperatives, local moneylenders used to extend causal credit to meet the occasional needs of the rural folk and they played a subordinate role in the economy of country-side. Their operations being[5] simple, informal and free from delays and having personal approach and rapport with villagers, the moneylenders were proved to be invaluable assets in rural areas. However, the rapid development of commerce and trade, the introduction of established law and permanent civil courts and the enactment of such measures as the Contract Act, opened up a golden age for the moneylenders. Even after the establishment of so many credit agencies, the banking system in the country, till recently neglected the rural sector as it considered loans to agriculture was highly risky and farmers lack security except land. The moneylenders snatched this opportunity by lending money on exorbitant interest rates and earned enormous profits. It was thus found, even in 1970's, when the organized banking structure increasingly decided to involve in financing the rural sector, 60 per cent of production credit of rural areas was still met by the village moneylenders. Surely, they have been catering to the needs of millions, but on unfavourable terms.

With their strong socio-economic hold in the village and lack of comparative alternative lending institution of organized type, the moneylenders can and often do resort to various malpractices due to the help-lessens, ignorance and necessity of the borrowers. Some of the malpractices followed by the moneylenders may be summarized as stated below[6] :

- Demand for an advance rent at the time of giving loan and deduct the total interest for the year from the principal but make the borrowers sign the bonds to the effect that the full amounts have been met.
- Claiming illegal deductions from the amount of loans given to cultivators. They may be for charity, temple, document writing and Girak Khulai i.e. for opening the purse.

- Obtaining bonds and promissory notes from their debtors on false pretences and insert in them sums larger than actually lent.
- Getting of thumb impressions on blank papers with the object of inserting arbitrary amount at a later date.
- Changing the records in register and maneuver the accounts.
- Taking conditional sale-deeds relating to borrowers' land or house as a sort of insurance against the possibility of failure to repay the principal.
- Charging exorbitant interest rates, which may be anything from 40 to 400 per cent a year and that too on a compound rate.
- Non-issue of receipts on payment of interest and principal.
- Advance contracts for tied sale of output only through the money lenders resulting in a sale price below the market price; and
- Having free services or normal pay from debtors, thus reducing borrowers to the status of serfs or semi-serfs.

As regards collecting dues from the unfortunate borrowers, moneylenders in rural areas have several controls in their possession[7]. With the socio-economic environment prevailing in the villages, it becomes easy for the local moneylenders to reinforce their octopus hold over the poor clients. Factors such as loss of face or caste disapproval or pressure on borrowers through panchayats exercise considerable formal and informal power. Several sociologists like Bailey, Gough, Berteille, etc., pointed out in their studies that the dominant upper class can exercise compelling measures against borrowers from so-called lower classes. In the words of A.Bottomley, "local moneylenders may even resort to violence when a farmer does not pay... Last, but far from least among the factors reinforcing the private moneylenders' position is the element of social coercion"[8]. These coercive measures are generally in the form of payment of fines to the temple funds operated by the high caste Brahmins and at the extreme, evictions of peasants from the lands traditionally cultivated by them. Thus the poor villagers are permanently trapped in the net of moneylenders because of the vicious circle of poverty in which their expenses exceed their income every year[9]. They have to keep borrowing from them for various purposes like production, consumption, religious ceremonies, etc. as the bulk of our peasants are at subsistence level with virtually no surplus[10], they have to obtain credit to buy seeds and fertilizers, to install pump set or dig a canal or to raise next crop, etc. The social ceremonies, traditions and cultural practices which prevail in rural areas also force the rural people to spend extravagantly on marriages, funeral rites, ornaments and so on. These expenses naturally end up in more debt to moneylender. Frequent occurrences of drought, flood cyclone, hailstorm, conflagration, locust and other devastating natural calamities compel a bulk of rural population to borrow. Moreover, the high interest rates charged by money lenders, the past debts and the litigations among the villagers contribute to the growth of indebtedness. In this way, the poor villagers will continue to be steeped in debt either because their economic activity is inherently non-viable or their working life has been overtaken by a series of personal misfortunes. The drag of debt burden, thus accumulated, saps the energy of the cultivators, affects adversely their efficiency and destroys innovative tendencies for improved methods of cultivation. It ultimately culminates in the loss of property and transfer of land from farmers to moneylenders and also results in servitude of the debtor to the money lenders.

Since the earliest times, State has taken measures, both positive and pervasive, to solve the problem of rural indebtedness. The pervasive measures are regulative in nature and legislative in action. In the first place, they include fixing the interest rates on legal terms, reducing the effective burden of land revenue, increasing irrigation facilities, increasing means of communication and transportation and marketing facilities, etc. Secondly, by passing several Land Alienation Acts, the Government attempted to protect the assets of the farmers from passing into the hands of the moneylenders. Thirdly legislative action has been taken in many states in India in order to restrict and regulate the activities of moneylenders. The regulation has taken place in three forms: (i) Reduction of debts through conciliation, (ii) Compulsory scaling down of debts and (iii) Regulation of money lender's business by checking down their accounts, licences, etc. As a result of all these legislative and regulatory measures, though the money lenders have lost some of their stronghold in the rural areas, they are still able to carry out unscrupulous activities due to the extreme neediness of the peasants. It was, thus realized that no control over moneylenders would be successful unless a strong institutional agency is organized to fulfill the financial needs of the cultivators with the same efficiency. So, the Government had adopted positive measures side by side by setting up various institutional organizations to provide the credit needs of the rural areas. It was against this background that cooperatives and other institutional agencies made their appearance on the rural credit scene.

The Cooperative Movement

The idea of using co-operation in India as a means of combating rural indebtedness and as an instrument for alleviating the suffering of the rural masses by supplying credit was first suggested by Sir Frederick Nicholson in 1897. Before this, Taccavi loans were the only main channel of credit for rural development. These loans were, however, unpopular, as they were granted only for specified purposes. There was also a great deal of rigidity in the mode of collection, endless delays due to red-tapism in distribution and vexatious exactions by petty official underlings. With its rapid implementation of rules and regulations and indifferent attitude of the bureaucracy, the loans proved a total failure[11].

Under the circumstances, the Government used the cooperatives as the most effective method of uplifting and modernizing the rural poor by providing adequate credit facilities with cheaper interest rates. The Cooperative Societies Act of 1904 gave[12] an impetus to the formation of agricultural credit cooperatives. The Act of 1912 made an attempt of extending the cooperative organisation to non-agricultural credit as well. The Maclegan Committee of 1915, thoroughly examined the developments in the sphere of cooperation and provided the organizational foundation by advising the three-tier structure of cooperative credit. The All-India Rural Credit Survey Committee (1952) recommended an integrated credit scheme with state partnership for the formulation of comprehensive multipurpose cooperatives having the objective of linking the production with marketing of inputs and outputs, processing and warehousing activities. It has been formulated for the benefit of the rural producer, in a programme for the organisation on a cooperative basis of such other economic activities as are of important to him as cultivator, agricultural labourer or handicraftsman.

Thus the cooperative movement in India was introduced as a State Policy. Apart from progress in building up the structure, cooperatives were strengthened during the successive five year plans through Government share capital contribution and other financial assistance such as managerial subsidies, risk fund contributions, grants-in-aid-cum-loans for augmenting stabilization funds, term loans for maintenance of NODC, etc. Further, an interesting change in the functioning of the cooperative credit system was brought about with the introduction of the "crop loan system".[13] Under which quantum of credit to be provided is determined with reference to the production cost and disbursement of credit is made as far as possible in 'kind' and thereby linking it with marketing and processing. Another important innovation in the cooperative credit structure is that of stabilization arrangements which envisages conversion of dues under short-term production loans into medium-term loans and medium-term loans into long-term. This will be allowed whenever natural calamities like floods, droughts, pests, etc., result in failure of crops, impairing the repaying capacity of borrowers. Under the circumstances, fresh production finance for the next crop is also made eligible, besides postponing the recovery of dues.

Types of Cooperatives

The cooperative credit structure in India mainly consists of three types[14] (i) short and medium term agricultural credit societies, (ii) long-term agricultural credit societies, and (iii) non-agricultural credit societies. The short and medium term credit structure is federal in character based on three-tier pattern with the apex banks or the State Cooperative Banks (SCBs) at the State level, the District Central Cooperative Banks (DCCBS) at the district level and the Primary Agricultural Credit Societies (PACS) at the village level. There will be general affiliation between SCBS and DCCBS on the one hand and between DCCBs and PACS on the other. It is revealed that generally the apex banks depend upon the RBI and the NABARD and the State Governments for their funds which they loan out to DCCBS and they in turn to PACS. These institutions constitute an effective machinery functioning as balancing centres within the movement and supplementing the internal financial resources by borrowing outside. Here again the PACS form the basis of the financial structure and are considered "the kernel" of the cooperative movement itself.[15] This unit epitomizes the vitality and service potential of the cooperation and links the farmer in the remote village with the money market of the country. It is the most ideal agency suited to institutionalize provision of credit and inputs for agricultural development as well as the real competitors of the moneylenders. Apart from getting loans from DCCBs, the PACS may raise their own funds to lend directly to member cultivators. The very essence of the system lies in the collective responsibility and vigilance of the member borrowers. Thus, the PACS are the ultimate links in the flow of organized funds to the cultivators.

In order to provide long-term credit, a separate structure consisting of State Land Development Banks (SLDBS) as the apex institutions at the State level and Primary Land Development Banks (PLDBS) or branches of SLDBS at the Taluk / Block level has been built up. The PLDBS like the PACS are field level cooperative institutions which provide credit to individual borrowers. There are also non-agricultural cooperative credit societies mainly catering to the needs of artisans and small industrialists.

In pursuance of the recommendations made by National Commission on Agriculture,[16] a number of Farmers Service Societies (FSSs) are functioning at the base level as a new cooperative society from the year 1971. These societies are expected to provide not only short and medium loan requirements of the farmers but also to undertake the supply of inputs, custom and repair services, marketing of produce, sale of consumer goods, etc. There are also large sized multipurpose societies (LAMPS) working as a special type of institutions at the grass root level to take care of the needs of weaker sections.

Progress and Performance of Cooperative Banks

Credit cooperatives have registered significant progress since the implementation of the 'integrated credit scheme' suggested by the Committee of Direction of the Rural Credit Survey. Recently, at the end of June 1984, the broad network of the three-tier cooperative structure catering to the rural credit needs consisted of 28 State Cooperative Banks with 474 branches, 349 central cooperative banks with 8,396 branches and 92,000 Primary Agricultural Credit Societies with a membership of 67 million membership stood at 23 million constituting 37.7 per cent of the total membership. There were also 19 State/Central Land Development Banks and 873 Primary Land Development Banks. Further details of the progress of cooperative credit movement between 1975-76 and 1983-84 are shown in Table.1.

Table–1 reveals that cooperative banks achieved significant progress between the period 1975-76 and 1983-84. The loans issued by the State Cooperative Banks had gone up from Rs. 1,515 crores in 1975-76 to Rs. 4,444 crores in 1983-84 registering a growth of 193 per cent. During the same period, the loans outstanding increased from Rs. 894 crores to Rs. 2,916 crores or by 226 per cent and the loans overdue from Rs. 44 crores to Rs. 178 crores or by 304 per cent.

Table 1
Progress of Co-operative Credit Movement in India
(Cooperative Year) (July-June)

(Amount in Crores of Rupees)

Co-operative Institutions	*1975-76*	*1983-84*
State Cooperative Banks		
Number (Actuals)	26	28
Loans issued	1,515	4,444
Loans outstanding	894	2,916
Loans overdue	44	178
Central Cooperative Banks		
Number (Actuals)	344	349
Loans issued	1,722	5,110
Loans outstanding	1,428	4,707
Loans overdue	460	1,567
Primary Agricultural Credit Societies		
Number (000's)	139	92
Membership (000's)	39,521	66,669
Total loans issued	1,024	2,499
Total loans outstanding	1,302	3,498
Loans overdue	562	1,238*
State/Central Land Development Banks		
Number (Actuals)	19	19
Loans issued	205	439
Loans outstanding	1,069	2,236
Loans overdue	64	283**
Primary Land Development Banks		
Number (Actuals)	890	873
Loans issued	26,22,347	N.A
Loans outstanding	136	N.A
Loans overdue	576	N.A

* Taken as short-term loans
** Includes interest overdue

Source:
1. RBI : Progress of Co-operative credit Societies in India, 1977-78, pp. 3-4.
2. RBI: Annual Report on Trend and Progress of Banking in India, 1979-80 and 1984-85 issues.

The loans issued by the Central Cooperative Banks, at the same time, went up from Rs. 1,722 crores to Rs. 5,110 crores or by 197 per cent while loans outstanding from Rs. 1,428 crores to Rs. 4,707 crores or by 230 per cent and loans overdue from Rs. 460 crores to Rs. 1,567 crores or by 241 per cent.

In the case of Primary Agricultural Credit Societies, loans advanced has increased from Rs. 1,024 crores to Rs. 2,499 crores or by 144 per cent and loans outstanding from Rs. 1,302 crores to Rs. 3,498 crores or by 169 per cent during the same period.

As for the State/Central Land Development Banks, loans issued, outstanding and overdues increased by 114 per cent, 109 per cent and 342 per cent respectively.

Table-2 and Table-3 give us the information regarding the share of different institutions in institutional finance for agriculture.

Table 2
Percentage Share of Different Institutions in Institutional Finance for Agriculture

Type of Loan / Lending Institutions	*1975*	*1979*	*1985*
Short-term Loans			
Cooperatives	84.9	70.6	95.5
Commercial banks*	9.8	29.4	N.A
Government	5.2	N.A	4.5
Term-Loans			
Cooperatives	58.4	43.8	82.5
Commercial Banks	25.9	40.3	N.A
Rural Electrification Corporation Ltd.	15.7	15.9	17.5

* Includes RRBs for the year 1979 and 1985
N.A Not Available
Source:
1. Agricultural Finance Corporation : A Study of Regional Rural Banks, Bombay, 1981, p.24.
2. RBI: Report on Currency and Finance, 1984-85, Economic Review, Vol. I, pp.210-11.

It is visible from Table-2 that the percentage share of cooperatives in institutional finance for agriculture was 84.9 per cent as per short-term loan and 58.4 per cent for long-term loans in the year 1975. These shares were gone down considerably during the year 1979 as to 70.6 per cent and 43.8 per cent respectively. Comparatively the share of commercial banks for short-term and long-term loans were gone up from 9.8 per cent and 25.9 per cent to 29.4 per cent and 40.3 per cent during the same period. As for the year 1985, the share of cooperatives appear to be higher as the information about

Table 3
Institutional Finance for Agriculture

(Amount in Crores of Rupees)

Direct/Indirect Loan	*Loans Outstanding at the End of June*	
	1975	1985*
Direct Finance		
Short-term Loans		
PACS (Primary Agricultural Credit Societies) (105.0)	903.7	2750.0E
State Government Department Loans	N.A	N.A
Scheduled Commercial Banks	246.2	N.A
Regional Rural Banks	N.A	673.0
Total Short-term Loans (I)	1149.9	3423.0
Medium and Long-term Loans		
PACS (Primary Agricultural Credit Societies)	272.9	3544.0
Land Development Banks	983.5	2477.0
Scheduled Commercial Banks	317.4	6161.7**
Total Medium & Long -term Loans (II)	1573.7	12182.7
Total Direct Finance (I+II)	2723.6	15605.7
Indirect Finance		
Short-term Loans		
State Cooperative Banks	176.7	1250.0
Central Cooperative Banks	118.4	945.0
Scheduled Commercial Banks	98.4	N.A
Regional Rural Banks	-	32.0
Total Short-term Loans (I)	393.5	2227.0
Medium-term Loans		
Scheduled Commercial Banks	181.2	N.A
Rural Electrification Corporation Ltd.	240.7	1674.5
Total Medium-term Loans (II)	421.9	1674.5
Total Indirect Finance (I+II)	815.4	3901.5

*As on March 31, 1985

RE - Revised Estimates
R - Revised
NA - Not Available
E - Estimates
** Data relating to public sector relate to short-term finance provided by RRBs and other commercial banks through PACS.

Source: RBI: Report on Currency and Finance Economic Review, Vol.I, 1974-75, p.149 and 1984-85, p.211.

commercial banks is not available. The shares of Government and Rural Electrification Corporation on all years proved to be in significant.

A further division of outstanding loans of different institutions for agriculture into direct and indirect channels are shown in Table. 3. Accordingly between 1975 and 1985, the institutional finance for agriculture from all sources, including cooperatives has been increasing.

Furthermore, cooperatives are expected to extend[17] Rs. 5540 crores, Rs.500 crores and Rs. 1030 crores respectively as for the short-term, medium-term and long-term loans by the end of the Seventh Plan.

On the whole there was not only a general expansicn of the credit movement but also an increase in the proportion of borrowings from the cooperatives. Thanks to the policy of State partnership in the share capital and the process of amalgamation of a number of weak Central cooperative banks, many of the cooperative financing banks are stronger today. The cooperative Movement in India thus has made tremendous progress covering more than 95 per cent of the villages numbering 5.80 lakhs and brining with in its fold nearly 50 per cent of the country's population and 47 per cent of the rural population. It also provides more than 40 per cent production credit and 50 per cent of investment credit to weaker sections with built up vertical and horizontal connections and integration, thus coordinating varieties of agricultural activities and operations and planning improvements in operational efficiency of personnel, etc. In spite of all this remarkable progress, monopoly of agricultural finance by cooperatives proved to be a mixed blessing. While the objective of institutionalization of rural credit and reducing the hold of non-institutional credit agencies was party fulfilled, some grime evils also crept in, proving the limitations of cooperatives to meet the challenges posted by the rural sector in the field of finance.

Weaknesses of Cooperative Bank

The performance of cooperatives in India is often considered inelastic, dilatory and inadequate largely owing to the unchallenged influence of privileged few and they were said to have failed in gaining the confidence of rural masses. As a result, they could neither mobilize savings in villages, nor could they inculcate the banking habit among the rural folk. Further, they were unable to meet the increased credit needs of the rural sector which were augmented in the wake of Green Revolution. The main weaknesses of cooperatives are as follows.[18]

(i) Even after a lapse of eight decades, the coverage of villages through active societies (PACS) is not cent per cent and there has been considerable regional imbalances and disparities in the overall progress of cooperatives. They vary rather widely from State to State. The total loans disbursed by cooperatives during 1981-82 were Rs. 195 crores in Punjab and Rs. 199 crores in Kerala. At the same time loan disbursement in comparatively biger States was relatively meager – Rs. 25 crores in Bihar, Rs. 95 crores in Rajasthan and Rs. 77 crores in Tamilnadu. The disbursement of loans in North-Eastern States like Assam, Tripura, Nagaland, Meghalaya, Manipur and Arunachal Pradesh is very small. Thus, the cooperative credit movement is weak in Northern and Eastern States but it is strong in Western and Southern States.

(ii) Many of cooperative societies in the villages are either dormant or working inefficiently. In 1976, the All-India average figure of dormant PACS out of all PACS constituted 8.6 per cent. In later years it has gone up to 15 per cent. This percentage is as high as 60 in Assam and as low as 22 in Orissa. The financial weakness of many societies led to their poor absorptive capacity and much of the financial assistance from Central agencies could not have been disbursed by PACS which in turn limited the scope for augmenting the share capital and reserves of the society. Ultimately the number of PACS themselves has declined from 2.12 lakhs in 1960-61 to 92 thousands by the end of June 1984.

(iii) The problem of loan administration and the ability to delay reflected in the rising proportion of overdues. The outstanding dues in respect of short-term and medium-term loans stood at 45 per cent and 37 per cent in 1975-76.[19] In spite of statistical confirmation that loans were advanced for productive purpose alone, the cooperative fact of overdues confirms the fear that it is quite possible that some part of the money was diverted for unproductive purposes.

(iv) Another disappointing aspect is that though the working capital of the PACS had increased from Rs. 547 crores in 1965-66 to Rs.2920 crores in 1978-79, the major part has not come out of deposit mobilization by PACS, but by borrowing from DCCBS which in turn from the apex banks. It is extremely disheartening that public deposits should constitute only a minor fraction of working funds of PACs, which means a major failure of the societies, who were supposed to promote thrift among members and mobilize deposits for mutual help of the members.

(v) The cooperatives, particularly PACS have suffered from incompetent, ignorant and non-performing management.[20] Their incapacity to mobilize local resources has compelled them to rely on external aid and assistance all along, while lack of a sense of business management and administrative inefficiency led to insolvency of many cooperatives and to their poor recovery performance. Dates of repayments as fixed by them created inconveniences for the cultivators. Cases of book adjustments of old loans through renewals which overstated the amount of repayment were frequent. Lack of organisation in their credit structure was also responsible for the fragmented approach of cooperatives towards finding solutions to rural problems and in many cases coordination was lacking between PACS and DCCBS and also between credit and non-credit societies.

(vi) A great deal of favouritism and nepotism as well as communalism are involved in granting of loans. As a result, diversion and misuse of loans are common among the borrowers particularly in the States of Rajasthan, Orissa, Kerala, Bengal, Tamilnadu, Punjab and Uttar Pradesh. Nearly 28 per cent of the cooperative credit was diverted to purposes other than those for which it was given in 1979.[21] Further, financing of commercial crops was more favoured having a frown on consumption credit.

(vii) The inefficiency and high-handedness of the managing committees turned the cooperatives into the closed shops of the affluent sections by paying only lip-service to the poor and socially oppressed communities. A substantial amount of credit is disbursed mainly to the same members, year after year, with very few new entrants enjoying these facilities. Small and marginal farmers are conspicuous non-beneficiaries and there is a distinct gap as far as the non-cultivator sections are concerned. The very fact that the RBI has compelled not so long as to suggest that the cooperatives should aim at providing at least 20 per cent of their total credit for this class of farmers shows the relative neglect of their needs. The statistical picture supports this view. At the end of 1984, though PACS were supposed to cover 95 per cent of villages the proportion of borrowing membership to total membership was only 33.7 per cent, which has steadily declined from 51 per cent in 1961-62.

(viii) The cooperative societies have become a powerful tool in the hands of politicians[22] who are using the vast funds available at concessional rates for securing their political ends. This harmful development in rural financing since 1969 has disturbed economic balance in the rural economy making it extremely advantageous for big farmers. By virtue of their wealth and influence in the village they resort to exploitative productive operations such as manipulating lending accounts, charging exhorbitant interest rates etc. Thus the cooperatives have become no better than the money lending system.

(ix) Both SCBS and CCBS have also failed in mobilising urban savings to any significant extent and their contributions were limited in certain States. For example, the CCBS were able to mob1lise two-thirds of their deposits in four States namely, Maharashtra, Gujarat, Punjab and Uttar Pradesh. The chief reason[23] for this none-too encouraging performance of SEBS and CCBS is that they have to compete with relatively efficient and financially better off commercial banks.

(x) The performance of LDBS was often considered to be ineffective on account of the delay involved and technical staff to be maintained in assessing the value of land and examining its title deeds. Further, the policies and procedures followed by these banks hardly benefitted the small and medium farmers.

(xi) The revitalised cooperative structure i.e. the FSS are also unable to provide the desired integration between credit and marketing to the desired extent and their performance is low.

(xii) A study of cooperative legislation from 1904 up to recent legislation reveals a gradual increase of State patronage and interference in the movement. Such cases of Government interference at the cost of the rest of the community have been called into question by some writers and got tremendous opposition from landlords and private traders. Again, there was a fear, in the anxiety to fulfill the quantitative targets, the cooperative movement was emerging as an important inflationary agent. Thus the process of the movement increasingly based upon extent of fresh injection year by year of funds from RBI, leaned heavily on official and bureaucratic support and sponsorship and miserably failed in replacing the moneylender.

It was against this background that commercial banks have entered in the field of rural finance.

In 1950-51 commercial banking in India was almost a non-entity in the Rural Credit scene. It was always viewed an urban-based industry which grew in isolation with the rural economy.[24] The commercial banks were started and developed by the big industrialists and business men whose activities were concentrated mainly in the metropolitan cities and port towns. Hence, the villages and rural interiors of the country were left neglected. The inadequate guarantee and security in farm advances and the uncertainty about the return of principal and interest led to the poor performance of commercial banks in this field.

The Green Revolution, which had provided a breakthrough in agricultural production, has, however, changed the whole perspective of rural banking. There was and is a rising demand for modern input whim include irrigation facilities and mechanised farming operations. It was felt then that cooperatives by themselves alone would not be in a position to commensurate all the credit requirements of an expanding agricultural sector. It was feared by many that agricultural growth in our country may be hampered by the inadequacies and weaknesses of the cooperative credit structure. Figuratively, the All-India Rural Credit Review Committee (1969) estimated[25] that about a sum of Rs. 4,000 crores would b required for meeting the short-term and long-term credit needs of agriculture during the Fourth Plan period. As the cooperative movement with its inherent limitations was expected to provide about Rs.750 crores by way of short-term credit and the like amount by way of medium and long-term credit by 1973-74. This would leave a large portion of credit demand to be met by other agencies including moneylenders. It was against this historical setting that the "Multi-Agency Approach" to agricultural finance has been considered and the entry of commercial banks in the sphere of rural areas has been accepted by the Government. In this gigantic function, the public sector banks were directed by the RBI not merely to fulfil the credit gap, but also to assist the weaker sections of the community in a big way.

The Rural Orientation Process

Initial efforts to make commercial banks in India to provide rural credit may be traced back to the nationalisation of Imperial Bank of India.[26] In 1956, the State Bank of India had already begun in the direction of provision of finance for agriculture indirectly via introduced 1n 1968 by monetary authorities, very little amount has been lent by the commercial banks to the agricultural sector less than 2 per cent of total bank credit and the failure of modern banking to penetrate into rural areas remained a persistent problem.

The nationalization of 14 major banks in 1969[27] marked several tall promises and has been widely applauded to be a far reaching measure aimed at carrying banking message to the door steps of rural masses. It has become a potent weapon in the hands of the Government which decided that the resources of the public sector banks should supplement those of the cooperative banks in the supply of farm credit. This was sought to be attained through large and rapid expansion of bank offices, particularly in the rural and semi-urban areas, vigorous mobilisation of deposits and larger deployment of credit to the hither to neglected sectors of the economy-agriculture, small industry, retail trade and small business, professional and self-employed, etc. In addition, major commercial banks were asked to direct their efforts to evolve a three dimensional strategy-area based, occupation based and weaker sections oriented. Through financial assistance, the banks were expected to involve largely in the economic life of the Villages and help in the regeneration of the rural economy. Though these unconventional tasks did result in additional burden on the banking industry, yet they shouldered these responsibilities with exemplary adaptability. The progress made by commercial banks in India since nationalisation in their operations is detailed in Table-4.

It can be observed from Table-4 that the total branches of commercial banks have grown from 8,262 in June 1969 to 41,182 in March 1983. Centre-wise, the number of rural branches went up from 1,832 to 21,932, semi-urban branches from 3,322 to

Table 4
Centre-wise Distribution of Branches, Deposits and Credit of Scheduled Commercial Banks

(Amount in Crores of Rupees)

	June 1969			*March 1983*		
	Branches	*Deposits*	*Credit*	*Branches*	*Deposits*	*Credit*
Rural	1,832(22.2)	145(3.1)	54(1.5)	21,932(53.3)	4,599(12.4)	2,629(10.6)
Semi Urban	3,322(40.2)	1,024(22.0)	407(11.3)	8,969(21.8)	8,598(23.2)	4,207(17.0)
Urban	1,447(17.5)	1,209(25.9)	722(20.0)	5,535(13.4)	9,186(24.8)	5,486(22.2)
Metropolitan	1,661(20.1)	2,287(49.0)	2,426(67.2)	4,746(11.5)	14,612(39.5)	12,415(50.2)
Total	8,262(100.0)	4,665(100.0)	3,609(100.0)	41,182(100.0)	36,995(100.0)	24,737(100.0)

Source: RBI : Report on currency and Finance, Economic Review, Vol. I, 1976-77 and 1982-83 Issues

8,869, urban branches from 1,447 to 5,535 and metropolitan branches from 1,661 to 4,746 during the same period. However, it is to be noticed that even though the aggregate number of branches at all centres have gone up, the share of branches to total have grown only in rural centres but not in other centres. Thus while the share of rural branches to total branches increased from 22.2 per cent in 1969 to 53.2 per cent in 1983, the share of semi-urban, urban and metropolitan offices decreased from 40.2 per cent to 21.8 per cent, 17.5 per cent to 13.4 per cent and 20.1 per cent to 11.5 per cent during the same period. This illustration shows the efforts of commercial banks[28] in strengthening their branch network in rural hinterland.

The strengthening of branch network along with improvement in the old branches (i.e. the branches that were in existence in June 1969) and the introduction of attractive deposit schemes and liberal lending rates tailored to the need of every section of population yielded results in terms of increase both in deposits and advances. The aggregate deposits of commercial banks thus increased from Rs.4,665 crores in 1969 to Rs.36,995 crores in 1983, showing an increase of 8 times while total credit of the banking industry went up from Rs.3,609 crores in 1969 to 24,737 crores in 1983, with an increase of 7 times. The point noteworthy here is, although 'the rural and semi-urban centres show the lowest percentage shares in total deposits and advances in comparison to the share of urban and metropolitan ones the overall trend of deposit and advances remained increasing in the former than the later case. Thus, the percentage of deposits of rural areas to the total went up from 3.1 per cent in 1969 to 12.4 per cent in 1983 or by 32 times and the advances from 1.5 per cent to 10.6 per cent or by 49 times. This trend shows the liberal credit expansion of commercial banks in backward rural centres and its ability in popularizing banking habit among the rural folk.

Another important achievement of nationalization has been reflected in the flow of credit to the priority sectors which comprised a large number of agriculturists, small scale industrialists, road and water operators, retail traders, small businessmen, professional/self employed persons and other small borrowers. The progressive increase in credit deployment to the priority sectors of the economy between the period 1969 and 1985 could be seen from Table-5

Table 5
Advances by Public Sector Banks to Agriculture and Other Priority Sectors

(Accounts in '000) (Amount in Rs. Crores)

	June 1969		September 1985	
	Account	Amount	Account	Amount
Agriculture	164	162.33(5.4)	15176	8174.30(18.2)
a) Direct	160	40.21(1.3)	14168	6799.35(15.1)
b) Indirect	4	122.12(4.1)	1008	1374.95(3.1)
Small Scale Industries	51	251.07(8.3)	1488	6803.24(15.1)
Others	45	27.57(0.9)	6263	4230.66(15.1)
Total advances to priority sector	260	440.97(14.6)	22927	19208.65(42.7)
Total advances	N.A.	3016.76(100.0)	N.A	44983.65(100.0)

Figures in brackets indicate percent to total credit.
N.A. : Not Available
Source : Varshaneya, J.S. "Bank Nationalisation and After", Yojana, Vol. 30, No. 13, July 16-31, 1986, p.6.

Table-5 illustrates that credit to priority sectors by the banking system rose from Rs.441 crores in June 1969 to Rs.19,208 crores in September 1985 and loan to total credit, the priority sector credit increased from 14.0 per cent to 42.7 per cent during the same period. Among priority sector advances, agriculture get the major share. Between the period 1969 and 1985, its percentage share has gone up from 5.4 per cent to 18.3 per cent. Small scale industries share increased from 8.3 per cent to 15.1 per cent and the share of others from 0.9 per cent to 9.4 per cent.

Further, commercial banks are expected to extend[29] agricultural credit to the tune of Rs.2,500 crores as for short-term loans and Rs. 3,000 crores as for medium-term loans by the end of Seventh Plan.

Furthermore, in order to meet the varied objectives of nationalisation, the commercial banks made a dynamic endeavour to formulate and introduce various innovative and novel credit schemes aimed at developing the necessary infrastructure coupled with reorientation of approach to lending from asset base to project base. Firstly, the "Lead Bank Scheme" was introduced in 1969 to demarcate the responsibilities of individual banks in developing banking infrastructure and providing financial facilities.[30] Accordingly, all districts excluding the metropolitan cities were allotted to different banks. Each of these banks was expected to play a lead role or as a consortium of banks and other financial institutions of its area in promoting the development schemes in coordination with various agencies of Central and State Governments. Secondly, under area approach, the State Bank of India had set up "Agricultural Development Branches", to finance exclusively the farmers. These branches were to be located after taking careful survey of the area and assessing the potential credit absorption capacity in consultation with State Governments. By the end of 1974, there were 177 branches of such type. The "Village Adoption Scheme (VAS)" which constitutes another important programme of area approach, envisages[31] the adoption of cluster of villages within a manageable distance by branches to prepare and implement schemes for meeting the credit requirements of all sections of community, after making a detailed survey of the resource potential available at the end of June 1983 commercial banks had adopted 1,41,042 villages and financed 5 million agricultural loan accounts involving a total amount of Rs.1557 crores. Thirdly, with a view to filling the credit gaps that existed in the areas of some of financially and administratively weak DCCBS, a scheme for financing of Primary Agricultural Credit Societies was formulated by the RBI in 1970.[32] Accordingly, by the end of December 1974, 360 branches of 21 commercial banks had taken over 2,693 primary societies. In addition, the banks were asked to set up Farmers Service Societies where the cooperative lobby did not object to their entry. Fourthly, with a view to assist the weakest among the weak the Scheme of "Differential Interest Rate (DIR)- was introduced 1n 1972[33] banks at a concessional rate of interest of 4 per cent per annum for starting any income generating viable project. The eligibility criteria for credit under the scheme stipulates that annual income of a person from all sources should not exceed Rs.2,000 in rural areas and Rs.3,000 in other areas. Of the total bank credit, the allotment of the scheme was 1 per cent between 1972 and 1985 the number of loan accounts under the scheme rose from 0.26 lakhs to 42.96 lakhs and loans outstanding from Rs.87.3 lakhs to Rs.465.72 crores. In addition~all these schemes, commercial banks have also been participating actively in financing various poverty eradication programmes.

In spite of several innovations brought in the field of rural financing by commercial banks, the policy makers, both at the Central Government as well as the RBI levels, at the time of bank nationalisation decided that the commercial banks should only supplement the efforts of cooperative credit institutions, and even assist them in the matter of meeting the credit needs of rural population. No doubt, the commercial banks have performed this function admirably" But this was only one-sided development considering the existence of credit gaps which are still persisting in rural areas. If we look at the system as a whole the working of commercial banks is not quite rural in attitude and temperament and they suffer from a number of weaknesses.

Inherent limitations of Commercial Banks

The entry of commercial banks in the field of rural finance has created more problems instead of fulfilling the objective for which they were brought in the field, namely supplementing rural credit which was felt inadequate. Some of the important problems experienced by commercial banks are as follows:

- Despite the fact that commercial banks have gone in a big way to cover rural areas, certain criticisms have been put forth regarding their rural branch expansion policy such as[34]
  - The banks appeared to be more concerned with fulfilling physical targets assigned, which they did by opening large number of branches in the final quarter of every calendar year with a view to avoid lapses.
  - There was an inflation of rural branch banks in view of classifying the branches opened in semi-urban areas as rural branches.

- Although almost all the blocks in the country have been covered under branch expansion programme average population per bank office in several backward States like Bihar, Orissa, Assam, etc., has been much higher than the national average.
- Most of the new bank offices have been located near sub-divisional or district towns and not in interior rural areas.[35]
- The rapid branch expansion in non-traditional areas has effected the earning capacity of the banking system and also increased its operational costs.

• Although direct finance to agriculture increased significantly during the period 1969-75, only six States namely Andhra Pradesh, Gujarat, Maharastra, Tamil Nadu, Karnataka and West Bengal shared 60 per cent of public sector bank credit for agriculture. The eastern and north-eastern regions, where the cooperative structure is precisely weak, received only 10 per cent of aggregate credit. This indicates that the process of imbalances surrounding a few islands of prosperities have been left untouched.

• The credit portfolio of commercial banks reveals its class nature and step-motherly treatment towards rural areas. It is obvious from the fact that in 1980, while the share of rural deposits of banks had been 12.5 per cent, the share of rural credit was only 10.6 per cent, which was a clear indication of rural exploitation. The C-D ratio for rural branches (56.9 per cent) was below the national average (66.9 per cent) indicating the thereby the commercial banks have used rural branches as 'deposit centres' rather than for the deployment of resources in rural areas.

• Lack of sufficient deposits from rural areas was another problem faced by commercial banks. For instance,[36] the total deposits of the banks were

Rs.13,111 crores in 1975. Of them, 69 per cent account for urban and metropolitan centres, which had a share of 338.8 per cent of total bank offices, while the rural and semi-urban centres account for just 31 per cent, even though they had a share of 66.2 per cent of total branches. Accordingly, deposits per office in rural areas worked out to mere Rs.32 lakhs whereas in urban centres it was Rs.139 lakhs i.e., four times as larger deposits s a rural branch. Therefore, it is unprofitable exercise for a commercial bank to penetrate into rural areas to remain non-viable for a long time.

- The rural branches of commercial banks are generally starved of requisite staff which has come in the way of building up necessary business potential.[37] Because of their urban culture, show piece ethos. managerial hierarchy and the consequent high cost structure, the banks were not proving the appropriate agencies for large distance rural financing through a scattered network of rural branches. They appeared to be strangers on the rural scene because of their highly paid officials and lack of necessary local knowledge and contacts. Their methods and approach to the rural needs and problems of credit have generally remained unsuited 1n the context of typical socio-economic environment prevailing in these areas. Thus, the security-oriented commercial banks have found wedded as they are, to present problems and systems, that surviving rural business is expensive and many rural branches uneconomic.
- The commercial banks seem to be disregarding the relatively small borrowers in rural areas and concentrating on the well-to-do farmers. The class structure with feudal set up and capitalist sway which were one of the reasons for the failure of cooperatives also come in the working of commercial banks. The more affluent farmer with his political leverage and high credit rating, enjoy easier access to bank credit.

And the beneficiaries of the lending by commercial banks were mostly the plantation estate owners and big commercial farmers.[38] For example at the and of 1978 out of total credit purveyed by commercial banks, the share of big landlord of above 10 acre each constituted 60.8 per cent, whereas the small farmers with land holdings of below 2.5 acres each could get only 9.4 per cent. Again this inadequate portion of credit was subjected to numerous instances of benami transactions.

Apart from agriculture, the small scale industry has also been bereaved of its due share from commercial banks. Much of their allotted amounts had been kept away in favour of big borrowers.

- The innovative schemes introduced by commercial banks for the regeneration of the village economy were not much successful. In spite of its bright record of absolute figures, the village adoption scheme was unable to reach the goal of assisting the cultivator with small incomes and also failed in achieving the objective of all-round development of the adopted village.[39] The agricultural development branches set up by the State Bank of India, on the other hand erred on high operational costs, while the performance of societies took over by the commercial banks through effectively linkage was no better as compared to operative financed by cooperative banks. There Seems to be an entanglement and reservation in the dealings between both the sides namely, the commercial banks and the primaries ceded to them.
- Among the branches of commercial banks coordination was found to be lacking, resulting in overlapping and duplication of finance and hence financial indiscipline both on the part of the lenders and borrowers alike. Besides the cooperative banks not only resented the competition from commercial banks but also the scheme to resuscitate and strengthen PACS through

their adoption of villages. Further, there is the general and strong apathy of the rural people to accept inventions and innovations. Communication gap, lack of safe vault and inconvenience of remittance funds are the other big hurdles in the working of the commercial banking system.

Institutional Credit Gap

The institutional credit gap estimated[40] by the All-India Rural Credit Survey Committee at Rs.4,000 crores could not be met by the existing credit infrastructure during the earlier seventies. Although cooperative institutions and commercial bank together pumped in about Rs.1,500 crores, a large credit gap between demand and supply still persisted to be bridged.

The Working Group on cooperation appointed by the Union Ministry of Agricultural and Irrigation for formulation of the Fifth Five Year Plan estimated the credit needs for seasonal agricultural operation of the country as a whole would be around Rs.3,000 crores and Rs.2,400 crores would be needed for meeting the medium and long-term credit requirements thus totaling to Rs.5,400 crores by 1978-79. It was contemplated that the volume of short-term credit to be advanced by cooperatives and commercial banks would be about Rs. 1,700 crores thereby leaving a credit gap of Rs. 1,300 crores to be met elsewhere.

Further, a detailed exercise undertaken by the National Commission on Agriculture (1976) revealed that by 1985, the short, medium and long-term credit needs of the marginal and small farmers would be of the order of Rs. 4,690 crores.

Still further, the All-India Debt and Investment Survey (1976) has estimated[41] the total liabilities of rural households with holdings less than 5 acre at Rs.1,910 crores. Out of this the institutional share accounted for roughly about a third at Rs.665 crores (such as cooperatives at Rs. 525 crores at Rs. 100 crores) and the non-institutional sources at about two thirds or Rs. 1,245 crores. Assuming that these liabilities have been incurred over a period of three years, the annual indebtedness would work out at Rs. 415 crores from non-institutional sources. Further assuming that about Rs. 103 crores or about 25 per cent was advanced towards non productive consumption expenditure of avoidable nature, the credit gap that was likely to be created as a result of credit flow from non-institutional sources would be about Rs. 312 crores a year.

In addition to all this, the Sivaraman Committee (Expert Committee on Consumption Credit) estimated[42] that the consumption credit gap of rural population as a result of village moneylenders at Rs. 295 crores - Rs. 170 crores of landless labourers and Rs. 125 crores for small farmers holding less than 5 acres of land.

After about five years of nationalization it was realized that commercial banks were also not in a position to meet the challenge of filling credit gaps and conveying banking facilities to the door step of every rural entrepreneur. Owing to this and the failure of other financial institutions in supplying credit sufficiently, the rural people have been and are still falling prey to unscrupulous moneylenders who lend money only at exhorbitant interest rates. The share of institutional credit, altogether, in the year 1975 was estimated[43] at somewhat over a third of rural credit requirements. The increasing credit gap assumed added significance then both in view of a quantitative rise in credit demand and more essentially in the light of demand that has accompanied in result of modernization of agriculture and the new technological induction which in turn necessitated provision for institutional credit. This need was felt by the Government of India to think in terms of providing a different institutional framework for meeting the credit needs of small farmers and the less privileged sections in rural areas. This was the rational for the emergence of Regional Rural Banks.

The Banking Commissions Proposal

The real beginning for setting up of rural banks was put forward by the Banking Commission in its report in 1972. The Banking Commission was appointed by the Government of India under the Chairmanship of R.G. Saraiya in February 1969 to enquire into the operational efficiency of the entire banking system in the country with particular reference to commercial banks. The terms of reference of the Commission included.[44] A comprehensive survey of the existing commercial banking structure and to make various recommendations for improving and modernizing its methods and procedures and also for extending its geographical and functional coverage, and secondly to revise the working of cooperative banks and to make suggestions with a view to ensuring a coordinated development of commercial and cooperative banks.

After investigating deeply into the prevailing credit system, the Banking Commission expressed serious doubts on the capabilities of commercial banks for giving adequate coverage to the rural sector in the foreseeable future. It observed, "In the total scheme for bridging the credit gaps in agricultural sector, the major difficulty is that the cooperative banking sector which has a wide organisation at the field level is unable to mobilise deposits. While the commercial banks which are able to mobilize deposits in a substantial manner, are unable to provide credit to agriculture owing to their lower coverage of rural sector and their lack of knowledge of problems of lending to this sector.[45] The Commission believed that, "In the large and complex situation in the field of rural credit in India, there will remain large gap even after the maximum possible branch expansion has been tried by commercial banks.[46] This gap was explained not only in quantitative terms for meeting the needs of rural credit but also for diffusing the banking habits among the rural folk. The Commission was of the opinion that in a country like India where diversities are around, any single type of financial institution would not be appropriate to meet the credit needs of rural people and therefore suggested that all possible alternatives should be tried. In this context, the Banking Commission has proposed the establishment of a chain of 'rural banks' in places where cooperative credit structure was not working well. Such banks, according to the Commission, could be created in one of the following three possible ways[47] (i) by converting viable primary agricultural societies into 'rural cooperative banks', (ii) by structuring a primary agricultural society as a subsidiary of a commercial bank, (iii) by formation of 'rural subsidiary bank' to be promoted by a commercial bank. Here the case for specially sponsored rural banks was based on the ground that cooperatives would not succeed in every region of the country, whereas opening of branches of commercial banks in rural areas has its own limitations.

The Banking Commission defined a rural bank as a primary banking institution established to serve a compact group of villages by performing banking and some non-banking functions with the objective of developing village areas. Some of the salient features[48] of the 'rural bank' as proposed by the Banking commission are as follows:

(a) An agency of rural bank should basically be a bank accepting deposits from public and giving credit to the farmers and other rural entrepreneurs. It should work as a public commercial bank without preferential or differential treatment to any person or group. The agency is to be given separate entity and status and the right to generate its own funds like any other institution.

(b) The specified jurisdiction of such bank serves a compact group of villages covering a population ranging from 5,000 to 20,000 and in sparsely populated area it could cover as big an area as a development block.

(c) Regardless of the organisational set up of Rural bank its minimum paid up capital should not be less than Rs.50,000/-. Where a Rural Bank is set up as a subsidiary of a commercial bank, its authorized capital should be Rs.1,00,000/- of which 50 per cent should be fully paid up and the balance by the people in the local area of operation serves a compact group of villages covering a population raging from 5,000 to 20,000 and in sparsely populated area it could cover as big an area as a development block.

(d) The banking and non-banking functions of the rural bank include, mobilizing savings by means of various deposit providing short-term and long-term loans to the farmers and other rural entrepreneurs, implementing programmes of supervised credit and giving ancillary banking services to local people maintaining godowns and warehouses: supplying agricultural inputs; assisting in marketing of farm products and giving general help in overall development of villages.

(e) On rural bank representation of the local people should be on the principle of one man - one vote. The sponsoring bank should control the voting power and nominate the majority of directors in the Board of that bank. Several other forms of controls on members are also suggested so that the shareholders, the borrowers and depositors would have tangible interests in the bank.

The pattern of rural banks discussed so far, however, called for imperative changes in the banking legislation both at the Centre and the State levels. Acknowledging the practical difficulties which would be met in starting such rural banks, the Commission laid down priorities for opening such banks and a phased plan for their expansion. It recommended particularly for a limited number of rural banks which would be subsidiaries of commercial banks during the first experimental phase of 5 years.

Establishment of Regional Rural Banks

No action was taken by the Government of India on the proposal put forward by the Banking Commission for installing a chain of rural banks. Any need for establishing such banks felt by policy makers in Government remained passive for three years. It was only in July 1975, when the Prime Minister of the country announced a package of economic measures called -The Twenty Point Economic Programme" that the idea of setting up of -rural banks came into reality.[49] The main theme of the programme was ameliorating the lot of the weaker sections of the rural society. Among many issues a renewed emphasis has been laid on the availability of credit for agricultural production under this programme. Point 5 of the programme related to this: "Plan for liquidation of rural indebtedness: legislative measures for moratorium on recovery of debts from landless labourers small or marginal farmers and rural artisans". It also included provision for alternative sources of credit and setting up of rural banks.

Accordingly, in July 1975 ordinances were issued in several States on the basis of guidelines from Central Government to enable the rural households with less than income of Rs.2,400 per year either to redeem their debt obligations or interest duties on advances through moratorium for specified periods. Also guidelines were delivered[50] appropriate action should he taken down to ensure that the debts of margin 1 farmers holding up to 2.5 acres of un-irrigated land should be taken as totally repaid and those of small farmer holding between 2.5 and 5 acres of such land should be scaled down for the same borrowers, the Government recommended a moratorium on the recovery of debts through courts for a period of one year. Further, it suggested that the debts of those holding irrigated lands should also be scaled down in particular state in question. In pursuance of these directives, several State Governments enacted legislation for complete liquidation of rural indebtedness which included moratorium, legislation and scaling down of debts from unorganized sources. The discrimination in giving relief was made on the basis of different categories of borrowers from the poorer sections of rural community such as small and marginal farmers, landless labourers, rural artisan and so on.

Further, in view of the debt relief legislation passed, it was expected that a dangerous vaccum would be created for meeting the credit needs of weaker sections as the traditional sources of credit were either dried up or would demand extortionately high interest rates on loans to cover the risk of non-payment within the purview of law. It was in this context that the Government of India strongly conceived the idea of setting up of rural banks as a part and follow-up action of the New Economic Programme. In pursuance of this view, it appointed on July 1, 1975, Working Group on Rural Banks under the Chairmanship of M. Narasimham 'to examine in depth the setting of new rural banks as subsidiaries of public sector bank to cater to the to the credit needs of rural people'. The Group submitted its report within a short period of one month, on June 30, 1975.

The Group in its report, identified various weaknesses of cooperative credit agencies and the commercial banks and felt that the existing in institutions, as they were structured would not be able to fill the regional and functional gap in the rural credit institutional system within a reasonable period of time, even with such adaptation, reorganization and restructuring as may be considered. It, therefore, saw an urgent need to try new experiment especially in the credit starved rural areas of the country.

In this connection, the Working Group felt that; "the field of rural credit is so vast and its problems are so varied and complex and the area of un satisfied demand so great at there is always scope for experimentation and innovation to try out new ideas, to fashion new instruments of policy and to evolve new institution for efficient and effective dispensation of credit. In a country of the size and regional diversity as ours no single pattern, be it commercial banking or cooperative credit, can be expected to meet all the emerging requirements in all areas".[51]

These observations drove the Working Group to envisage a new institution, rural banks, which combine the good features of both cooperative and commercial banks, namely, "The local feel and familiarity with rural problems which cooperatives possess and the degree of business organization, ability to mobilize deposits, access to central money markets and a modernized outlook which the commercial banks have".[52] The Working Group, thereby recommended for the establishment of rural banks on rural basis. While recommending the formation of Rural Banks the Group emphasized that, "the role of the new institutions would be to supplant and not supplement the other institutional agencies in the field".[53] In order to avoid overlapping with credit institutions which are working satisfactorily and over financing the same borrowers, the Group suggested to set up a few such banks in selected areas to serve on pilot basis.

Accordingly, the first five Regional Rural Banks were established by the Government of India on 2nd October, 1975 (The Gandhi Jayanthi Day), covering nine districts and being located in four States, at Mordabad and Gorakhpur in Uttar Pradesh, Bhiwani in Haryana, Jaipur in Rajasthan and Malda in West Bengal.

Conclusion

In India, rural credit is a two-fold problem of inadequacy and unsuitability that has long been continually faced by rural population, particularly the rural poor who can raise their incomes only when they have adequate access to credit and inputs. Since earlier times, the privates agencies, especially the village money lenders dominated the rural credit scene. The banking industry then was totally neglecting the rural areas as it considered loans to agriculture as highly risky and lack adequate security except land. The moneylenders used this opportunity by lending money on exorbitant interest rates and earned huge profits. With their strong socio-economic hold in villages, they used to resort to various malpractices at the time of advancing loans and coercive measures at the time of collection. The burden of indebtedness of this category has become heavier with lapse of time and rural debt more or less has come to be recognized as a misery or catastrophe.

But, ever since the historic All-India Rural Credit Survey Committee (1950-51) made important observations on rural credit scene and stressed the need for replacing moneylenders by an ideal rural credit system which ensures greater flow of institutional credit to the rural poor, significant changes took place in that sphere. The Government of India, thereafter, experimented several type of rural credit institutions and agricultural credit programmes at action level, having a significant positive bias towards weaker sections. The multiple credit requirements of rural sector could not for obvious reasons be met by any single institutional agency. A multi-agency approach has, therefore, been viewed as a better alternative, especially in the wake of Green Revolution and modernization of agriculture which started taking place remarkably since 1960's.

The cooperative movement had its beginning in the first decade of this century. The cooperative banks are ideally suited rural oriented financial institutions but not an organized ones. In modern times, they have received greater importance to finance the villages notably after the introduction of the 'integrated' credit scheme with State Partnership'. The main attributes of cooperatives are non-exploitative character, voluntary membership, democratic decentralization and self-imposed curbs on profit. As an instrument of development combining the advantages of private ownership and public good, they rendered useful services to the rural community and lessened the influence of moneylenders to some extent. In spite of them, the cooperatives failed to cope up with the credit requirements of rural population to the desired levels. The benefits of banks have gone to big farmers and the distribution was uneven–not much of it has flown to backward States. They revealed that their capacity to shoulder further responsibilities is rather minimal, especially in view of the shortage of their own funds and accumulating over dues.

Commercial banks entered the field of rural finance much later with the introduction of social controls in 1968. Following the nationalization of major commercial banks in July 1969, they have pursued their efforts in rural lending with vigorous enthusiasm. Massive branch expansion was launched with a thrust in rural areas and the share of rural offices in total offices have more than doubled. Credit to priority sectors has also gone up, significantly to agriculture. The introduction of schemes–lead bank, village Adoption, Differential Interest Rate and Financing of Cooperatives have resulted in an expanding role played by these banks in rural areas. However, in spite of remarkable success, the functioning of commercial banks marked high cost structure and lack of rural knowledge and bias. Besides, they used rural branches as 'deposit centres' and neglected the rural interiors and their population. With their urban-oriented staff they failed to develop a linkage with the rural culture.

At the end of June 1975, cooperative agencies and commercial banks together were deemed to have met about 40 per cent of the total farm credit and there was still a wide institutional credit gap of 60 per cent to be met. The cooperatives were clearly too weak to furnish an alternative source of credit. The rural branches of commercial banks were too restricted to fill up the credit gap effectively in time. Thus, taking into consideration the increasing credit gap in rural areas and the virtual neglect of the weaker sections of rural society by the existing financial infrastructure, the Government of India seriously contemplated to devise a new alternative source of finance. It was, therefore, decided to establish 'rural banks' as a new institution which combines the best features of both cooperative and commercial banks and avoid their weaknesses. Besides, the rationale for new rural banks was also emerged by considerations of lowering the cost of rural banking and operating such banks with local staff in an environment which the rural poor would find most homely.

The process for formation of rural banks was first inspired with the proposal of the Banking Commission in its report in 1972. The implementation of the Twenty Point Economic Programme which aimed at 'Liquidation of rural indebtedness' necessitated the opening of rural banks in rural areas to fill the credit gaps created by the eviction of moneylenders. The working Group on Rural Banks (1975), appointed by the Government of India to study in depth the necessity of rural banks, firmly recommended for formation of such banks, besides stating the limitations of existing credit structure in meeting the credit gap, even with modification and restructuring. Accordingly, the first five Regional Banks were set up in the country on October 2, 1975.

Footnotes

1. Nicolson, Frederick : "Report Regarding the Possibility of Introducing Land and Agricultural Banks in the Madras Presidency", Vol.1, Reserve Bank of India, Bombay, Reprint 1960, p.3.

2. Desai, Vasant : *Op.cit.*,pp.66-67.
3. Reserve Bank of India : "All-India Rural Credit Survey", Vol.II, Bombay, 1954, p.167.
4. Reserve Bank of India : "All India Debt and Investment Survey 1971-72 -Indebtedness of Rural Households and Availability of Institutional Finance", Bombay, 1977, p.4.
5. Darling, M.L. : "The Punjab Peasant in Prosperity and Debt", Oxford University Press, Bombay, 1932, p.204.
6. Government of India : The Indian Central Banking Enquiry Committee Majority Report, New Delhi, 1931, p.77.
7. Ghatak, Subrata : "Rural Money Markets in India", Macmillan Company of India Ltd., Delhi, 1976, p.16.
8. Bottomley, A ; "Monopoly Profit as a Determinant of Interest Rates in Underdeveloped Rural Areas", Oxford Economic Papers, Vol.16, No.3, October 1964, pp.432-33.
9. Wadhva, Charan, D : *Op.cit.*,p.2.
10. Natarajan, B: "Banking and Rural Debt Redemption", The Banker. Vol.XXIII, No.9, November 1976, pp.31-38.
11. Yegna Narayana Aiyer, A.K : "Co-operation and Indian Agriculture", The Bangalore Printing and Publishing Co. Ltd., Bangalore, 1951, pp.14-15.
12. Eleanor, M. Hough : "The Cooperative Movement in India", Oxford University Press, Bombay, 1966, p.48.
13. "Introduction to Indian Agriculture and the Role of Cooperative Credit and Banking Institution", The Banker Vol. XXXII, No. 13, December 1985, pp. 13-17.
14. Choubey, B.N. "Principles and Practice of Cooperative Banking in India", Asia Publishing House, Bombay, 1968, p.15.
15. Memoria, C.B.: "Rural Credit and Agricultural Co-operation in India", Kitab Mahal, Delhi, 1983, p.147.
16. Government of India: "Interim Report of the National Commission on Agriculture", December 1971.
17. Government of India: The Seventh Five Year Plan, 1985-90, Vol. II, p.18.
18. Battacharya, Kalyan: "Financial Intermediation and Rural Development: Role of Cooperative Credit in Agricultural Development", The Indian Economic Journal, Vol. 26, No.2, October-December 1978, pp.13-20.
19. Reserve Bank of India: "Statistical Statement s Relating to Cooperative Movement in India", Vol. I, 1975-76.
20. Reserve Bank of India: "Report of the Committee on Integration of Cooperative Credit Institutions", Bombay, 1976, pp.26-27.
21. Memoria, C.B.: *Op.cit.*, p. 167.
22. Mathur, B.S.: "Cooperation in India (A Critical Analysis of the Cooperative Movement in India's Planned Economy)" Sahitya Bhawan, Agra, 1974, p. 172.
23. Goyal, O.P. : "Financial Institutions and Economic Growth in India", Life and Light Publishers, New Delhi, 1979, p.378.

24. Thingalaya, N " "Banks and Rural Development : Some Crucial Issues", Pigmy Economic Review, Vol. 27, No. 3, October 1981, p.1
25. Reserve Bank of India: "Report of the All-India Rural Credit Review Committee", Bombay, 1969, p.88.
26. Saxena, D.N. : "Commercial Banking in the Current Development Strategy in India", S.L.N. Sinha (Ed)., Reform of the Indian Banking System, Orient Longman Ltd., Madras, 1973, p.129.
27. Six more banks were nationalized in April 1980.
28. It was further revealed that out of every 100 new branches opened in the period after nationalisation as many as 48 have been opened in rural ares. This was indeed a big step forward.
29. Government of India: The Seventh Five Year Plan, Vol. II, Op. Cit.
30. Varshneya, J.S." "Bank Nationalisation and After", Yojana, Vol.30, No. 13, July 16-31, 1986, p.6.
31. *Ibid.*
32. Choubey, B.N. : "Institutoinal Finance for Agricultural Development", Shubada Saraswata, Pune 1977, pp. 132-45.
33. "Progress of Indian Banking–First Decade of Nationalisation", United Commercial Bank Review, Vol. XXIV, No. 2-3, April/ June/ September 1980, p.23.
34. Reserve Bank of India: "Functioning of Public Sector Banks–Report of the Committee", 1978, Ch.3, pp.17-18.
35. 62nd Report of the Estimates Committee : "Extension of Credit Facilities to Weaker Sections of Society and for Development of Backward Areas", Sixth Lok Sabha 1977-78, p.63.
36. Shetty, Sundara : "Neglect of Rural Credit", Southern Economist, Vol. 16, No. 16, December 15, 1977, p.23.
37. Shetty, S.L. : "Performance of Commercial Banks since Nationalisation of Major Banks, Promise and Reality", Economic and Political Weekly, Vol. XIII, No. 31, August 1978, p.1415.
38. Reserve Bank of India: "Report of the All India Rural Credit Review Committee", *Op.cit.*,p.336.
39. Chauhan, A.B. and Deobhankar, S.G. : "Restructuring of Commercial Banks in India, Some Thoughts", Lok Udyog, Vol. XV, No. 6, September 1981, pp.21-25.
40. "Issues Before Regional Banks", Bank of Baroda Weekly Review, Vol. 13, No. 30, July 25, 1975, pp.1-3.
41. Natarajan, B: "Banking and Rural Debit Redemption", The Banker, Vol. XXIII, No. 9, November 1979, pp. 31-38.
42. "Need for integrating rural credit institutions", The Capital, Vol. CLXXVII, 1 July 1976, p.16.
43. Narasimham, M. : "Rural Credit and Regional Rural Banks", Southern Economist, Vol. 14, No. 11, October 1975, p.15.
44. Government of India: "Report of the Banking Commission", 1972, p.3.
45. *Ibid.*, p.174.
46. *Ibid.*
47. *Ibid.*, p.166.

48. Sharma, D.P. : "Rural Bank", "Rural Banking in India" M.R. Toshi and D.P. Sharma (Ed.), Oxford & IBH Publishing Co., Delhi, 1975, pp.108-118.
49. Hanif, M.W.: "25 Point Socio-Economic Programme" S. Chand, & Co. Ltd. Delhi, 1977, p.26.
50. Wadhava, Charan, D: *Op.cit.*,p.13.
51. Government of India: "Report of the Committee (Working Group) on Rural Banks", New Delhi, 1975, p.9.
52. *Ibid.*, pp.9-10.
53. *Ibid.*, p.13.

4

The Working of Regional Rural Banks in India

"To the millions of small farmers, artisans and other self-employed persons a bank can be a source of credit which is the very basis of any effort to improve their meager economic lot".

Indira Gandhi [1]

Introduction

The Regional Rural Banks (RRBs) were set up in the country under the Regional Rural banks Ordinance, 1975, promulgated[2] by the President of India on 26th September, 1975. The working Group on Rural Banks constituted by the Government of India on 1st July, 1975 examined in detail the existing structure and functioning of both cooperative and commercial banks and brought into light their relative strengths and weaknesses. The Group envisaged a novel institution, Regional Rural Banks, which combines the local knowledge, rural bias, spirit of service and dedication to the rural people which are characteristics of the cooperative banks and the adequacy of resources, management expertise and operational efficiency of the commercial banks.

The Government of India, with certain modifications accepted the recommendations of the working group and the first five Regional Rural banks came into existence on 2 October 1975 as a new institutional framework for rural credit, supplementary to existing one but having a different identity. Subsequently, the regional Rural Banks Act, 1976 was passed on 9th February 1976 replacing the earlier ordinance. Also a

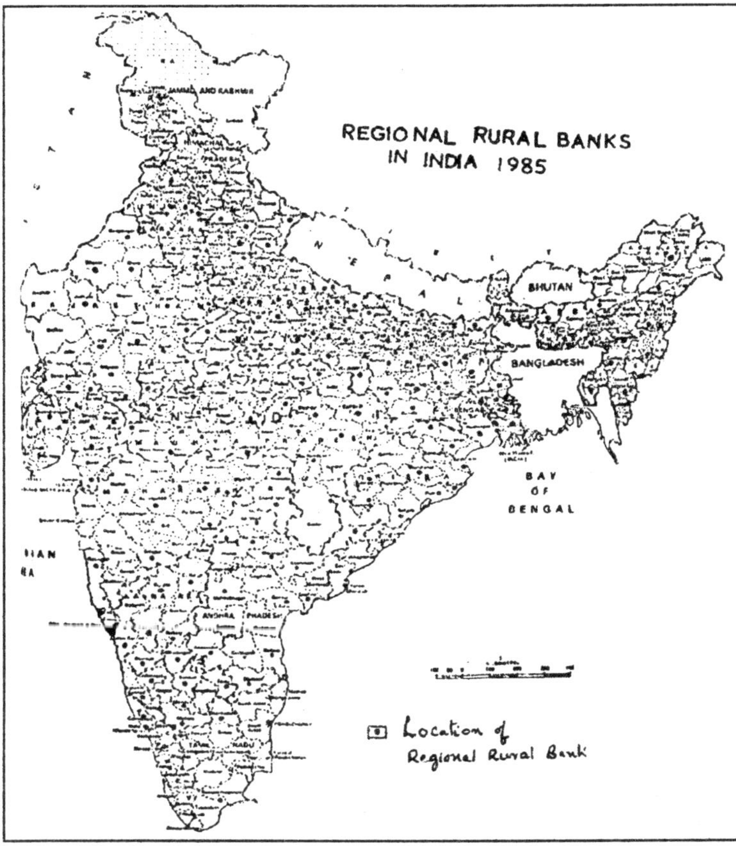

Regional Rural Banks in India 1985

Steering Committee was appointed by the Government of India to formulate and coordinate their policies at the national level.

Today, the Regional Rural Banks, which were mainly brought into existence to bring about a revolutionary change in the rural world of India by wiping out its indebtedness and bridging the credit gaps, have already finished their first decade of survival. During this short span of a decade, the Regional Rural Banks have carved out a niche for themselves among the rural financing agencies. They have also achieved tremendous and impressive progress in terms of number of branches, amount of deposits and advances and number of districts covered. More significantly, they have been helping the economically backward people in meeting their credit requirements for production and consumption. Apart from opening the special credit windows for the weaker sections, the Regional Rural Banks are also making available necessary inputs for agriculture and enabling the rural poor to adopt subsidiary occupations which will go a long way in tackling the ticklish problem of unemployment. Moreover, being a banking institution, they are also mobilizing rural savings and thus cultivating the banking habit among the rural folk. So, by successfully serving the poorest among the poor and having creative, innovative and developmental banking functions with a different philosophy from that of traditional cooperative commercial banks, the Regional Rural Banks are trying to establish their image of a "Small-man's Bank".

The present chapter analyses the important provisions of Regional Rural Banks Act and evaluates the progress and performance of Regional Rural banks in India during the period 1975-85 with relevant official statistics. Indeed, the chapter constitutes a statistical analysis of the working of the Regional Rural Banks in India involving a lengthy coverage.

Important Provisions of the Regional Rural Banks Act, 1976

There were no major changes in the Regional Rural Banks Act of 1976 and the Regional Rural Banks Ordinance of 1975 except clarifications[3] on certain issues. Thus, the Act of 1976 which was deemed to have come into force from 26th September 1975 provided for the incorporation, regulation and working of the Regional Rural Banks. The main features of the scheme for setting of Regional Rural Banks as adopted by the Government of India, are as follows:

Objective

The Regional Rural Banks were set up mainly "with a view to developing the rural economy by providing, for the purpose of development of agriculture, trade, commerce, industry and other productive activities in the rural areas, credit, and other facilities particularly to the small and marginal farmers, agricultural labourers, artisan and small entrepreneurs, and for matters connected therewith and incidental thereto"[4]

Jurisdiction

Each Regional Rural Bank will operate within specified districts in a State and that of its branches within the local limits specified within the districts. Generally, each Regional Rural Bank for its area of operation will have a compact area of one to five districts with homogeneity in agro-climatic conditions and rural clientele with a commonality of problems. Its branch office will cover one to three blocks and be in a position to finance five to ten Farmers' Service Societies. Most commonly, the Regional Rural Banks were to open their branches in the unbanked and under banked centres where the primary agricultural credit societies and commercial banks are weak and impotent to cater to the needs of weaker sections.

Sponsorship

Each Regional Rural Bank will be sponsored[5] by a scheduled commercial bank (mainly by a public sector bank) in consultation with the concerned State and Central Governments and under-license from the Reserve Bank of India. The sponsor bank will provide assistance to the Regional Rural Banks in various ways. These include subscription to share capital, provision of managerial and other staff assistance to be mutually agreed upon within the period of first five years of existence. Financial support will also be given on mutually negotiable terms.

Capital Structure

The authorized and the issued capital of each Regional Rural Bank will be Rs.1 crore and Rs.25 lakhs respectively. Out of issued capital 50 per cent would be subscribed by the Government of India, 15 per cent by the concerned State Government and the balance viz., 35 per cent by the sponsor bank.[6]

Management Structure

The general superintendence, direction and management of the affairs and business of a Regional Rural Bank will be through a nine number board of directors. Of the nine directors, four are to be nominated by the Central Government including the Chairman, two by the State Government and the remaining three by the sponsor bank.[7] The strength of the Board could be raised to 15 with the approval of the Government of India. The Chairman is a full-time executive. Along with him, the nominated board of directors controls and regulates the affairs of Regional Rural Bank and also acts on business principle with due regard to public interest.

The structure of remuneration payable to the staff of the Regional Rural Banks prescribed by the Government of India in accordance with the salary structure of employees of the State Government and local authorities of comparable levels and status in the area of operation of Regional Rural Banks. The structure of remuneration is generally lower than that applicable to the staff of the sponsor bank.

Training Facilities

The Reserve Bank of India would arrange training facilities for the senior staff of the Regional Rural Banks like the Chairmen and branch managers at the Reserve Bank of India's college of Agricultural Banking, Pune. Staff training of junior cadre like accountants, field officers and clerks will be conducted at the zonal training centres of their sponsoring banks under the overall supervision of College of Agricultural Banking.

Banking Business

Every Regional Rural Bank has the status of a scheduled commercial bank. As such, the Regional Rural Banks are permitted to undertake all banking business activities as defined in Clause (b) of Section (5) of the Banking Regulation Act of 1949 and may engage in one or more forms of business as specified in Sub-Section (1) of Section (6) of the said Act. Every Regional Rural Bank is required to undertake the business of mobilizing deposits and granting of short-term and medium-term loans and advances directly only to the small and marginal farmers, agricultural labourers, rural artisans, small entrepreneurs and persons of small means engaged in any productive activity or indirectly through the medium of cooperative societies or the Farmers' Service Societies (FSSs). They can provide loans both for production and consumption purposes within the specified limits.

Refinance Facilities

The Regional Rural Banks can obtain[8] refinance from the Reserve Bank of India under Section 17 (3B) of the Reserve Bank of India Act, 1934 at 2 per cent below the bank rate on par with facilities available to cooperative banks. The actual extent of refinance, within the overall limit would de end upon the quantum of actual advances of the Regional aural Banks to the eligible categories of borrowers. Pending the scrutiny of applications for regular limits, each Regional Rural Bank has been allowed to apply for an adhoc refinance limit of Rs.10 lakhs which would ease, once regular limit is fixed.

Special Concessions and Privileges

In order to enable the Regional Rural Banks in their initial stages of infancy the Reserve Bank of India (RBI) has granted a number of concessions and privileges for conducting their banking business. They are as the following[9] :

(a) Cash reserves can be maintained at 3 per cent of the total demand and time liabilities as against 6 per cent made available to the other scheduled commercial banks.

(b) The statutory liquid assets to be maintained by Regional Rural Banks has been fixed at only 25 per cent as against 35 per cent in the case of the other banks.

(c) The Region Rural Banks are exempted from the purview of directive requiring scheduled commercial banks to maintain with RBI, 10 per cent of the incremental demand and time liabilities.

(d) The Regional Rural Banks are allowed to offer half a per cent more rate of interest on its deposits over the rate offered by scheduled commercial banks. The rates payable on deposits, however, on par with those offered by District Central Cooperative Banks (DCCBs) but half a per cent lower than the rates by village level cooperatives i.e., the primary agricultural credit societies (PACS) or on par with them in specified cases in their respective area of operation.

(e) The RBI has allowed the facility of free transfer of funds in multiples between Head Office of Regional Rural Banks and their respective branches through the offices of public sector banks operating in the area covered by Regional Rural Banks.

(f) The RBI has also made facilities to enable the Regional Rural Banks to be financed from the two special funds of the Government of India, namely, from the National Agricultural (Long-term operations) fund and the National Agricultural Credit, (Stabilisation) Fund.

(g) Facilities provided by the Deposit Insurance Corporation of India have been extended to the Regional Rural Banks to protect the interests of deposits on insurance up to Rs.20,000 and

(h) The Regional Rural Banks are deemed to be cooperative banks for the income-tax purposes. As such, they are not liable to pay tax under the Income Tax Act of 1974.

Immediately after the establishment of Regional Rural Banks, Steering Committee (SC) had been set up by the Government of India at the national level to work out the details of the Regional Rural Banks' Scheme, to monitor its progress and to provide guidelines from time to time. Later on the Committee had been reconstituted several times in last ten years, first under 'the operational control of the RBI[10] and ore recently under the aegis of NABARD.[11] As an advisory body for tendering expert opinion on the organisational and operational aspects of Regional Rural Banks the Steering Committee, during the years discussed several matters which included inter aria (1) identifying of areas (districts) for the establishment of new Regional Rural Banks in different parts of the country[12], (ii) looking after organisational matters such as local participation in management, appointment of Chairman, composition of board, attendance at the Board meetings of Regional Rural Banks, etc., (iii) Working out operational matters, such as feasibility of enlarging the scope of lending policies, etc. (iv) Periodical review of existing concessions and relaxations in regard to liquidity requirements (v) procedures and policies in respect of recruitment/training/promotion of staff and (vi) matters relating to State level coordination committee meetings, advances against gold/silver ornaments, etc. In addition to all these, in its latest meetings held after the formation of NABARD, the Steering Committee has considered the question of enlarging the scope of lending by Regional Rural Banks and decide that the image of Regional Rural Banks as a small man's bank should be preserved", It further prescribed[13] that Regional Rural Banks' loaning policies should be directed to serve the weaker sections.

With a view to bringing about uniformity in certain matters and ensuring that administrative and staff problems of Regional Rural Banks located in a State are sorted out by internal consultations, the Government of India decided in consultations with Steering Committees, to set up State-level co-ordination committees for the Regional Rural Banks located in each State. Inter alia, the Committee would consider and make recommendations to the central government on staff matters such as service rules, pay scales, extension of facilities, allowances, etc., available to the corresponding cadre of the State Government to the employees of the Regional Rural Banks.

The Evolution of Regional Rural Banking

The evolution of the Regional Rural Banking in India is the result of the recommendation of several committees and groups entrusted with the work of shaping their development.

A Review Committee was appointed by the Reserve Bank of India under the Chairmanship of Prof M.L. Dantwala in June 1977 to evaluate the performance of Regional Rural Banks in the light of objectives for which they were set up in India and to indicate their precise role in the rural credit structure and also to make recommendations on the scope, methods and procedures for their functioning and other related matters. The Dantwala Committee submitted its report to the Reserve Bank of India in February 1978. The Report contained[14] an excellent background survey and an expert assessment of the functioning of the Regional Rural Banks based on detailed studies on 12 selected Regional Rural Banks.

The Committee, in its report, strongly recommended that the Regional Rural Banks should be made an integral part of the rural credit structure. This was based on Committees finding[15] that within a short span of two years, the Regional Rural Banks have demonstrated their capacity to serve the purpose for which they were set up., The Regional Rural Banks the Committee opined, have established their image as a new type of institution catering to the credit needs of a class of borrowers (i.e., the poorest of the poor) to whom institutional credit was hitherto not available. The superiority of RRBs as an agency of rural credit over the rural branches of commercial banks as derived from their relatively lower cost of operating, simplicity and low profile, local participation in its management (with due safeguards against domination by vested interests), feel and familiarity of the local staff and close association of the district-level agricultural and rural development agencies and personnel"[16] pointing out that the regional Reserve Bank of India Rural Banks are well-suited for the purpose of filling the credit gap in the rural sector, the Committee observed: "The Committee is definitely of the view that the RRBs with some modifications in their organisation and functions can become a very useful component in the totality of rural credit structure. In fact we are convinced that such an institution is needed to make good some of the inadequacies in the existing rural credit system".[17]

In order to allay the fears of the cooperatives on the implications of the Review Committee's recommendation for making RRBs an integral part of 'the rural credit structure the Committee has stressed that "the cooperative credit structure will not be disturbed at the base level." The reorganised primary agricultural credit societies (PACS) and farmers service societies (FSSs) where ever they can be effectively organised will constitute the base of the rural credit structure. the RRBs however, with the approval of the cooperative leadership and State Government can help to strengthen the retail level cooperative societies by routing their credit through them.

Further, the Review Committee clarified that -the RBBs would function at the intermediate level". That is the RRB system should be extended to such areas where the district credit cooperative bank (DCCBs) are not able 'to adequately serve the primary societies (PACS) within their jurisdiction. In the words of the Committee, "We feel that 'the credit gap, both quantitative and qualitative is so large that given a spirit of understanding both the RRBs and DCCBs can function side by side without a clash of interest. The competition from the RRBs which the DCCBs will face will be no more acute than what they are facing today from the commercial banks and their rural branches. Further more, "Diversification of agricultural activity through horticulture animal husbandry, forestry, etc., will swell the demand for credit which the cooperatives alone will not be able to met".[18] The Review Committee, therefore, came to the conclusion that "the RRBs can make a substantial of contribution towards improving the quality and quantity of credit flows to the rural areas by becoming an integral part of the rural credit structure.[19] In this connection, the Committee emphasised that the programme for the establishment of RRBs need to be accelerated, the most relevant criterion for their extension being the state of the cooperative credit structure at the district 1evel. It envisaged, thus; that over a period of time, there will be total replacement of rural branches of commercial banks by RRBs and their branches in the command areas of RRBs.

The major recommendations made by the Dantwala Committee relating to the organisation and functioning of RRBs[20] are as follows :

(a) Normally a RRB should cover a population of 10 to 15 lakhs. From the angle of financial viability and managerial efficiency the number of branches per district for each RRB will be between 50 to 60. Thus each RRB branch would serve a population of 20,000 and an area covered by five reorganised primary agricultural credit societies.

(b) There is no longer any need for central Government control over RRB through the Steering Committee. 'There should be an appropriate organisational set up in the Reserve Bank to look after RRB work.[21]

(c) The authorised and paid-up capital of RRB should be Rs. 1 crore and Rs.25 lakhs respectively. The composition of share capital should be as follows : Reserve Bank of India : 25 per cent, sponsoring bank 40 per cent, State Government is percent and local participation 20 per cent.

(d) Each RRB should have a Board consisting of eight members (including one RBI official) plus the Chairman.

(e) While the RRBs should cater predominantly to the needs of weaker sections of rural population, they should be allowed to take up financing of large borrowers to a limited extent and also extend all typist of banking services.

(f) At least 60 per cent of loans should be earmarked for the benefit of small farmers, rural artisans and other rural people.[22] There should also be a graded scale of finance to different categories of borrowers, paying due attention to their repaying capacity.

(g) Uniform rate of interest should be followed by all credit institutions catering to the credit requirements of rural community.

(h) The relaxation and concessions offered by the RBI should be continued at least for the first five years from the inception of RRB.

(i) The task of training should be decentralised entrusting responsibilities for training of the personnel of the RRBs primarily by the sponsor banks.

The RBI has accepted the Committee's view that RRBs should be made an integral part of rural credit structure. In pursuance of decisions taken on the recommendations of the Committee, a steering committee was constituted in the RBI to look after the work relating to RRBs and to suggest guidelines on the follow-up action on Dantwala Committee Report.

The Working Group on Multi- Agency Approach in Agricultural Finance under the Chairmanship of C.E. Kamath (which was appointed by the RBI in August 1976) has made some relevant observations on the role of Regional Rural Bank. According to it, the setting up of RRBs was a recent development of significance in the rural credit field. Along with the cooperatives and commercial banks, the existence of RRBs as part of the multi-agency approach to financing agriculture has now become an accepted fact. The role of the RRB, however, is to supplement and not to supplant the other institutional agencies in the field. The Group was of 'the view[23] that in providing credit for agriculture and allied activities, the prime role would have to be that of cooperatives, the commercial banks/ RRBs playing a supplementary role. Until the cooperatives at the field level are well-established and placed on a viable footing, the commercial banks/RRBs it pointed out, will have to supplement the credit disbursal of weak cooperatives and also finance other rural development activities that are normally undertaken by cooperatives. Here, the Kamath Group has emphasized the need for area demarcation for various credit agencies on geographical basis. It suggested[24] certain criteria to be adopted for the purpose, including strict regulation over the future branch expansion of commercial banks/RRBs to prevent necessary proliferation of branches in the rural and semi-urban areas where the cooperative network is fairly adequate.

The Kamath Group further recommended that the RRBs in their direct loaning should not enter into competition with cooperatives inter se. It clearly preferred the RRBS to the commercial banks for the future expansion of banking in rural areas "because they are better suited to direct financing of farmers owing to their low cost structure and rural ethos"[25] It also favoured the idea of allowing the RRBs to allocate a part of their loans to large and medium sized farmers.

The Committee on the functioning of the public sector banks under the Chairmanship of James Raj found the new institution of the RRBs to be useful and preferred its expansion in the rural areas to the expansion of the rural branches of commercial banks. It suggested that, "wherever and whenever RRBs are well-established, offices of commercial banks in the operating rural areas of RRBs may be taken over by RRBs and their power of lending may be widened to include not only small borrowers but also others[26]

In the comprehensive review of the institutional credit set up, the Committee to Review the Arrangements for Agriculture and Rural Development. (CRAFICARD), which submitted its Report in March 1981 has found[27] the institution of RRBs especially suitable for rural development work. The Committee has therefore, recommended that RRBs should continue to confine their operations to the weaker sections and preference should be given to RRBs in regard to licensing of branches in the rural areas. Other important recommendations of the Committee are[28] as follows :

(a) The RBI should take necessary steps to facilitate the transfer of eligible business of rural branches of commercial banks to RRBs when such proposals are presented.

(b) RRBs losses in the initial years should be made good by their shareholders and the equity capital of RRBs ay also be raised suitably.

(c) Emoluments of the staff of RRBs should continue to be determined with due regard to State Government Pay Scales.

(d) Facilities from sponsor banks to RRBs should continue for a period of 10 years in each case.

(e) The experts concerned with agricultural development may be nominated on the Board of RRBs.

(f) The control, regulation and promotional responsibility relating to RRBs should be transferred from the Government of India to RBI/NABARD.

(g) Since the RRBs serve the weaker sections exclusively, facilities of concessional refinance from RBI should continue.

Refinancing Facilities

During their ten years of existence, the Regional Rural Banks have continued to avail refinance facilities (introduced on 6th October 1976) and other important guidelines on policy matters from the RBI and recently from NABARD after its formation in 1982. The amount of refinance availed to Regional Rural Banks by the RBI is given in Table-1.

Table 1
Refinance Facilities from Reserve Bank of India to Regional Rural Banks

(Amount in Crores of Rupees)

Year Ending July-June	*Refinance Limits Sanctioned*	*Outstanding Refinance*	*Sanctioned to Number of RRBs*
1976-77	9.9	4.1	17
1977-78	21.72	16.91	33
1978-79	N.A	N.A.	N.A.
1979-80	75.64	67.38	45
1980-81	119.64	111.40	52
1981-82	177.00	162.00	82

* Year ending May 1982

N.A. Not Available

Source: Reserve Bank of India : "Annual Report on Trend and Progress of Banking in India", Various issues from 1975-76 to 1981-82.

For the refinance year 1976-77 (July-June), credit limits aggregating Rs.9.9 crores were sanctioned to 17 Regional Rural Banks. The amount outstanding against these limits was Rs.4.1 crores. These figures had gone up considerably in the following years as the number of Regional Rural Banks and their duties towards rural areas extended. Thus during 1981-82 (year ending May, limits aggregating Rs. 177 crores to over 82 Regional.

Rural Banks were sanctioned and the outstanding against these limits were Rs. 162 crores.

The policy of refinance in respect of the Regional Rural Banks for the year 1981-82 was reviewed [29] since some of the Banks had shown their ability to mobilize sufficient resources. Accordingly, the Regional Rural Banks which have deposits of Rs. 5 crores and above at the end of March, 1981 should maintain their own involvement not less then 25 per cent of their outstanding loans and advances while other Regional Rural Banks may continue to maintain their old level of 15 per cent. At the same time the RBI's share of refinance of 50 per cent continued to be the same to all banks.

However, in order to ensure that Regional Rural Banks employ their deposit resources to the minimum extent possible in extending loans, it was decided that for the purpose of providing refinance during 1982-83, Regional Rural Banks were divided into three categories and Regional Rural Banks under each category would require to show minimum involvement as follows.

Eligibility Criteria	*Minimum Involvement (in terms of percentage to outstanding loans)*	*Maximum Refinance from RBI (as percentage of total eligible loans)*	*Maximum Refinance from Sponsor Banks (percentage)*
As on March 31, 1982			
RRBs with outstanding loans of Rs. 8 crores and above	30	40	30
RRBs with out standing loans of less than Rs. 8 crores but in existence for 5 years and before	20	50	30
All other RRBs	15	50	35

Source: Reserve Bank of India : "Report on Currency and Finance", 1981-82, Economic Review, Vol.I, pp.160-161.

Subject to the above, minimum involvement of a Regional Rural Bank and the refinance limit from RBI will be determined in each individual case, taking into account the deposit resources of the bank, the amount kept with the sponsor bank by way of deposits and the realistic lending programme.

The RBI has allowed[30] the Regional Rural Banks to recover/ levy service and other charges in the manner of stamp duty, registration fee on documents, legal charges (but not exceeding Rs. 20 per loan case), once for all service charges and expenses connected with recovery proceedings upto certain limits. Further, they have been advised to make every effort for availing maximum refinance from the Agricultural Refinance and Development Corporation (presently merged into NABARD), and Industrial Development Bank of India (IDBI) in view of the automatic refinance facility available in respect of the financing of rural artisans and small/cottage industries unit. With a view to make the involvement of Regional Rural Banks deeper in the area of Rural Development, they have also been advised[31] by the RBI to make their policy flexible in regard to requests from fresh loans from their borrowers who are unable to repay their short-term agricultural loans for reasons beyond their control (besides natural calamities) conversion facilities were also asked to give to the small and marginal farmers and the guarantee cover of DICGC subject to certain co stipulations. In addition, sanctioning of loans for non-agricultural purposes provided for the protective borrowers whose pre-investment income did exceed up to Rs. 4,000. Also, with a view to help the Regional Rural Banks to increase their loan business and cater to the credit needs of the smallest among the small borrowers, they have been permitted to grant loans to eligible borrowers at 4 per cent under the Differential Interest Rate Scheme (DRI).

Following the recommendations of the Working Group on the development of the Scheduled Castes and the Scheduled Tribes, Regional Rural Banks have been asked to formulated their credit plans taking into account the needs of these communities to draw up special banking schemes to ensure a large flow of credit to them for self-employment. The RBI also issued guidelines for the preparation of District Credit Plans (DCPs) and involving in providing credit assistance to identified beneficiaries under Twenty-Point Economic Programme.[32] Integrated Rural Development Programme (IRDP) and other special programmes, Concessional finance to the physically handicapped persons were also asked to be made available through Regional Rural Banks for purchase of artificial limbs, hearing aids, wheel chairs, etc., subject to a maximum of Rs.2,500 per borrower.

NABARD has become the major refinancing agency for the Regional Rural Banks since 1982 as it took over the erstwhile functions and responsibilities of the Agricultural Refinance and Development Corporation (ARDC) and Rural Planning and Credit Cell of the Reserve Bank of India.

Two types of loans and advances granted by Regional Rural Banks are eligible[33] for refinance from NABARD under the composite credit limit, viz., advances of agricultural purposes and loan advances including handloom weavers, small entrepreneurs and persons of small means engaged in industry, business, services and other productive activities. While sanctioning the limits, factors such as the banks' resources, branch expansion programme, projected realistic lending programme, share allowed under Annual Action Plan (AAP), Schematic lending, etc., are taken into consideration.

However, with quite a few Regional Rural Banks having passed the nascent stage of development and having acquired the necessary knowledge and expertise, the NABARD's refinancing policy underwent a change[34] during 1984-85. Under the new policy, Regional Rural Banks which have completed five years of existence as on 1 July 1984, are required to apply for separate limits[35] under short-term and medium-term. Other Regional Rural Banks are, however, eligible for a composite limit as hitherto. While the composite/short-term refinance is provided from RBI under general line of credit, the medium-term (non-schematic) refinance is out of NABARD's NRC (LTO) Fund.[36] Depending on their age and level of business, the quantum of refinance available to Regional Rural Banks under the composite/short-term ranges between 40 to 50 per

Table 2
Refinance Facilities from NABARD to Regional Rural Banks

(Amount in Crores of Rupees)

Year End of June-July	Short-term Refinance: Limits Aggregating	Short-term Refinance: Outstanding	Sanctioned to Number of RRBs	Schematic Refinance: Limits Aggregating	Schematic Refinance: Outstanding	Sanctioned to number of Schemes
1982-83	227	189	97	177	120	478
1983-84	271	242	108	219	149	554
1984-85	203	183	126	445	347	892

Source:
RBI: (1) "Report on Currency and Finance", 1983-84, Economic Review, Vol.I, p.183.
(2) "Report on Currency and Finance", 1984-85, Economic Review, Vol.I, p.219.

cent, while the five year old Regional Rural Banks are, however, eligible for a fixed 60 per cent refinance under medium term (non-schematic) limit.

The following table reveals the extent of refinance facilities extended by NABARD to Regional Rural Banks during 1982-83 to 1984-85.

It is obvious from Table-2 during 1983-84, the NABARD had sanctioned limits aggregating Rs.271 crores to 108 Regional Rural Banks as against Rs.227 crores to 97 Regional Rural Banks during 1982-83. Outstanding refinance of these banks at the end of June 1964 amounted to Rs.242 crores as against Rs.189 crores in June 1983.

With regard to schematic refinance, 554 schemes involving NABARD's commitment of Rs.219 crores were sanctioned to Regional Rural Banks and drawals amounted to Rs.149 crores in June 1984 compared with 458 schemes involving commitment of Rs.177 crores and drawals of Rs.120 crores as at the end of June 1983.

However, during 1984-85, under the revised refinance policy, the NABARD had sanctioned short term / composite limits of Rs.203 crores to 126 Regional Rural Banks and the outstanding against it was Rs.183 crores. At the end of June 1985" 892 schemes involving NABARD's commitment. of Rs.445 crores were sanctioned to Regional Rural Banks as long-term finance and the drawal against this amounted to Rs.347 crores. Over 56 Regional Rural Banks have become eligible for separate limits under the new policy. Accordingly, the NABARD had sanctioned medium-term (non-schematic) limit aggregating Rs.40.6 crores to 19 Regional Rural Banks and the outstanding against it was Rs. 24.7 crores.

In addition to all this; certain amount of financial discipline has also been introduced by the NABARD over Regional Rural Banks. Accordingly, Regional Rural Banks whose over dues exceed 60 per cent of the demand are not sanctioned upto enhanced limits, The applications of such banks are considered to the extent of their outstanding under previous year's limit, after taking into account the special recovery efforts made by them.

Further, to increase the Regional Rural Bank's involvement in Schematic lending and enable them to formulate viable schemes independently NABARD decided[37] to provide on request, assistance to Regional Rural Banks from its Research and Development Fund (RD Fund) for setting up Technical, Monitoring and Evaluation cells by way of grants on tapering basis up to five years from January 1985. The qualifications of the technical officers to man the cell have also been relaxed so that Regional Rural Banks may be able to attract qualified personnel to meet their requirements of technical staff.

Furthermore, NABARD has been actively involving in the organisation of new Regional Rural Banks and monitoring the working of Regional Rural Banks. The BIRD (Bankers Institute for Rural Development) organised two courses during 1983-84 with a total capacity of 54 participants for the benefit of participants from Regional Rural Banks. It has also been decided that regional training centres are to be set up in other parts of the country to supplement the training facilities at NABARD in a large measure to Regional Rural Banks.

The sponsor banks continued to provide managerial and financial support to Regional Rural Banks as stipulated under the Regional Rural Banks Act. The aggregate amount of refinance availed by the total Regional Rural Banks from their sponsor banks was Rs.205.48 crores as at the end of December 1985 as against Rs.178.6 crores as at the end of December 1984 and Rs.99 crores at the end of December 1983, respectively.

Structure and Coverage

India made a modest beginning with five Regional Rural Banks in October 1975. introducing in four States, covering 11 districts and sponsored by different public sector banks. In the very next year the speed of setting up of these banks rose sharply totaling to 40 covering 15 States sand 84 districts. However, this tempo was not kept up in the succeeding three years (8 banks in 1977, 3 in 1978 and 9 in 1979) as there appeared to be some reservations and reconsiderations about the speed with which new Regional Rural Banks are to be opened.

In view of the strong support and favourable recommendations by the Review Committee on Regional Rural Banks in 1977, once again; there had been a giant forward step in the number and coverage of Regional Rural Banks as could be seen from Table-3.

The number and coverage of Regional Rural Banks were good in the year 1976. With a considerable setback during the period 1977-79, the Regional Rural Bank movement in India got momentum from the year 1990 in which 25 new RRBs were set up aggregating the total number of RRBs in the country to 85 with a coverage of 17 States and 144 districts. During the next year ending 1981, the number of RRBs have gone up to 107 with a coverage of 19 States and 182 districts. In the next two years ending 1983, their number further increased to 150 with a coverage of 21 States 2 Union Territories and 265 districts.

Table 3
Structure of Regional Rural Banks in India : 1975-85

Year at the End of December	*No. of Regional Rural Banks*	*No. of Districts Covered*	*No. of States Covered*	*No. of Sponsoring Banks*
1975	6	11	5	5
1976	40	84	15	16
1977	48	99	16	16
1978	51	102	16	18
1979	60	114	17	18
1980	85	144	17	18
1981	107	182	19	19
1982	124	214	19	23
1983	150	265	23*	23
1984	173	307	23*	24
1985	188	333	23*	26

Note: * Including two Union Territories.

Source:
1. AFC : "A study of Regional Rural Banks", Bombay, 1981, pp.41-42.
2. RBI : Report of the Committee to Review Arrangements for Institutional Credit for Agriculture and Rural Development (CRAFICARD), Bombay, 1981, pp.109-113.

The Government of India planned[38] to take up the expansion programme of RRBs at an accelerated speed during the Sixth

Plan period (March 1980-85) and fixed up a target of establishment of 170 Regional Rural Banks covering 270 districts by the end of the plan. This target was well achieved in advance as the number of RRBs have gone upto 173 covering 307 districts by the end of December 1984. However during the year ending December 1985, the number of RRBs in the country stood at 188 covering 333 districts and almost all Indian States (except Sikkim), besides 2 of the 9 Union Territories. The number of sponsor banks were 26.

Thus, the number of Regional Rural Banks have grown remarkably over 31 times during the decade and the number of districts covered gone up by 30 times while the number of States covered as well as sponsor banks increased by 5 time each.

Further, out of the 188 Regional Rural Banks surviving by the end of December 1985, 6 RRBs had completed a period of a decade, 34 RRBs had completed a period of 9 years, 8 RRBs 8 years, 3 RRBs 7 years, 9 RRBs 6 years, 25 RRBs 5 years, 23 RRBs 4 years, 16 RRBs 3 years and 26 RRBs 2 years. There were also 23 RRBs of just one year old and over 15 RRBs are recently born about a few months back.

The State-wise and year-wise establishment of Regional Rural Banks is provided in Table-4.

It can be seen from the table that from the beginning, the backward States of Uttar Pradesh, Bihar, Madhya Pradesh, Rajasthan, Orissa and Andhra Pradesh accounted for setting up of greater number of RRBs. The spread of these banks was also equally good in some of the developed States like Karnataka.. Maharashtra, Gujarat and West Bengal. However the number of RRBs were only minimum in some of the major States like Punjab and Tamil Nadu where the prevailing cooperative movement is strong. In recent years the spread of these banks extended to 2 Union Territories.

Thus at the end of December 1985, Uttar Pradesh was leading with maximum number of RRBs i.e., 39 banks (20.7 per cent of the total) with a coverage of 51 districts (15.3 per cent of the total), followed by Madhya Pradesh and Bihar having 23 RRBs (12.2 per cent) covering 42 districts (12.6

Table 4

State-wise Establishment of Regional Rural Banks in India : 1975-85

Name of the State/ Union Territory	*1975*	*1976*	*1977*	*1978*	*1979*	*1980*	*1981*	*1982*	*1983*	*1984*	*1985*
	As at the End of December										
Andhra Pradesh	-	3	3	3	3	4	5	10	12	12	14
Assam	-	1	1	1	1	2	5	5	5	5	5
Bihar	1	4	7	7	10	16	17	17	17	20	22
Gujarat	-	-	-	1	2	2	3	4	5	9	9
Haryana	1	2	2	2	2	2	2	2	2	3	4
Himachal Pradesh	-	1	1	1	1	1	1	1	1	1	2
Jammu & Kashmir	-	1	1	1	1	3	3	3	3	3	3
Karnataka	-	3	3	3	4	4	5	6	8	12	13
Kerala	-	2	2	2	2	2	2	2	2	2	2
Madhya Pradesh	-	3	4	5	6	11	13	15	19	22	23
Maharashtra	-	1	1	1	1	1	1	2	5	7	9
Manipur	-	-	-	-	-	1	1	1	1	1	1
Meghalaya	-	-	-	-	-	-	-	1	1	7	1
Nagaland	-	-	-	-	-	-	-	-	1	7	1
Orissa	-	4	4	4	5	8	8	9	9	9	9
Punjab	-	-	-	-	-	-	-	-	3	3	3
Rajasthan	1	3	3	4	4	5	5	7	9	13	14
Tamil Nadu	1	-	1	1	1	1	1	1	1	1	2
Tripura	-	1	1	1	1	1	1	1	1	1	1
Uttar Pradesh	2	8	10	10	10	17	27	29	35	36	39
West Bengal	1	3	4	4	4	4	7	8	8	9	9
Arunachal Pradesh	-	-	-	-	-	-	-	-	1	1	1
Mizoram	-	-	-	-	-	-	-	-	1	1	1
All India	6	40	48	51	60	85	107	124	150	173	188

Source:

1. RBI :"Statistical Tables Relating to Banks in India", 1975-80 Issues.
2. RBI :"Report on Currency and Finance" Statistical Statements, II Volumes, 1980-81 to 1984- 85 Issues.

per cent) and 22 RRBs (11.7 per cent) covering 37 districts (11.1 per cent), respectively.

Whereas 14 RRBs (7.5 per cent of the total) each have been set up in Andhra Pradesh and Rajasthan, Karnataka has got 13 (6.9 per cent) and 9 (4.8 per cent) each have been set up in Gujarat, Maharashtra and Orissa and West Bengal. 5 RRBs in Assam, 4 in Haryana, 3 each in Jammu & Kashmir and Punjab 2 each in Himachal Pradesh, Kerala, Tamil Nadu and 1 each in Manipur, Meghalaya and Nagaland have been established. One each also had been set up in the Union Territories of Arunachal Pradesh.

Table 5

Sponsor Bank-wise Distribution of Offices of Regional Rural Banks (As at the End of December 1983)

Name of the Sponsor Bank	*No. of RRBs*	*Rank*	*No. of Districts Covered*	*Rank*	*No. of Bran-ches*	*Rank*
State Bank of India	30	1	66	1	2085	1
State Bank of Bikaner and Jaipur	3	11	5	11	165	17
State Bank of Hyderabad	4	10	4	12	120	18
State Bank of Mysore	2	12	4	12	191	15
State Bank of Saurashtra	3	11	5	11	81	20
Allahabad Bank	7	9	8	8	492	10
Andhra Bank	2	12	2	13	103	19
Bank of Baroda	19	3	28	5	1078	3
Bank of India	16	5	27	6	868	6
Bank of Maharashtra	2	12	7	9	264	13
Canara Bank	8	8	11	8	676	9
Central Bank of India	23	2	38	2	1643	2
Corporation Bank	1	13	2	13	40	24
Dena Bank	4	10	7	9	210	14
Indian Bank	2	12	2	13	66	22
Indian Oversease Bank	3	11	6	10	297	12
New Bank of India	1	13	2	13	12	25
Punjab National Bank	17	4	31	3	1047	4
Syndicate Bank	10	7	17	7	970	5
Union Bank of India	14	10	6	10	390	11
United Bank of India	11	6	29	4	803	7
United Commercial Bank	11	6	17	7	686	8
Vijaya Bank	1	13	1	14	-	-
Bank of Rajasthan Ltd.	1	13	1	14	58	23
Jammu & Kashmir Bank Ltd.	2	12	6	10	188	16
The U.P.State Cooperative Bank Ltd.	1	13	1	14	70	
All India	188		333		12606	

Source: NABARD: "Statistics on Regional Rural Banks"

Table-5 provides the sponsor bank-wise coverage of Regional Rural Banks in India.

The State Bank of India accounted for sponsoring highest number of Regional Rural Banks and covering greater number of districts from the beginning of the scheme itself. According to Table-5, by the end of December 1985, the State Bank of India along with its subsidiaries [39] has sponsored 42 out of a total of 188 MBs and covered 66 districts out of a total of 333 RRB districts in the country.

This was followed by Central Bank of India sponsoring 23 RRBs (covering 38 districts; Bank of Baroda - 19 RRBs (covering 28 districts); Punjab National Bank-17 RRBs (covering 31 districts); Bank of India - 16 RRBs (covering 27 districts); and United Bank of India and United Commercial Bank - 11 RRBs each, led others in sponsoring more Regional Rural Banks. Whereas 10 RRBs have been sponsored by Syndicate Bank, 8 by Canara Bank, 7 by Allahabad Bank, 4 each by Dena Bank and Union Bank of India, 3 by Indian Overseas Bank, 2 each by Andhra Bank, Bank of Maharashtra, Indian Bank and Jammu and Kashmir Bank Ltd., and 1 each by Corporation Bank. Vijaya Bank, Bank of Rajasthan Ltd., The U.P. State. Co-operative Bank Ltd., and New Bank of India.

Among the subsidiaries of State Bank of India" State Bank of Travancore, State Ban of Patiala and State Bank of Indore, have not yet opened any Regional Rural Banks. Among the public sector banks, the Oriental Bank of Commerce and the Punjab and Sind Bank have also not opened any Regional Rural Banks.

The District-wise analysis of Bank in India is given in Table-6.

A look at the above table reveals that as at the end of December 1985, 90 Regional aural Banks had a jurisdiction of 1 district each, another 68 RRBs had 2 districts each, 21 RRBs had 3 districts each, over 6 RRBs had 4 districts each and 1 RRB with a jurisdiction of seven districts[40] and another 1 with 8 districts[41] have covered over 333 districts (or 77 per cent of the total districts) out of a whole of 433 districts in the country[42] and thereby its population.

Table 6
District-wise Distribution of Regional Rural Banks
(As at the End of December 1985)

Name of the State/Union Territory	Total No. of Districts in the State/Union Territories	No. of Districts Covered by RRBs	Rank Order	Total Number of Banks* having: One Dist. Each	Two Dist. Each	Three Dist. Each	Four Dist. Each	Five Dist. Each	Six Dist. Each	Seven Dist. Each	Eight Dist. Each	Total Number of Banks
Andhra Pradesh	23	19	5	10	3	1	-	-	-	-	-	14
Assam	17	12	9	-	3	2	-	-	-	-	-	5
Bihar	38	37	3	14	3	3	2	-	-	-	-	22
Gujarat	19	15	7	3	6	-	-	-	-	-	-	9
Haryana	12	9	11	-	3	1	-	-	-	-	-	4
Himachal Pradesh	12	4	16	1	-	1	2	-	-	-	-	2
Jammu & Kashmir	14	10	10	-	1	-	-	-	-	-	-	3
Karnataka	19	19	5	7	6	-	-	-	-	-	-	13
Kerala	14	5	15	-	1	1	-	-	-	-	-	2
Madhya Pradesh	45	42	2	5	17	1	-	-	-	-	-	23
Maharashtra	30	16	6	5	3	-	-	1	-	-	-	9
Manipur	6	8	12	-	-	-	-	-	-	-	1	1
Meghalaya	5	3	17	-	-	1	-	-	-	-	-	1
Nagaland	7	7	13	-	-	-	-	-	-	1	-	1
Orissa	13	13	8	6	2	1	-	-	-	-	-	9
Punjab	12	6	14	-	3	-	-	-	-	-	-	3
Rajasthan	27	27	4	4	7	3	-	-	-	-	-	14
Tamil Nadu	16	5	15	1	-	-	1	-	-	-	-	2

Contd.

Name of the State/Union Territory	Total No. of Districts in the State/Union Territories	No. of Districts Covered by RRBs	Rank Order	Total Number of Banks* having								
				One Dist. Each	Two Dist. Each	Three Dist. Each	Four Dist. Each	Five Dist. Each	Six Dist. Each	Seven Dist. Each	Eight Dist. Each	Total Number of Banks
Tripura	3	3	17	-	-	1	-	-	-	-	-	1
Uttar Pradesh	57	51	1	29	8	2	-	-	-	-	-	39
West Bengal	16	15	7	5	2	2	-	-	-	-	-	9
Arunachal Pradesh	10	4	16	-	-	-	1	-	-	-	-	1
Mizoram	3	3	17	-	-	1	-	-	-	-	-	1
All India	420	333		90	68	21	6	1		1	1	188

Note: *Computed

Source:

1. Government of India : "India", 1985.
2. NABARD : "Statistics on Regional Rural Banks"

Table 7

Region-wise Expansion of Regional Rural Banks in India : 1980-85

Name of the Region	*1980*	*1981*	*1982*	*1983*	*1984*	*1985*
			Number of Regional Rural Banks			
Northern Region	28(32.94)	39(36.45)	42(33.87)	53(35.33)	59(34.10)	65(34.57)
North-Eastern Region	4(4.71)	6(5.61)	8(6.45)	11(7.33)	11(6.36)	11(5.85)
Eastern Region	28(32.94)	33(30.84)	34(27.42)	34(22.67)	38(21.97)	40(21.28)
Western Region	14(16.47)	16(14.95)	21(16.94)	29(19.34)	38(21.97)	41(21.81)
Southern Region	11(19.94)	13(12.15)	19(15.32)	23(15.33)	27(15.61)	31(16.49)
All India	85(100.00)	107(100.00)	124(100.00)	150(100.00)	173(100.00)	188(100.00)
			Number of Regional Rural Banks			
Northern Region	49(34.03	59(32.42)	68(31.78)	86(32.45)	96(31.27)	107(32.13)
North-Eastern Region	8(5.56)	18(9.89)	22(10.28)	38(14.34)	38(12.38	40(12.01)
Eastern Region	45(31.25)	52(28.57)	54(25.23)	54(20.38)	63(20.38)	65(19.52)
Western Region	21(14.58)	29(15.93)	38(17.76)	51(19.25)	69(22.15)	73(21.93)
Southern Region	21(14.58)	24(13.19)	32(14.95)	36(13.58)	42(13.68)	48(14.41)
All India	144(100.00)	182(100.00)	214(100.00)	150(100.00)	307(100.00)	333(100.00)
			Number of Regional Rural Banks			
Northern Region	938(28.61)	1399(29.18)	1950(31.50)	2627(33.70)	3515(34.31)	4369(34.66)
North-Eastern Region	86(2.62)	138(2.88)	182(2.94)	239(3.07)	361(34.31)	511(4.06)
Eastern Region	1030(31.41)	1671(34.85)	2089(33.74)	2326(29.84)	2697(26.33)	3230(25.62)
Western Region	401(12.23)	589(12.28)	780(12.60)	1077(13.81)	1661(16.21)	2133(16.92)
Southern Region	824(25.13)	998(20.81)	1190(19.22)	1526(15.26)	2011(19.63)	2363(18.74)
All India	3279(100.00)	4795(100.00)	6191(100.00)	7795(100.00)	10245(100.00)	12606(100.00)

Note :Figures in parentheses are percentages to total.
Source: RBI: "Report on Currency and Finance", Statistical Statements, II Volumes, Issues from 1980-81 to 1984-85.

Again of the total number of 333 districts covered by the 188 Regional Rural Banks functioning in different parts of the country, over 53 per cent of the districts fall in the above said 5 backward States namely Uttar Pradesh (15.3 per cent) Madhya Pradesh (12.6 per cent) Bihar (11.1 per cent), Rajasthan (8.1 per cent) and Andhra Pradesh (5.8 per cent.).

The region-wise growth of Regional Rural Banks is shown in Table-7.

For years, the Northern, Eastern and Western regions were leading in establishing Regional Rural Banks while the Southern and North-Eastern Regions lagged behind. At the end of the year 1985, 65 RRBs (35 per cent of the total) covering 107 districts are concentrated in the Northern region while 41 RRBs (22 per cent) covering 73 districts were operating in the Western region. They were followed by Eastern region with 40 RRBs (21 per cent) covering 65 districts, Southern region with 31 RRBs (16 per cent) covering 49 districts and North-Eastern region with a minimum of RRBs (6 per cent) covering 40 districts.

Branch Expansion

Ono of the major achievements of Regional Rural Banks had been the rapid expansion of branch network in the rural and backward areas of the country" most of them being unbanked and under banked centres. There was also noticeable increase in the number of districts covered by the RRB branches and thereby significant improvement in their population coverage. The details of year-wise and quarter-wise branch expansion of Regional Rural Banks is furnished in the accompanying table.

To start with there were only 17 RRB branches by the end of December 1975. In 1976, they increased to a huge total of 503 showing an increase of 2.959 per cent. After this initial ambitious enlargement, there were periods when branch expansion waxed and waned. However, once it was agreed that RRBs should be made an integral part of the rural credit structure, the network of RRBs expanded regularly and vigorously in very nook and corner of the country. Thus, in

1971 the RRB branches rose to 1,187 or by 236 per cent (over 1976); in 1978 to 1,762 or by 148 per cent, in 1979 to 2,420 or by 137 per cent; in 1980 3,279 or by 135 per cent; in 1981 to 4,795 or by 143 per cent in 1982 to 6,191 or by 129 per cent, in 1983 to 7795 or by 126 per cent, in 1984, to 10,245 or by 131 per cent; and in 1985 to a massive total of 12,606 or by 123 per cent.

Table 8

Branch Expansion of Regional Rural Banks in India 1975-85

As at the End of	*Number of Branches*	*Per RRB Branches*
December 1975	17	2.83
June 1976	112	3.61
December 1976	503	12.57
June 1977	767	15.98
December 1977	1187	24.73
June 1978	1405	29.27
December 1978	1762	34.55
June 1979	1990	35.54
December 1979	2420	40.33
June 1980	2735	37.47
December 1980	3279	38.58
June 1981	3784	37.10
December 1981	4795	44.81
June 1982	5393	46.22
December 1982	6191	49.93
June 1983	6812	47.97
December 1983	7795	51.97
June 1984	8724	53.87
December 1984	10245	59.22
June 1985	12139	66.33
December 1985	12606	67.05

Source:

1. RBI : "Annual Repot on Trend and Progress of Banking in India", Various Issues from 1975-70 to 1984-85.
2. NABARD : "Statistics on RRBs", Op.cit.

If we look at the overall increase the RRB branches increased by 652 per cent between the period 1976-80 and by 384 per cent between the period 1980-85 and by 2,506 per cent between the period 1976-85.

Side by side, the average number of branch offices per RRB has also grown steadily during the period 1975-85. It increased from a mere 3 in 1975 to 25 in 1977, which further rose up to 40 in 1979, 45 in 1981, 52 in 1983 and 67 in 1985.

The branches of Regional Rural Banks form 21.2 per cent of the offices of all commercial banks at the end of February 1985 as against 8.3 per cent in June 1980 while the rural/semi-urban branches of RRBs in February 1985 constituted 30.3 per cent of the rural/ semi-urban branches of all commercial banks as against 11.5 per cent in June 1990 Of the 3 600 new offices opened by commercial banks[43] during July 1984 to February 1985, as many as 2,033 (or 56.5 per cent of the total) were accounted for Regional Rural Banks.

But the most distinctive feature of this branch expansion programme of Regional Rural Banks has been the coverage of the rural, backward and other long neglected areas of the country in comparison to urban-oriented expansion of commercial bank branches. Table-9 shows the population group-wise distribution of Regional Rural Banks in India during the period 1976-85.

Almost all the years of its existence, the Regional Rural Banks have opened more than 90 per cent of its offices only in rural areas. While the semi-urban areas got the second preference, the urban areas have been allotted only a few branches, though the shares of both these centres have been decreasing during the years in preference to rural branches. Thus by March 1985 out of a total of 11,451 operating branches as many as 10,769 (94 per cent of the total) were in rural areas, 627 (5.5 per cent) in semi-urban areas and 54 (0.5 per cent) in urban areas. In comparison, the commercial banks have opened 57.5 per cent of its branches in rural areas, 19.5 per cent in semi-urban areas, while the urban and metropolitan centres have got 12.5 per cent and 10.5 per cent respectively at the end of February 1985.

Another commendable and praiseworthy feature of the branch expansion programme of Regional Rural Bank has been its coverage of unbanked and underbanked areas in every nook and corner of the Country. Table-10 crystallises the fact about the extent in which Regional Rural Banks have been trying to convey its message to the hitherto neglected areas and its population.

Table 9
Population Group-wise Distribution of Regional Rural Banks' Offices in India, 1976-85

Population Group	*June 1976*	*June 1977*	*June 1978*	*June 1978*	*June 1980*
Rural	94(83.9)	688(88.2)	1275(90.7)	1813(92.2)	2473(92.3)
Semi-Urban	13(11.6)	75(9.6)	110(7.9)	131(6.7)	181(6.8)
Urban	5(4.5)	17(2.2)	20(1.4)	21(1.1)	24(0.9)
Metropolitan/ Part Town	-(-)	-(-)	-(-)	-(-)	-(-)
Total	112(100.0)	780(100.0)	1405(100.0)	1965(100.0)	2678(100.0)
	June 1981	*June 1982*	*June 1983*	*June 1984*	*June 1985*	*Percentage Share of Commercial Banks' offices in Rural Areas February 1985*
	3326(92.6)	4748(92.8)	5988(93.0)	7853(93.9)	10769(94.0)	57.5
	241(6.7)	330(6.5)	382(6.0)	456(5.5)	456(5.5)	19.5
	30(0.8)	38(0.7)	42(1.0)	50(0.6)	50(0.6)	12.5
	1(-)	1(-)	1(-)	1(-)	1(-)	10.3
	3598(100.0)	5117(100.0)	6413(100.0)	8360(100.0)	11451(100.0)	

Note: Figures in brackets are percentages to total

Source:

RBI: (a) "Report on Currency and Finance", Economic Review, Vol.I, 1976-77, p.103
(b) "Report on Currency and Finance", Economic Review, Vol.I, 1978-78,p.138
(c) "Report on Currency and Finance", Economic Review, Vol.I, 1981-82, p.156.
(d) "Report on Currency and Finance", Economic Review, Vol.I, 1982-83, p.190.

Excepting the initial the initial two years, the percentage coverage of unbanked centres by Regional Rural Banks branches stood at more than 90 per cent, in all the years of its existence, while a minimum of offices opened in banked areas. This may hold a new economic order in the backward areas of the country and help the weaker sections to avail of banking facilities. Thus, out of 668 new offices opened by RRBs in 1976-77 as many as 517 were established in unbanked centres. In 1978-79, 524 out of 560; in 1980-81, 818 out of 920; in 1982-83 1,238 out of 1,296; and in 1984-85, 1,943 out of 2,033 were opened in unbanked centres.

Table 10
Opening of New Offices by Regional Rural Banks, 1975-85

Year Ending July, June	*New Offices Opened by RRBs*	*Of which in Unbanked Centres*	*Banked Centres*	*Total No. of Bank Offices as at the End of the Year*	*Number of Banks as at the End of the Year*
1975-76	112	79(70.5)	33(29.5)	112	-
1976-77	668	517(77.4)	151(22.6)	780	48
1977-79	625	560(89.6)	65(10.4)	1405	48
1978-79	560	524(93.6)	36(6.4)	1965	56
1979-80	713	645(90.5)	68(9.5)	2678	73
1980-81	920	818(88.9)	102(11.1)	3598	102
1981-82	1519	1399(92.1)	120(7.9)	5117	121
1982-83	1296	1238(95.5)	58(4.5)	6413	142
1983-84	1947	1868(95.9)	79(4.5)	8360	162
1984-85*	2033	1943(5.6)	90(4.4)	10393	177

* As at the end of February 1985.
Note: Figures in brackets are percentages to total.
Source: Compiled from RBI's "Annual Report on Trend and Progress of Banking in India", 1975-76 to 1984-5.

At the end of December 1985, Uttar Pradesh had the largest number of Regional Rural Bank offices at 2,745 (or 21.8 per cent of the total) followed by Bihar with 1,173 offices (14.1 per cent of the total) and Madhya Pradesh with 1,400 branches (11.1 per cent). The number of offices varied between 1,000 and 800 in Andhra Pradesh, Karnataka and Rajasthan: between

800 and 600 in Orissa and West Bengal; and between 600 and 200 in Maharashtra, Assam, Gujarat, Kerala, Jammu and Kashmir and Haryana. The number of branches of the rest of the States range below 200.

The year-wise and State-wise distribution of Regional Rural Bank offices is given in Table-11.

It indicates that the States, over the years, which have the largest number of operating offices, have the largest number of operating offices, have also had the greater share in opening new offices. It could be seen for the latest year ending 1985, of the total 2,361 new branch offices opened, 21.1 per cent (498) of them new opened in Uttar Pradesh; 12.4 per cent (293) in Bihar, 11.5 per cent (271) in Rajasthan; 11.3 per cent (268) in Madhya Pradesh; 1.6 per cent (169) in Andhra Pradesh and 6.3 per cent (148) in Karnataka.

The Northern region was dominating (Table-7) with 4,369 branches (35 per cent of the total branches), while the North-Eastern region lagged behind with a minimum of 511 branches (4 per cent of the total) at the end of 1985. The Eastern region had 3,230 branches (26 per cent), the Southern region had 2,363 branches (19 per cent) and the Western region had 2,133 branches (17 per cent).

Sponsor bank-wise table (Table-5) shows that only 4 banks were having more than 1,000 branches under the control of their respective operating RRBs in 1985. They were the State Bank of India (2,085 or 17 per cent of the total branches), the Central Bank of India (1,643 or 13 per cent), the Bank of Baroda (1,078 or 9 per cent) and the Punjab National Bank (1,041 or 8.3 per cent).

Further, out of the total[44] 188 Regional Rural Banks in the country in 1985, only one RRB (the Marathwada Grameena Bank of Maharashtra) had 216 operating branches, while 9 RRBs had[45] varied number of offices between 200 and 150, 24 RRBs had the range between 150 and 100; 81 RRBs between 100 and 50 and over 68 RRBs had below 50 operating branches. In addition, there were also 5 young RRBs awaiting to open their account.

Table 11
The Year-wise and State-wise Distribution of Regional Rural Bank Offices, 1975-85
(As at the End of December)

Name of the State Union Territory	*1975*	*1976*	*1977*	*1978*	*1979**	*1980*	*1981*	*1982*	*1983*	*1984*	*1985*
Andhra Pradesh	-	52	155	232	240	309	373	436	578	816	985
Assam	-	10	18	30	34	55	87	124	158	223	320
Bihar	3	39	122	210	266	622	996	1200	1298	1480	1773
Gujarat	-	-	-	2	9	43	57	76	114	175	288
Haryana	2	40	45	55	63	69	123	135	168	181	214
Himachal Pradesh	-	1	11	21	22	39	50	60	79	87	90
Jammu & Kashmir	-	20	35	38	42	68	112	160	197	238	259
Karnataka	-	30	78	131	156	260	328	421	604	818	966
Kerala	-	8	68	96	117	171	197	225	230	247	262
Madhya Pradesh	-	29	89	131	151	269	431	589	813	1132	1400
Maharashtra	-	3	28	44	49	89	101	115	150	354	445
Manipur	-	-	-	-	-	-	1	4	9	16	22
Meghalaya	-	-	-	-	-	-	-	3	11	30	39
Nagaland	-	-	-	-	-	-	-	-	-	4	8
Orissa	-	43	122	146	159	226	380	484	568	689	764
Punjab	-	-	-	-	-	-	-	-	11	79	107
Rajasthan	2	49	90	159	169	226	227	336	475	683	954
Tamil Nadu	-	-	25	50	55	84	100	108	114	130	150
Tripura	-	5	22	24	24	31	50	51	61	64	77
Uttar Pradesh	6	130	218	306	337	516	837	1255	1697	2247	2745

Contd.

Name of the State Union Territory	*1975*	*1976*	*1977*	*1978*	*1979**	*1980*	*1981*	*1982*	*1983*	*1984*	*1985*
West Bengal	4	44	71	87	97	182	295	405	460	528	693
Arunachal Pradesh	-	-	-	-	-	-	-	-	-	4	12
Mizoram	-	-	-	-	-	-	-	-	-	20	33
All India	17	503	1172	1762	1990	3279	4795	6191	7795	10245	12606

Note:

* Year as at the end of June

Source:

1. RBI :"Report on Currency and Finance", Economic Review, Various Issues from 1974-75 to 1984-85.
2. RBI : Annual Report on Trend and Progress of Banking in India", Various Issues from 1974-75 to 1984-85.

Deposit Mobilisation

With the remarkable improvement in the number of Regional Rural Banks and tremendous expansion in their branch network and number of districts covered, impressive progress has been achieved in the sphere of deposit mobilisation. Table-12 gives the year-wise growth of deposits of RRBs and also the number of deposit accounts.

The total deposits of RRBs were Rs.0.2 crores in 1975. By the end of December 1976 they amounted to Rs.7.6 crores. In 1978 the have gone up to Rs.74.9 crores; in 1980 to 199.8 crores; in 1982 to Rs.502.3 crores; in 1984 to Rs.959.9 crores; and in 1985 to a peak of Rs.1,285.8 crores.

Simultaneously, deposits per RRB and per branch also went up during the decade 1975-85. The average deposit per AAB which was Rs. 3.33 lakhs in 1975 has gone up to Rs. 68.75 lakhs in 1977. Again in 1979 it rose to Rs. 205.33 lakhs; in 1981 to Rs.314.02 lakhs: in 1983 to Rs.451.90 lakhs and in 1985 to Rs.683.95 lakhs.

In the same way deposits per branch increased from Rs. 1.18 lakhs in 1975 to Rs.2.78 lakhs in 1977; which further rose up to Rs.5.09 lakhs in 1979 to Rs.7.01 lakhs in 1981, to Rs.8.70 lakhs in 1983; and to Rs.10.20 lakhs in 1985.

Thus, during the period 1976-85, there has been an impressive increase in the amount of RRBs deposits as follows: (i) overall deposits increased over 169 times (ii) deposits per RRB went up by 36 times and (iii) deposits per branch raised about 7 times.

The Regional Rural Banks were also able to bring into its fold an admirably larger number of depositors as could be gauged from Table-12. The number of depositors of all Regional Rural Banks in the country increased from 1,94,998 to 37,00,557 during the period 1976-80; and from 37,00,557 to 1,61,24,412 during the period 1980-85. At the same time, number of depositors per RRB rose from 4,875 to 43,536 during the period 1976-80 which again went up from 43,536 to 85,768 during the period 1980-85. Likewise, deposit accounts per branch also have grown up to 1,279 in 1985 as against 1,129 in 1980 and 388 in 1976.

Table 12
Growth of Deposits of Regional Rural Banks, 1975-85

Year at the End of December	*Total Deposits (Rs. in Crores)*	*Total No. of Deposit Accounts*	*Per RRB Deposits (Rs. in Lakhs)*	*Per Branch Deposits (Rs. in Lakhs)*	*Per RRB Deposit Accounts*	*Per Branch Deposit Accounts*
1975	0.2	N.A	3.33	1.18	N.A	N.A
1976	7.6	194998	19.00	1.51	4874.95	387.67
1977	33.0	805243	68.75	2.78	16775.90	678.38
1978	74.9	1672780	146.86	4.25	32799.61	949.36
1979	123.2	N.A	205.33	5.09	N.A	N.A
1980	199.8	3700557	235.09	6.09	43535.96	1128.56
1981	336.0	5502222	314.02	7.01	51422.64	1147.49
1982	502.3	7636149	405.05	8.11	61089.19	1233.43
1983	677.8	9808718	451.90	8.70	65391.45	1258.33
1984	959.9	12834728	554.88	9.37	74189.18	1252.78
1985	1285.8	16124412	683.95	10.20	85768.15	1279.11

N.A.: Not Available

Source :

1. RBI : "Committee to Review Arrangements for Institutional Credit for Agriculture and Rural Development (CRAFICARD)", Bombay, 1981, pp.109-113.
2. NABARD : "Statistics on Regional Rural Banks", December, 1985.

Thus the growth registered in deposit accounts during 1976-85 is as follows: (i) total number of deposit accounts increased 83 times, (ii) accounts per RRB exceeded about 18 times and (iii) accounts per branch office rose only 3 times.

So, from the above analysis, it can be said that the Regional Rural Banks have made satisfactory progress towards inculcating saving habits with the banking system in their areas of operation particularly at locations which were unbanked or under banked. The Regional Rural Banks, therefore, were able to establish their image of a 'small-man's bank'.

Table 13
Growth of Deposits of Regional Rural Banks : Year-wise and State-wise

Name of the State/ Union Territory	*Deposits as at the End of the Year*					
	1980	*1981*	*1982*	*1983*	*1984*	*1985*
Andhra Pradesh	26.46	35.48	51.88	64.90	85.66	111.06
Assam	2.18	7.25	10.36	17.16	23.61	31.34
Bihar	25.16	53.38	82.72	110.73	157.09	198.50
Gujarat	1.66	2.66	4.73	6.43	9.51	15.05
Haryana	5.10	10.03	11.57	19.45	28.79	40.13
Himachal Pradesh	3.42	5.50	7.75	11.38	15.64	20.57
Jammu & Kashmir	3.42	6.27	10.27	12.40	18.33	23.48
Karnataka	3.47	18.77	29.11	41.79	62.80	90.30
Kerala	13.22	15.25	22.91	24.39	35.05	44.14
Madhya Pradesh	10.79	16.45	25.52	40.28	62.38	88.73
Maharashtra	8.25	5.57	8.22	8.28	15.98	28.86
Manipur	4.36	0.01	0.07	0.19	0.29	0.47
Meghalaya	-	-	0.07	0.35	0.88	2.11
Nagaland	-	-	-	-	0.05	0.20
Orissa	15.66	25.96	32.25	38.31	46.20	54.75
Punjab	-	-	-	0.33	1.54	6.01
Rajasthan	12.67	18.70	26.68	36.37	51.24	72.33
Tamil Nadu	4.91	7.31	9.61	11.32	15.61	16.80
Tripura	3.09	5.04	6.47	9.81	12.19	16.81
Uttar Pradesh	50.88	85.66	138.14	186.29	258.70	337.21
West Bengal	8.75	16.71	23.93	37.67	58.12	85.04
Arunachal Pradesh	-	-	-	-	0.07	0.30
Mizoram	-	-	-	-	0.23	1.63
All India	199.83	336.00	502.26	677.85	959.95	1285.82

Source: Compiled from RBI : "Report on Currency and Finance", Statistical Statements, II Volume, Various Issues from 1980-81 to 1984-85.

The State-wise and year-wise mobilisation of deposits by Regional Rural Banks are illustrated in Table-13.

Over the years, four States, namely, Uttar Pradesh, Bihar, Andhra Pradesh and Karnataka accounted for mobilising higher levels of deposits for RRBs. For instance, in 1985, Uttar Pradesh mobilised total deposits amounting to Rs.337.21 crores (or 26.2 per cent of the total), while Bihar mobilised Rs.198.50 crores (or 15.4 per cent). This was followed by Andhra Pradesh (Rs.111.06 crores or 8.6 per cent) and Karnataka (Rs.90.30 crores or 7 per cent) respectively. These four States also account for greater number of deposit accounts.

Classification of Regional Rural Banks on the basis of their deposits, at the end of December 1985 is as follows:

Amount of Deposits	*Number of Regional Rural Banks*
Below Rs. 1 crore	31
Between Rs. 1-5 crores	72
Between Rs. 5-10 crores	37
Above Rs. 10 crores	43
Nil	5
Total	188

Out of a total of 188 operating RRBs at the end of 1985, about 43 RRBs had deposits above Rs. 10 crores, 37 RRBs had deposits between Rs. 10-5 cores, 72 RRBs between Rs. 5-1 crores and over 31 RRBs had deposits below Rs. 1 crore.

The Region-wise operations of Regional Rural Banks are provided in Table-14.

The Northern and Eastern regions were able to mobilise larger amounts of deposits for Regional Rural Bank. During the period 1980-85, the percentage share of Northern region remained almost constant at 39 per cent of the total deposits in the country, while the Eastern region maintained its second position of above 25 per cent in all the years. The case of Southern region was a discouraging one. Its hare in mobilising deposits had been decreasing year after year i.e., from 28 per cent to 20 per cent during the 1980-85 period. About the position in Western and North-Eastern regions, though their

Table 14
Region-wise Operations of Regional Rural Banks in India (1980-85)
(As at the End of December)

(Amount in Crores of Rupees)

Name of the Region	*1980*	*1981*	*1982*	*1983*	*1984*	*1985*
			Deposits			
Northern Region	75.54(37.80)	126.16(37.55)	194.41(38.71)	226.24(39.28)	354.24(38.99)	499.73(38.86)
North-Eastern Region	5.27(2.64)	12.30(3.66)	16.90(3.38)	27.51(4.06)	37.31(3.89)	52.86(4.11)
Eastern Region	49.57(24.81)	96.05(28.59)	138.89(27.65)	186.71(27.54)	261.41(27.23)	338.29(26.31)
Western Region	14.07(7.04)	24.68(7.34)	38.47(7.66)	54.99(8.11)	87.87(9.15)	132.65(10.32)
Southern Region	55.38(27.71)	76.81(22.86)	113.51(22.60)	142.39(21.01)	199.12(20.74)	262.30(20.40)
All India	199.83(100.00)	336.00(100.00)	502.26(100.00)	677.85(100.00)	959.95(100.00)	1285.82(100.00)
			Credit			
Northern Region	60.66(24.92)	108.86(26.77)	172.49(29.89)	226.27(30.14)	332.01(30.72)	415.10(29.49)
North-Eastern Region	5.04(2.07)	11.09(2.73)	18.33(3.18)	23.99(3.19)	32.48(3.01)	46.75(3.32)
Eastern Region	55.93(22.98)	98.74(24.29)	150.31(26.04)	210.57(28.04)	291.18(26.94)	360.87(25.64)
Western Region	15.13(6.21)	30.21(7.43)	45.11(7.82)	58.20(7.75)	97.93(9.06)	146.13(10.38)
Southern Region	106.64(43.82)	157.69(38.78)	190.86(33.07)	231.82(30.88)	327.19(30.27)	438.82(31.17)
All India	243.38(100.00)	406.59(100.00)	577.11(100.00)	750.84(100.00)	1080.77(100.00)	1407.67(100.00)
			Credit-Deposit Ratio			
Northern Region	80.3	86.3	88.7	85.0	93.7	83.1
North-Eastern Region	95.6	90.2	108.5	87.2	87.1	88.4
Eastern Region	112.8	102.8	108.2	112.8	111.4	106.7
Western Region	107.5	122.4	117.5	105.8	111.5	110.1
Southern Region	192.6	205.3	168.1	162.8	164.3	167.3
All India	121.8	121.0	114.9	110.8	112.6	109.5

Note: Figures in parentheses are percentages to total.
Source: RBI: "Report on Currency and Finance", I Volume,Various Issues from 1980-81 to 1984-85.

deposit mobilisations were very insignificant compared to All India picture, their share to total had been increasing from 7 to 10 per cent and 3 to 4 percent respectively.

Loans and Advances

A review of the advances made by the Regional Rural Banks in India during the decade 1975-85 reveals that significant progress has been achieved in this sphere also. Table-15 provides the information on year-wise growth of advances of RRBs while Table-16 illustrates State-wise picture on the same matter.

The outstanding loans provided by Regional Rural Banks were a mere Rs.0.1 crore in 1975. They increased to Rs. 7.5 crores in 1976. In 1978 they further went up to RS.117.6 crores; in 1980 to Rs.243.4 crores; in 1982 to Rs.577.1 crores in 1984 to Rs.1080.8 crores and in 1985 to a massive total of Rs.1407.7 crores.

Simultaneously advances per RRB and per branch have also gone up during the period 1975-85. The outstanding advances per RRB, which was Rs.1.67 lakhs in 1975, went up to Rs.82.50 lakhs in 1977, which again increased to Rs.279 lakhs in 1979, to Rs.379.99 lakhs in 1981; to Rs.500.56 1akhs in 1983, and to Rs.748.76 lakhs in 1985.

In the same way, outstanding advances per branch registered an increase of Rs.11.17 1akhs in 1985, as against Rs.9.63 lakhs in 1983, Rs.8.48 lakhs in 1981, Rs.6.92 lakhs in 1979; Rs.3.34 lakhs in 1977 and Rs.0.59 lakhs in 1975.

Thus, during the decade 1975-85, there has been an increase in advances as follows : (a) overall advances increased nearly 171 times, (b) advances per RRB grew around 40 times and (c) advances per branch enlarged over 8 times.

The total number of loan accounts, which are also an important measure to judge the spread of banking facilities, have also increased substantially to a bulk of 70,12,524 at the end of December 1985 as against 21,16,740 in 1980 and a mere 100,039 in 1976. At the same time, the number of borrowers per RRB and per branch during the 1976-85 period improved from 2.5 thousands to 37.3 thousand and from 199 to 556

Table 15
Growth of Advances of Regional Rural Banks: 1975-85

Year at the End of December	*Total Outstanding Advances (Rs. in Crores)*	*Total No. of Loan Accounts*	*Per RRB Outstanding Advances (Rs. in Lakhs)*	*Per Branch Outstanding Advances (Rs. in Lakhs)*	*Per RRB Loan Accounts*	*Per Branch Loan Accounts*
1975	0.1	N.A	1.67	0.59	N.A	N.A
1976	7.5	100039	18.75	1.49	2500.97	198.88
1977	39.6	497684	82.50	3.34	10368.42	419.28
1978	117.6	1219731	230.00	6.67	24122.49	698.21
1979	167.4	N.A.	279.00	6.92	N.A	N.A
1980	243.4	2116740	286.33	7.42	24902.82	645.54
1981	406.6	2912630	379.99	8.48	27220.84	607.43
1982	577.1	3686316	465.41	9.32	29490.53	595.43
1983	750.8	4496525	500.56	9.63	29976.83	576.85
1984	1080.8	5811872	624.72	10.55	33594.64	567.29
1985	1407.7	7012524	748.76	11.17	37300.66	556.28

N.A.: Not Available

Source:

1. Agriculture Finance Corporation : "A Study of Regional Rural Banks", Bombay, 1981, pp.41-42.
2. RBI : "Report on Currency and Finance", Statistical Statements, II Volumes, from 1980-81 to 1984-85 issues.

respectively. Hence growth in loan accounts has been as follows : (i) total number of accounts increased 70 times, (ii) accounts per RRB increased 15 times and (iii) accounts per branch rose around 3 times.

Table 16
State-wise and Year-wise Advances of Regional Rural Banks

(Amount in Crores of Rupees)

Name of the State Union Territory	*Deposits as at the End of the Year*					
	1980	*1981*	*1982*	*1983*	*1984*	*1985*
Andhra Pradesh	47.66	67.50	77.38	90.90	126.05	177.42
Assam	1.45	3.89	6.40	8.64	14.56	22.91
Bihar	19.53	44.78	67.91	94.74	133.78	171.09
Gujarat	0.58	1.27	2.21	3.98	7.63	12.35
Haryana	6.02	12.71	15.28	19.19	25.45	32.92
Himachal Pradesh	1.74	2.58	3.99	5.86	8.48	10.62
Jammu & Kashmir	1.88	3.63	5.43	7.62	9.81	12.41
Karnataka	23.36	38.37	56.06	75.51	116.75	153.27
Kerala	23.88	34.92	40.05	44.55	58.97	78.22
Madhya Pradesh	10.51	20.70	31.59	43.14	70.94	102.57
Maharashtra	4.04	8.24	11.31	11.08	19.37	31.21
Manipur	-	0.01	0.05	0.24	0.44	0.58
Meghalaya	-	-	0.01	0.10	0.43	0.91
Nagaland	-	-	-	-	0.80	0.16
Orissa	27.80	38.13	56.49	75.73	99.57	112.83
Punjab	-	-	-	0.30	1.12	4.64
Rajasthan	19.20	30.46	42.45	55.90	72.50	91.35
Tamil Nadu	11.74	16.90	17.38	20.85	25.42	29.91
Tripura	3.59	7.19	11.87	14.99	16.71	20.84
Uttar Pradesh	31.82	60.08	105.31	137.40	214.62	263.15
West Bengal	8.60	15.83	25.90	40.09	57.82	76.95
Arunachal Pradesh	-	-	-	-	0.01	0.05
Mizoram	-	-	-	-	0.25	1.31
All India	243.38	406.59	577.11	750.84	1080.77	1407.67

Source: Complied from RBI : "Report on Currency and Finance", Statistical Statements, II Volume, Various Issues from 1980-81 to 1984-85.

From Table-16 it can be observed that, by December 1965, over 51 per cent of total outstanding loans of all Regional Rural Banks in India were concentrated only in 5 States, namely, Uttar Pradesh (18.7 Per cent) Andhra Pradesh (12.6 per cent), Bihar (12.1 per cent), Karnataka (10.9 per cent) and Madhya Pradesh (7.3 per cent). The same States, excluding Bihar, also account for having greater number of loan beneficiaries in comparison with other states.

A region-wise analysis of Regional Rural Banks, as could be seen from Table-14 illustrates the fact that the Southern States were ahead in lending credit constituting 31 per cent of total advances in 1985, though it had declined consistently from 44 per cent from 1980. However, the cases of Northern (increased from 23 to 29 per cent), Eastern (increased from 23 to 26 per cent) and Western (increased from 6 to 9 per cent) regions were also appeared to be hopeful considering the fact that their percentage share had been increased year by year during the above said period while the position of North-Eastern region remained at an insignificant level. The Bank-wise performance of RRBs is as follows:

Outstanding Loans	*Number of Regional Rural Eanks*
Below Rs. 1crore	45
Between Rs. 1-5 crores	60
Between Rs. 5-10 crores	31
Above Rs. 10 crores	47
Nil	5
Total	188

At the end of December 1985, out of a total of 188 Regional Rural Banks in the country, over 47 RRBs had outstanding advances of above Rs.10 crores 31 RRBs had advances between Rs.10-5 crores 60 RRBs had between Rs.5-1 crore and over 45 had below Rs.1 crore advances.

As a small man's bank, the Regional Rural Banks are catering to the credit needs of extremely needy, helpless and vulnerable section of the rural society viz., the small farmers, marginal farmers, agricultural labourers, rural artisan and so on. The bulk of the loans almost all of them, have been restricted to the benefit of these target groups. Table-17 confirms this view.

Accordingly, the percentage share of weaker sections in the total direct advances of Regional Rural Banks remained consistently constant at over 90 per cent during all the years from 1976-85. This shows the extent of devotion of Regional Rural Banks to serve the weaker sections and help the common man to enjoy the banking facilities without much effort.

Table 17
Share of Weaker Sections in the Total Advances of Regional Rural Banks

(Rupees in Crores)

Year	*Total Advances*	*Advances to Small and Marginal Farmers/ Agricultural Labourers/ Rural Artisans and Others*	*Percentage of Col. 3 to 4*
1976-77	19.58	17.64	90.1
1977-78	52.27	48.40	92.6
1978-79	143.00	134.00	93.7
1979-80	181.00	164.00	91.0
1980-81	274.00	261.00	95.2
1981-82	436.00	415.00	95.2
1982-83	603.00	579.00	96.0
1983-84	809.00	781.00	96.5
1984-85	1048.30	968.60	92.4

Source: RBI: "Report on Currency and Finance", Volume I, Various Issues from 1975-76 to 1984-85.

The purpose-wise classification of direct advances of Regional Rural Banks for the years 1983 and 1985 is provided in Table-18.

The table illustrates that in June 1983, out of a total direct advances of Rs.600.55 crores in 37,66,836 accounts provided by Regional Rural Banks, Rs.108.50 crores in 9,48,854 accounts were given for short-term crop loans. The term loans constituting agricultural investments plus allied activities stood at Rs.273.05 crores in 12,83,441 accounts. Besides agricultural loans, the RRBs were also issued non-agricultural credit and the bulk of which went to retail trade/small business including self-employment amounting to Rs.144.26 crores in 9,56,870 accounts. The rural artisans along with village and cottage industries had got Rs.34.86 crores in 2,76,447 accounts, while Rs.2.58 crores in 33,113 accounts advanced as consumption loans and Rs.31.01 crores in 2,68,111 accounts were left to other purposes.

Table 18

Direct Advances of Regional Rural Banks: Purpose-wise Classification

(Amount Rupees in Crores)

Purpose	June 1983		December1985	
	No. of Accounts	Amount	No. of Accounts	Amount
Short-term loans (crop loans)	948854(25.19)	108.80(18.12)	1617968(23.25)	264.16(19.22)
Term Loans				
(a) Agricultural Investments	623961(16.56)	155.95(25.97)	1135268(16.31)	314.78(22.91)
(b) Allied Activities	659480(17.51)	117.10(19.50)	1195236(17.18)	236.60(17.22)
Retail Trade/Small business and Self-employment etc.	956870(25.40)	144.26(24.02)	1881896(27.04)	366.01(26.63)
Rural Artisans, Village and Cottage Industries	276447(7.34)	34.86(5.80)	526364(7.57)	79.91(5.82)
Consumption loans	33113(0.88)	2.58(0.43)	98876(1.42)	10.91(0.79)
Other purposes	268111(7.12)	37.01(6.16)	502783(7.23)	101.85(7.41)
Total	3766836(100.0)	600.55(100.0)	6958391(100.0)	1374.22(100.0)

Source:NABARD : "Statistics on Regional Rural Banks", 1983-1985 Issues.

Comparatively in 1985, the amounts and accounts of all the above said purposes have gone up considerably. Over 16,17,968 beneficiaries had got an amount of Rs.264.16 crores as short-term crop loans., Rs. 551.38 crores to 23,30,504 beneficiaries had been given as term loans1 Rs.366.01 crores to 18,81,896 borrowers for retail trade and small business including self employment; Rs.79.91 crores to 5,26,364 borrowers from rural artisan and village and cottage Industries Rs.10.91 crores to 98,876 borrowers for consumption and Rs.101.85 crores in 5,02,783 accounts for other purposes. The percentage loan increase in December 1985 over June 1983 for all these purposes were 243,202,254,229,423 and 275 respectively.

One noticeable fact here is that out of total direct advances lent to different borrowers in1985 or in 1983 nearly 60 per cent has been advanced towards agricultural purposes whereas the remaining 40 per cent was left to non-agricultural purposes. This clearly shows the dominance of farm loans in direct advances of RRBs and thereby their keen interest in modernising agriculture and development of the rural economy.

The purpose-wise and State-wise classification of direct advance of RRB in 1985 are mentioned in Table-19.

Further, another break up of year-wise and category-wise advances of Regional Rural Banks enable us to understand how far the RRBs have become successful in providing financial assistance to different customer groups of the poorer sections of rural society. The category-wise deployment of credit by Regional Rural Banks is given in Table-20.

The objective of RRBs in providing financial assistance to the small and marginal farmers and agricultural labourers has almost been fulfilled since they extended over 58 per cent of total advances consistently to this category during the decade 1975-85. The share of this group had grown by leaps and bounds from a mere Rs.11.60 crores in June 1977 to Rs.104.61 crores in December 1979 and further to Rs.180.34 crores in June 1991. This amount has further gone upto Rs.381.85 crores in June 1983 and further touched the peak of Rs.815.54 crores in

Table 19

Classification of Direct Advances of Regional Rural Bank as at the end of December, 1985 State-wise

(Amount in lakhs of Rupees)

Name of the States/Union Territory	Short-term (crop) Loans	Rank	Agricultural Investments	Rank	Allied Activities	Rank	Rural Artisans, Village and Cottage Industries	Rank
Andhra Pradesh	7594.01(28.75)	1	3384.51(10.75)	5	1471.18(6.22)	6	596.15(7.46)	7
Assam	163.21(0.62)	13	379.58(1.21)	13	400.86 (1.69)	14	122.74(1.54)	13
Bihar	713.41(2.70)	9	3785.27(12.02)	4	4322.18(18.27)	1	1192.73(14.93)	2
Gujarat	137.86(0.52)	14	383.44(1.22)	12	316.70(1.34)	17	110.69(1.39)	14
Haryana	48.13(0.18)	18	668.46(2.12)	10	1451.74(6.14)	7	148.17(1.85)	12
Himachal Pradesh	21.63(0.08)	20	64.09(0.20)	17	368.52(1.56)	16	109.69(1.37)	15
Jammu & Kashmir	77.47(0.29)	15	66.14(0.21)	16	514.24(2.17)	10	215.40(2.50)	10
Karnataka	4735.61(17.93)	2	2781.37(8.87)	6	2684.15(11.34)	3	371.79(4.65)	8
Kerala	2691.73(10.19)	4	664.91(2.11)	11	491.80(2.08)	11	252.38(3.16)	9
Madhya Pradesh	887.35(3.36)	8	3811.52(12.11)	3	1270.39(5.37)	8	772.62(9.67)	3
Maharashtra	472.84(1.79)	10	938.98(2.98)	9	455.45(1.92)	13	92.02(1.15)	16
Manipur	1.45(0.01)	21	3.60(0.01)	19	9.35(0.04)	20	5.71(0.07)	21
Meghalaya	53.90(0.20)	16	2.59(0.01)	21	3.86(0.02)	22	6.06(0.08)	20
Nagaland	0.80(-)	22	0.61(-)	22	6.63(0.03)	21	2.79(0.03)	22
Orissa	2662.20(10.08)	5	2232.51(7.09)	7	1571.02(6.64)	5	642.56(8.04)	5
Punjab	49.11(0.19)	17	37.31(0.12)	18	160.66(0.68)	18	48.41(0.61)	18
Rajasthan	391.00(1.40)	11	3875.46(12.31)	2	2419.29(10.32)	4	642.00(8.03)	6
Tamil Nadu	1171.20(4.43)	7	255.41(0.81)	14	452.70(1.91)	12	63.11(0.79)	17
Tripura	200.05(0.76)	12	165.63(0.53)	15	397.35(1.68)	15	194.22(2.43)	11
Uttar Pradesh	2779.98(10.52)	3	7009.07(22.27)	1	3775.41(15.96)	2	1624.78(20.23)	1
West Bengal	1524.18(5.77)	6	954.72(3.03)	80	1088.92(4.16)	9	746.60(9.34)	4
Arunachal Pradesh	1.67(0.01)	23	2.88(0.01)	20	-	-	0.24(-)	-

Contd.

Mizoram	37.00(0.14)	19	-	-	28.00(0.12)	19	30.00(0.38)	19
All India	26415.79(100.00)		31478.06(100.00)		23660.40(100.00)			

Contd.

	Retail Trade/ Small Business/ and Self-employees	Rank	Consumption Loans	Rank	Other Purposes	Rank	Total Direct Outstanding Advances	Rank
	1810.81(4.95)	8	202.05(18.52)	2	2318.63(22.76)	1	17377.34(12.64)	2
	873.59(2.39)	10	3.07(0.28)	14	207.81(2.04)	14	2150.86(1.57)	13
	6433.16(17.58)	2	46.44(4.26)	8	582.37(5.72)	6	17075.56(12.43)	3
	237.25(0.65)	17	19.67(1.80)	10	28.56(0.28)	18	1234.17(0.90)	16
	675.39(1.84)	11	5.00(0.46)	13	266.12(2.61)	11	3263.81(2.37)	10
	337.88(0.92)	15	0.36(0.03)	16	159.80(1.57)	13	1061.97(0.77)	17
	306.93(0.84)	16	-	-	60.20(0.59)	16	1240.38(0.90)	15
	1961.20(9.09)	7	92.81(8.51)	6	1436.79(14.11)	3	14073.72(10.24)	4
	3326.30(9.09)	3	167.47(15.00)	3	230.17(2.26)	12	7821.76(5.69)	8
	3113.08(8.51)	4	14.57(1.34)	11	292.28(2.87)	10	10161.81(7.39)	6
	672.12(1.84)	12	29.80(2.73)	9	130.98(1.29)	15	2792.19(2.03)	12
	35.58(0.10)	19	-	-	2.19(0.02)	21	57.88(0.04)	21
	21.66(0.06)	21	-	-	2.64(0.03)	20	90.71(0.07)	20
	3.94(0.01)	22	-	-	0.42(-)	22	15.19(0.01)	22
	2683.28(7.33)	5	1110.55(10.13)	4	1059.71(10.40)	4	10961.83(7.98)	5
	119.05(0.32)	18	-	-	49.82(0.49)	17	464.36(0.34)	18
	1436.64(3.92)	9	76.12(6.97	7	294.87(2.89)	9	9135.38(6.65)	7
	336.38(0.92)	14	1.43(0.13)	15	592.48(5.82)	5	2872.71(2.09)	11
	623.18(1.70)	13	92.41(8.47)	5	339.72(3.34)	7	2012.56(1.46)	14
	9000.57(24.59)	1	225.94(20.71)	1	1792.84(17.60)	2	26208.59(19.07)	1
	2562.71(7.00)	6	6.21(0.57)	12	330.89(3.25)	8	2214.23(5.25)	9
	0.25(-)	-	-	-	0.18(-)	23	5.22(-)	23
	30.00(0.08)	20	-	-	6.00(0.06)	19	131.00(0.10)	19
	36600(100.00)		1090.90(100.00)		10185.47(100.00)		137422.03(100.00)	

Source: NABARD: "Statistics on Regional Rural Banks", December, 1985, pp.14-23.

Table 20

Deployment of Credit by Regional Rural Banks : Category-wise

(Amount in Crores of Rupees)

Category	*June* 1977*	*June* 1978*	*December 1979*	*December 1980*
Small and Marginal Farmers and Landless Labourers (Agricultural purposes)	11.60(58.29)	40.04(60.71)	104.61(62.50)	N.A
Rural Artisans, Retail Trade, Village/Cottage Industries, Small Business including Self-employment, etc.	6.34(31.86)	21.12(32.02)	49.87(29.80)	N.A
Consumption Loans	0.03(0.15)	0.08(0.13)	0.91(0.50)	N.A
Indirect Loans Through Primary Agricultural Credit Societies/Farmers Service Societies	1.93(9.70)	4.71(7.14)	8.16(4.90)	N.A
Other purposes	-	-	3.86(2.30)	N.A
Total	19.90(100.0)	65.95(100.0)	167.41(100.0)	N.A

June 1981	*June 1982*	*June 1983*	*December 1884*	*December 1985*
180.34(59.60)	N.A	381.85(61.22)	644.07(59.59)	815.54(57.94)
81.61(27.00)	N.A	179.12(28.72)	315.22(29.17)	445.92(31.68)
1.48(0.50)	N.A	2.58(0.42)	9.30(0.86)	10.91(0.77)
16.08(5.30)	N.A	23.14(3.71)	32.52(3.01)	33.45(2.38)
22.94(7.60)	N.A	37.00(5.93)	79.66(7.37)	101.85(7.23)
302.45(100.0)	N.A	623.69(100.0)	1080.77(100.0)	1407.67(100.0)

N.A.: Not Available.

*Separate data on loans provided to other purpose are not available for the years 1977 and 1978.

Source:

1. RBI : "Functions and Working", 1983, p.218.
2. RBI : "Craficard" 1981, p.111.
3. NABARD : "Statistics on Regional Rural Banks", 1983-85 Issues.

December 1985. Side by side, the number of beneficiaries had increased remarkably from 1,50,000 in 1977 to 10,47.000 in 1979 and to 22,32,295 in 1983 and over 39.48,472 in 1985.

Along with agriculturists, another important category of borrowers of RRBs constitute the rural artisan and others from the side of village and cottage industries, retail trade, small business self-employment, etc. The loan outstanding of this category[46] stood in 81,000 accounts at Rs.6.34 crores in 1977; in 5,09,925 accounts at Rs.49.81 crores in 1979 in 12,33,317 accounts at Rs.179.12 crores in 1983 and in 24,08,260 accounts at Rs.445.92 crores in 1985. The percentage share of this category in total advances remained at 32 per cent both in 1977 and in 1985, though fluctuations occurred in between them.

The Regional Rural Banks were also providing consumption loans in the rural areas, but they constitute very negligible and insignificant amount in the total advances. Their share in the aggregate advances was only 0.77 per cent in 1985 as against 0.42 per cent in 1983 and against 0.50 per cent in 1977.

The amount of loans provided for other purposes constituted Rs.3.86 crores in 1979, Rs.22.94 crores in 1981, Rs.37.00 crores in 1983 and Rs.101.55 crores in 1985.

In addition to all the above categories, Regional Rural Banks have also granted indirect accommodation of loans to poorer sections through Farmers Service Societies and Primary Agricultural Credit Societies to the tune of Rs.33.45 crores in 1985 as against Rs.23.14 crores in 1983 and also Rs.8.16 crores in 1979 and Rs.1.93 crores in 1977.

The Regional Rural Banks have been specially established to cater to the financial needs of weaker sections. Even more they have been specifically instructed to make every effort to increase the coverage of beneficiaries under the New Twenty-Point Economic Programme and the IRDP. Along with other credit agencies, they were also asked to participate and implement the District Credit Plans.

According to available information, the RRBs were generally able to meet their share of commitments. Particularly, they have actively involved themselves in the implementation of IRDP. The total number of beneficiaries under the Programme were 4.25 lakhs in 1982. They increased to 7.84 lakhs in 1983 and 9.77 lakhs in 1984, but slightly decreased to 7.93 lakhs for the year 1985. Advances, on the other hand, which were Rs.100.28 crores in 1982, went up to Rs. 151.03 crores in 1983 and to Rs. 211.13 crores in 1984 and decreased to Rs. 180.93 crores in 1985.

Besides, RRBs also disbursed Rs.4.32 crores to 0.28 lakh beneficiaries under the DRI Scheme in 1985, as against Rs.6.65 crores to 0.48 beneficiaries in 1984 and also against Rs.6.89 crores to 0.57 lakh beneficiaries in 1983.

Table-21 gives the Inter-State variations of advances of RRBs under special programmes at the end of December 1985.

Accordingly, Uttar Pradesh (25 per cent), Bihar (24 per cent) and West Bengal (13 per cent) are the States in which greater amount of advances were given and larger number of beneficiaries were covered under the IRDP programme, whereas Karnataka (24 per cent) and Orissa (43 per cent) accounted for advances given heavily under the DRI Scheme.

Credit-Deposit Ratio

Credit-Deposit (C-D) ratio reveals the ratio of advances to the deposits collected. It was said to be[47] an important guiding principle for judging the operational efficiency of any financial institution. The year-wise C-D ratio of Regional Rural Banks is as follows:

Year	*Credit-Deposit Ratio*
1975	50
1976	99
1977	120
1978	157
1979	136
1980	122
1981	121
1982	115
1983	111
1984	113
1985	109

Table 21

Loans Issued by Regional Rural Banks under Special Programmes (January 1985 to December 1985)

(Amount in lakhs of Rupees)

Name of the State/ Union Territory	IRDP		DRI		Others		Total	
	No. of Accounts	Amount	No. of Accounts	Amount	No. of Accounts	Amount	No. of Accounts	Amount
Andhra Pradesh	20819(2.63)	749.12(4.14)	1663(5.91)	15.60(3.61)	99577(17.20)	2405.6118.79	1220598.72	3170.3310.12
Assam	23148(2.92)	502.07(2.77)	274(0.97)	3.23(0.75)	2163(0.37)	72.220.56	255851.83	577.521.84
Bihar	191150(24.11)	4372.33(24.17)	311(1.11)	2.07(0.48)	22147(3.82)	725.965.67	21360815.26	5100.3616.28
Gujarat	14800(1.87)	457.64(2.53)	287(1.02)	3.21(0.74)	1085(0.19)	27.240.21	161721.15	488.091.56
Haryana	9010(1.14)	293.28(1.62)	412(1.47)	13.92(3.22)	5578(0.96)	195.001.52	150001.07	502.201.60
Himachal Pradesh	3044(0.38)	73.00(0.40)	-	-	2817(0.49)	72.000.56	58610.42	145.000.42
Jammu and Kashmir	7716(0.97)	266.42(1.47)	789(2.81)	23.98(5.54)	824(0.14)	47.860.37	93290.67	338.261.08
Karnataka	28144(3.55)	819.78(4.53)	5170(18.40)	105.74(24.45)	37468(6.47)	853.496.67	707825.05	1779.015.68
Kerala	5463(0.65)	102.00(0.56)	3610(12.85)	29.62(6.85)	112454(19.42)	2252.6917.60	1215278.68	2384.317.61
Madhya Pradesh	96744(12.20)	2306.41(12.74)	485(1.73)	3.68(0.85)	46841(8.69)	1637.9112.79	14407010.29	3947.7812.60
Maharashtra	19855(2.50)	549.55(3.04)	-	-	3658(0.64)	119.370.93	23131.68	668.922.14
Manipur	185(0.02)	3.84(0.02)	470(1.67)	5.32(1.23)	598(0.10)	14.540.11	12530.09	23.700.08
Meghalaya	2(-)	0.01(-)	-	-	5104(0.88)	96.050.75	51060.36	96.060.31
Nagaland	-	-	56(0.20)	0.71(0.16)	363(0.06)	14.480.11	4190.03	15.190.05
Orissa	51127(6.45)	934.79(5.17)	11983(42.65)	187.25(43.30)	33914(5.86)	539.074.21	970246.93	1661.115.34
Punjab	4709(0.59)	125.80(0.70)	-	-	2010(0.35)	60.630.48	67190.49	186.430.60
Rajasthan	28800(3.63)	667.13(3.69)	128(0.45)	2.84(0.99)	1970(0.34)	63.760.50	308982.21	732.932.30
Tamil Nadu	7640(0.96)	177.97(0.98)	114(0.41)	4.29(0.99)	74768(12.19)	1387.6510.84	825225.89	1569.915.01
Tripura	14110(1.78)	240.28(1.33)	107(0.38)	0.59(0.14)	15538(2.68)	300.462.35	297552.12	541.331.73
Uttar Pradesh	205804(25.96)	4567.44(25.24)	1295(4.61)	22.16(5.12)	68881(11.89)	1493.7311.67	27598019.71	6083.3319.42
West Bengal	60691(7.65)	833.94(12.89)	680(2.42)	8.99(2.08)	41359(3.30)	422.743.30	1027.307.34	1315.674.23
Arunachal Pradesh	-	-	-	-	-	-	-	-
Mizoram	-	-	263(0.94)	0.09(0.02)	-	-	2630.02	0.09(-)
All India	792961(100.00)	18092.80(100.00)	28097(100.00)	432.49(100.00)	579117(100.00)	12802.24(100.00)	1400175100.00	31327.53(100.00)

Source: NABARD : "Statistics on Regional Rural Banks", December 1985, pp.9-12..

In the initial stages, the All-India Credit-Deposit ratio of Regional Rural Banks had shown an increasing trend. The C-D ratio of RRBs in 1975 was only 50 per cent. In 1976 it increased to 99, in 1977 to 120 and in 1978 it had reached the highest level at 157. From then on the C-D ratio of RRBs, showed a decreasing trend and started to fall year after year, from 136 in 1979 to 122 in 1980 and then to 121 in 1981, to 111 in 1983, to 113 in 1984 and to 109 in 1985.

The upshot of the above analysis indicates that RRBs should strive for the progressive improvement in their Credit-Deposit ratio. However, it was said by the supporters of Regional Rural Banks that the C-D ratios of these banks were definitely better than those of commercial banks which showed about 64.4 or rural areas during 1985. This high C-D ratio reveals that RRBs have been using more of their resources within the local areas they mobilised than in other areas. The Regional Rural Banks are therefore widely recognised as the development banks of rural Clientele and newer instrument of carrying the banking message to the rural areas on effective lines.

The Southern region had got the highest C-D ratio (Table-14), at 167.3 during 1985, followed by Western and Eastern regions with 110.7 and 106.7 respectively, while the North-Eastern and Northern region lagged behind at the ratios of 88.4 and 83.1.

Table- 22 illustrates the year-wise and State-wise Credit-Deposit ratios of RRBs.

One can notice widespread differences among the C-D ratios of different States during the period 1980-85. The States with higher C-D ratios well above the national level (109) in 1985 were Orissa (206), Tamil Nadu (178), Kerala (177), Karnataka (170), Andhra Pradesh (160), Rajasthan (126), Tripura (124), Manipur (123) and Madhya Pradesh (116). On 'the other hand, the States with C-D ratios much below the national level constituted Maharashtra (108), West Bengal (90), Bihar (86), Gujarat (82), Haryana (82), Uttar Pradesh (78), Punjab (77), Nagaland (77), Assam (73), Jammu & Kashmir (53), Himachal Pradesh (52) and Meghalaya (43). In the case of two Union Territories, Mizoram and Arunachal Pradesh the C-D was 81 and 18 respectively.

Table 22
Credit-Deposit Ratio of Regional Rural Banks: State-wise and Year-wise

Name of the State/ Union Territory	*As at the End of the Year*					
	1980	*1981*	*1982*	*1983*	*1984*	*1985*
Andhra Pradesh	180.1	190.2	149.2	140.1	147.2	159.8
Assam	66.5	53.7	61.8	50.3	61.7	73.1
Bihar	77.6	83.9	82.1	85.6	85.2	86.2
Gujarat	39.7	47.7	46.7	61.9	80.2	82.1
Haryana	118.0	126.7	132.1	98.7	88.4	82.0
Himachal Pradesh	50.9	46.9	51.5	51.5	54.2	51.6
Jammu & Kashmir	54.1	48.3	52.9	61.4	53.5	52.9
Karnataka	176.7	204.4	192.6	180.7	185.9	169.7
Kerala	221.3	228.9	174.8	182.7	668.2	177.2
Madhya Pradesh	127.3	125.8	123.8	107.1	113.7	115.6
Maharashtra	92.6	147.9	137.6	133.8	121.2	108.1
Manipur	-	100.0	71.4	126.3	152.7	123.4
Meghalaya	-	-	14.3	28.6	48.9	43.1
Nagaland	-	-	-	-	177.0	77.0
Orissa	177.5	146.9	175.2	197.7	215.5	206.1
Punjab	-	-	-	90.9	72.7	77.2
Rajasthan	151.5	162.9	159.1	153.7	141.5	126.3
Tamil Nadu	239.1	231.2	180.6	184.2	62.8	178.0
Tripura	116.2	142.7	183.5	152.8	137.1	124.0
Uttar Pradesh	62.5	70.1	76.2	73.8	83.0	78.0
West Bengal	98.3	94.7	108.2	106.4	99.5	90.5
Arunachal Pradesh	-	-	-	-	14.0	18.0
Mizoram	-	-	-	-	111.0	81.0
All India	121.8	121.0	114.9	110.8	112.6	109.5

Source: Compiled from RBI : Report on Currency and Finance, Statistical Statements, II Volumes, from 1980-81 to 1984-85.

Recovery Performance

The importance of timely recovery for maintaining an unrestricted flow of funds cannot be overemphasised, as recycling of funds is adversely affected by mounting overdues. The problem of overdues has been agency neutral and is common whether the agency is cooperatives, commercial banks or the Government.

In 1977, the Dantwala Committee estimated overdues of 8 Regional Rural Banks at 15.7 per cent. At the end of both December 1980 and 1981 overdues of RRBs remained at 17 per cent, while in the years 1983, 1984 and 1985 they continued to be at 25 per cent of total advances outstanding. The details of over dues of RRBs are shown in the following table.

Table 23
Overdues of Regional Rural Banks

Year Ending December	*Overdues Outstanding*		*Percentage of Overdues to Total Outstanding Advances*
	No. of Accounts	*Amount*	
1980	410877	41.47	17.04
1981	707847	68.11	16.75
1982	1061188	128.07	22.19
1983	1460528	191.72	25.53
1984	1670301	267.40	24.74
1985	2245176	351.93	25.00

Source: RBI: "Report on Currency and Finance", Statistical Statements, II Volumes, Various Issues from 1980-81 to 1984-85.

The classification of RRBs on the basis of their recovery performance at the end of June 1985 is as follows:

Recovery as Percentage to Demand	*Number of Regional Rural Banks*
More than 80 per cent	7
More than 70 per centUpto 80 per cent	20
More than 60 per centUpto 70 per cent	31
More than 50 per centUpto 60 per cent	40
More than 40 per centUpto 50 per cent	31
Up to 40 per cent	33
Nil	18
N.A.	3
Total	183

N.A: Not Available
Note: Calculated with the help of "Statistics on Regional Rural Banks", NABARD.

It is evident from the above illustration that only in 7 RRBs the recovery performance was above 80 per cent, while it was upto 40 per cent in 33 others.

Generally speaking the recovery has been about 48.4 per cent of a total demand of Rs.623.67 crores at the end of June 1985, the collections amounted to Rs.301.65 crores leaving an overdue amount of Rs.322.02 crores. The performance of recovery, however, varied among different States from as poor as 19.9 per cent to as high as 79.6 per cent. The State-wise recovery performance of RRBs is shown in Table-24.

Table 24
State-wise Recovery Performance of Regional Rural Banks for the year Ended June 1985

(Amount in Lakhs of Rupees)

Name of the State/ Union Territory	*Demand Amount*	*Collection Amount*	*Balance (Overdues) Amount*	*Percentage of Recovery to Demand (Col. 4 to 3)*
Andhra Pradesh	8543.80(13.70)	4236.45(14.04)	4307.35(13.38)	49.6
Assam	1184.83(1.90)	503.22(1.67)	681.61(2.12)	42.5
Bihar	6345.04(10.17)	2652.21(8.79)	2369.83(11.47)	41.8
Gujarat	398.32(0.64)	222.69(0.74)	175.63(0.55)	55.9
Haryana	1691.07(2.71)	879.28(2.91)	811.79(2.52)	52.0
Himachal Pradesh	367.08(0.59)	224.46(0.74)	142.62(0.44)	61.1
Jammu & Kashmir	546.95(0.88)	212.42(0.70)	334.53(1.04)	38.8
Karnataka	7697.14(12.34)	4432.10(14.69)	3265.04(10.14)	57.6
Kerala	5365.81(8.60)	3950.45(13.10)	1415 36(4.39)	73.6
Madhya Pradesh	3686.37(5.91)	1684.26(5.58)	2002.11(6.22)	45.7
Maharashtra	1351.37(2.17)	603.28(2.00)	748.09(2.32)	44.6
Manipur	18.32(0.03)	6.06(0.02)	12.26(0.04)	33.1
Meghalaya	34.05(0.06)	23.54(0.08)	10.51(0.03)	69.1
Nagaland	1.03(-)	0.37(-)	0.66(-)	35.9
Orissa	6154.44(9.87)	2284.19(7.57)	3870.25(12.01)	37.1
Punjab	40.43(0.06)	32.05(0.11)	8.38(0.03)	79.3
Rajasthan	3574.86(5.73)	1532.486(5.08)	2041.886(6.34)	42.9
Tamil Nadu	1802.16(2.89)	1132.22(3.76)	669.94(2.08)	62.8
Tripura	1235.78(1.98)	246.27(0.82)	989.51(3.07)	19.9
Uttar Pradesh	9021.97(14.47)	3836.94(12.72)	5185.03(16.10)	42.5
West Bengal	3289.03(5.29)	1464.95(4.86)	1834.48(5.70)	44.6
Arunachal Pradesh	1.05(-)	0.62(-)	0.43(-)	59.0
Mizoram	5.74(0.01)	4.01(0.01)	1.73(0.01)	69.9
All India	62366.64(100.00)	30164.62(100.00)	32202.02(100.00)	48.4

Note: Figures in parenthesis are percentages to total
Source: NABARD : "Statistics on Regional Rural Banks", December 1989, pp.29-33.

Staffing Pattern

The strength of the staff of Regional Rural Banks had increased markedly during the period 1976-85, as could be seen from Table-25.

Table 25
Staff Strength of Regional Rural Banks : Cadre-wise, 1976-85

Year at the End of December	Regional Rural Banks' Staff					
	Officers	*Clerical*	*Subordinate Staff*	*Total*	*Of which belonging to SC/ ST++*	*Total Trained Staff ++*
1976	565(5.92)	612(48.92)	74(45.16)	1251(100.00)	-	-
1977	1254(36.44)	1921(55.83)	266(7.73)	3441*(100.00)	-	-
1978	2669(41.36)	3364(52.12)	421(6.18)	6454**(100.00)	-	-
1979	3650(41.66)	4570(52.16)	541(6.18)	8761(100.00)	-	-
1980	5286(42.65)	6279(50.67)	828(6.68)	12393***(100.00)	-	-
1981	N.A	N.A	N.A	N.A	-	-
1982	N.A	N.A	N.A	N.A	-	-
1983*	12948(45.30)	12928(45.23)	2705(9.47)	28,581(100.00)	3572(12.50)	16019(56.05)
1984	18951(51.77)	17469(47.72)	190(0.52)	36610(100.00)	5307(21.04)	25221(68.89)
1985	22.870(51.27)	21417(48.02)	318(0.71)	44605(100.00)	7155(16.04)	33061(74.12)

Note: N.A.: Not Available

* Data for seven banks unavailable.

** Data for one bank unavailable.

***Data for five banks unavailable.+ Data as on June 1983

Source:

1. RBI : "Statistical Tables Relating to Banks in India", Various Issues from 1977 to 1980.
2. NABARD : "Statistics on Regional Rural Banks", 1983, 1984 and 1985 Issues.

The number of personnel of RRBs were 1,251 in 1976. It rose to 6,454 in 1978 showing an increase of 516 per cent over 1976. Again in 1980, their number has gone upto 12,393 or by 192 per cent. In June 1983, the figure jumped upto 28,581 registering an increase of 230 per cent over 1980 and in 1985 it further rose upto 44,605 or by 156 per cent over 1983.

Out of this total staff the position of officers had gone up from 565 to 22,870 (or by 4,047 per cent) during 1976-85. While the clerical staff went up from 612 to 21.417 (or by 3.499 per cent), the sub-ordinate staff increased from 74 to 318 (or by 430 per cent) during the same period.

Thus, the total staff of RRBs exceeded by 36 times during the 1976-85 period in which both the officer and clerical cadre rose about 40 times while the sub-ordinate staff increased at a minimum of 4 times.

Further, out of a total staff of 44,605 as on December 1985, 7,155 or 16 per cent of them belonged to Scheduled Caste/ Tribes and over 33,061 or 74 per cent of them have got training advantage. Thus, the Regional Rural Banks are providing employment opportunities to about 0.45 lakh people of the country. Further again, over 51 per cent of the total staff of the RRBs were only in four States namely, Uttar Pradesh (21.5 per cent), Bihar (11.6 per cent), Madhya Pradesh (9.7 per cent) and Andhra Pradesh (8.6 per cent) respectively. The illustration of State-wise staff strength of RRBs is provided in Table-26.

Operational Results

The adjoining tables provide the operational results of RRBs during 1976-85.

It is evident from Table-27 that the number of RRBs incurring losses had been increasing throughout the period 1976-85. They were 14 in 1976, 21 in 1977, 29 in 1978, 23 in 1979, 29 in 1980, 45 in 1981, 76 in 1982, 99 in 1983, 131 in 1984 and 139 in 1985. During the end of December 1985 only 34 RRBs, out of 188 RRBs in the country were running into profits which aggregated to Rs.318.72 lakhs, while the bulk of 139 RRBs running into losses which aggregated to Rs.2,787.74 lakhs and over 15 RRBs were working on no profit and no loss basis.

Table 26

State wise and Category wise Staff of Regional Rural Banks : (As at the End of December 1985)

Name of the State/ Union Territory	*Officers*	*Clearks*	*Subordinate Staff*	*Total*	*Of which belonging to SC/ST*	*Total Trained Staff*
Andhra Pradesh	2097(9.09)	1739(8.12)	22(0.92)	3840(8.61)	574(8.02)	3117(9.43)
Assam	641(2.80)	606(2.83)	11(3.46)	1256(11.56)	245(3.42)	506(1.53)
Bihar	2677(11.71)	2440(11.39)	39(12.26)	5156(11.56)	612(8.55)	3437(10.40)
Gujarat	417(1.82)	375(1.75)	13(4.09)	805(1.80)	109(1.52)	519(1.57)
Haryana	378(1.66)	438(2.05)	6(1.89)	822(1.84)	110(1.54)	708(2.14)
Himachal Pradesh	125(0.55)	195(0.91)	1(0.31)	321(0.72)	66(0.92)	241(0.73)
Jammu & Kashmir	479(2.09)	440(2.05)	15(4.72)	934(2.09)	26(0.36)	755(2.28)
Karnataka	2008(8.78)	2047(9.56)	19(5.97)	4074(9.13)	521(7.21)	3792(11.47)
Kerala	551(2.41)	1156(5.40)	4(1.26)	1711(3.84)	178(2.49)	1.599(4.84)
Madhya Pradesh	2463(10.77)	1833(8.56)	20(6.29)	4316(9.68)	827(11.56)	3592(10.87)
Maharashtra	696(3.04)	705(3.29)	12(3.77)	1413(3.17)	183(2.56)	926(2.80)
Manipur	23(0.10)	19(0.09)	5(1.57)	47(0.11)	5(0.07)	41(0.12)
Meghalaya	58(0.25)	64(0.30)	2(0.63)	124(0.28)	100(1.40)	63(0.19)
Nagaland	13(0.06)	14(0.07)	2(0.63)	29(0.06)	23(0.32)	9(0.03)
Orissa	1430(6.25)	-491(6.96)	32(10.06)	2953(6.62)	512(7.16)	1896(5.73)
Punjab	141(0.62)	129(0.60)	1(0.35)	271(0.61)	53(0.74)	186(0.56)
Rajasthan	1423(6.22)	1460(6.82)	10(3.15)	2893(6.49)	583(8.15)	2230(6.75)
Tamil Nadu	286(1.25)	335(1.56)	3(0.94)	624(1.40)	139(1.94)	520(1.57)
Tripura	243(1.06)	281(1.31)	2(0.63)	526(1.18)	180(2.52)	464(1.40)
Uttar Pradesh	5223(22.84)	4291(20.04)	69(21.70)	9583(21.84)	1458(20.38)	6980(21.11)
West Bengal	1459(6.38)	1288(6.01)	25(7.86)	2772(6.22)	532(7.42)	1369(4.14)
Arunachal Pradesh	9(0.04)	13(0.06)	2(0.63)	24(0.05)	11(0.15)	6(0.02)
Mizoram	48(0.21)	58(0.27)	3(0.94)	109(0.24)	108(1.51)	105(0.32)
All India	22870(100.00)	21417(100.00)	318(100.00)	44605(100.00)	7155(100.00)	33061(100.00)

Note: Figures in parentheses are percentages to total.

Source: NABARD : "Statistics on Regional Rural Banks", December 1985, pp.24-28.

Table 27
Operating Results of Regional Rural Banks, 1976-85

Item	*1976*	*1977*	*1978*	*1979*	*1980*	*1981*	*1982*	*1983*	*1984*	*1985*
Number of Regional Rural Banks functioning	40	48	51	60	85	107	124	150	173	188
Number of Banks earning profit	26	27	22	37	56	62	48	50	42	34
Amount of profit (Rs. in thousands)	10.92	33.42	63.81	147.35	227.72	312.68	352.67	356.55	37169.00	31872.00
Number of Regional Rural Banks Incurring losses	14	21	29	23	29	45	76	99	131	139
Amount of losses (Rs. in thousands)	2.51	26.68	54.45	62.84	103.58	221.51	561.98	964.53	153953.00	278774.00
Number of Regional Rural Banks earning no profit, no loss	-	-	-	-	-	-	-	1	-	15

Source:
1. "Economic Times", 15 October 1984.
2. NABARD : "Statistics on Regional Rural Banks", 1984-85 Issues.

Another disheartening fact which can be found from Table-28 is that over 69 per cent of the banks belonging to above the age of 5 years (59 being their number) were also incurring losses by the end of December 1985.

A perusal of Table-29 also reveals that the loss incurring banks largely belonged to the States of Uttar Pradesh (25). Madhya Pradesh (22), Bihar (14). Andhra Pradesh (11), Karnataka (10) and Rajasthan (13).

According to the information available from NABARD, over the years, the Regional Rural Banks as an organisation suffered heavy net 1osses.[48] Owing to continued losses some of these banks had eroded[49] their entire share capital and some others had eroded more than 50 per cent of their share capita1. The RRBs are thus heading for a massive deficit in their operations and if this process is allowed to drag on further, it is most likely to tell upon the very existence of these banks which were launched with much fanfare ten years ago and they cannot be forced to reckon within the development activity in the rural areas.

Viability

The Dantwala committee in 1977 drew up an objective criteria for the Viability of Regional Rural Banks. It was said that each Regional Rural Bank should become a profit making institution at a level of loan business of about Rs. 3 crores which could be expected to be reached in about 3 to 4 years. The introvertible fact is that though several RRBs were in existence for years and could achieve a business label of well over Rs.3 crores, they have fa1led[50] to reach the break-even point.

A more recent Reserve Bank of India's study on the viability of Regional Rural Banks made by an expert committee headed by M.Sivaraman, which submitted its report in May 1981 indicated[51] that a Regional Rural Bank would require about six years and a network of 70 branches to become viable and reach a business mark of Rs.8 crores keeping a margin of 5 per cent between its borrowing and lending rates. Since the Regional Rural Banks have only restricted areas of operation, the Committee opined that they have little scope for enhancing their earnings through commissions and exchange.

Table 28

Working Results of Regional Rural Banks (As at the End of December 1985)

Regional Rural Banks Set up Upto	*Number*	*Showed Profit*	*Loss*	*No of Profit No Loss*	*Regional Rural Banks with more than 5 years*	*Showed Profit*	*Loss*	*No Profit No Loss*
1975	6	3	3	-	-	-	-	-
1976	40	14	26	-	-	-	-	-
1977	48	17	30	1	-	-	-	-
1978	51	17	33	1	-	-	-	-
1979	60	18	40	2	-	-	-	-
1980	85	20	59	6	6	3	3	-
1981	107	21	79	8	40	14	26	-
1982	124	22	94	8	48	17	30	1
1983	150	22	116	12	51	17	33	1
1984	173	26	135	12	60	18	40	2
1985	188	34	139	15	85	20	59	6

Source: Computed with the help of NABARD : "Statistics on Regional Rural Banks"

Table 29
State-wise Working Results of Regional Rural Banks
(For the Year Ended December 1985)

Name of the State/ Union Territory	*Number of Profit Earning Banks*	*Number of Loss Incurring Banks*	*Number of Banks Earning No Profit No Loss*	*Total Number of Banks*
Andhra Pradesh	3	11	-	14
Assam	1	2	2	5
Bihar	7	14	1	22
Gujarat	2	7	-	9
Haryana	-	4	-	4
Himachal Pradesh	-	2	-	2
Jammu & Kashmir	1	2	-	3
Karnataka	3	10	-	13
Kerala	2	-	-	2
Madhya Pradesh	-	22	1	23
Maharashtra	1	8	-	9
Manipur	-	1	-	1
Meghalaya	-	-	1	1
Nagaland	-	-	1	1
Orissa	1	8	-	9
Punjab	-	3	-	3
Rajasthan	1	13	-	14
Tamil Nadu	1	-	1	2
Tripura	1	-	-	1
Uttar Pradesh	8	25	6	39
West Bengal	2	7	-	9
Arunachal Pradesh	-	-	1	1
Mizoram	-	-	1	1
All India	34	139	15	188

Source: NABARD : "Statistics on Regional Rural Banks".

On the other hand, the exclusion of the rich into the credit purview of Regional rural Banks because of lurking fear of dominance of RBB operations by them) had denied the deposits that might have been made by the rich farmers. Yet another constraint on 'their viability is that Regional Rural Banks are not allowed to undertake other banking activities on a regular basis in collaboration with their sponsoring banks. Hence, with the increase in cost of establishment, several Regional Rural Banks have been running at a loss.

Conclusion

The Regional Rural Banks were established in India with the sole objective of developing the rural economy by providing cheaper credit to rural poor, viz., the small farmers, marginal farmers, agricultural labourers, rural artisan and other small entrepreneurs. The Regional Rural Banks Act of 1976 provided for the incorporation, regulation and winding up of RRBs. It also contained important provisions of the scheme of RRBs such as the objective jurisdiction, sponsorship, capital structure, management structure, training facilities and special concessions and privileges offered.

The Steering Committee, which had been set up by the Government of India at the national level an advisory body to formulate and coordinate the policies and operational details of the RRB scheme, reconstituted several times during the last ten years and monitored its progress and provided guidelines to RRBs from time to time. Apart from that, the Regional Rural Banks had also been receiving refinance, exemption facilities and important policy guideline from the Reserve Bank of India and the NABARD along with their sponsoring banks.

The arrival, existence and suitability of Regional Rural Banks as part of the multi-agency approach to financing agriculture had been accepted and stressed by many committees. Particularly the RRBs have been made as 'an integral part of the rural credit structure' with the favourable recommendations of the high power Dantwala Committee on Regional Rural Banks.

The working of Regional Rural Banks in India had achieved a mixed record of success so far, during their first decade of existence in the country. On one side they have made spectacular progress on the following fronts :

- The number of Regional Rural Banks had grown up steadily over the decade with a coverage of 77 per cent of the total districts in the country and thereby its total population. But the Northern and Western regions had larger number of banks and branches concentrating in their States. The State Bank of India along with its subsidiaries sponsored many of the RRBs.

- The branch expansion of Regional Rural Banks had also been steady and continuous though there were periods when branch expansion slowed down and despite their geographical dispersion has been uneven, commendable progress has been achieved in 'this sphere. A large number of hither to un-banked centres and remote villages now appeared on the banking map. They had to face numerous odds and despite them they did well in opening branches in un-economic areas like rural, semi-urban, un-banked and backward areas and thereby they brought phenomenal increase in the number of bank branches in these areas.
- A significant improvement has been evidenced with regard to deposits collected by the RRBs indicating the strenuous efforts made to cultivate friendship with an overwhelming circle of common people hitherto far removed from the banking habit - farmers, small scale entrepreneurs, artisans, etc., from rural areas. Thus throughout the decade, there has been an uptrend in rural savings as well as in deposits not only in terms of aggregate for all the RRBs but also per RRB and more significantly per branch of RRB.
- The business of Regional Rural Banks had also grown faster and stronger day by day. Along with its growth, the number of beneficiaries served also increased considerably. A comparison of achievements in deposits and outstanding loans reveals that the growth in advances has been much faster than that in deposits. It further conveys that RRBs should recognise the need for the development of a sound deposit base so that they can serve the weaker sections in much better manner.
- The bulk of assistance of RRBs, both direct and indirect had gone to small farmers, marginal farmers, agricultural labourers, rural artisan and other small entrepreneurs in conformity with the objectives set before them. Particularly, the RRBs have made good

contribution to agriculture and rural development and thereby bringing income expansion and gainful employment opportunities in their respective areas. The RRBs, by contributing to these neglected sectors were also helping, in a way, to reduce the disparities among the areas, regions, States and individuals. Thus, the RRB, have successfully maintained their image of a Small mans Bank by carrying the banking services to the door-steps of rural masses.

- The Regional Rural Banks have fulfilled the target levels of integrated rural development programme and others in a satisfactory way. So, the RRBs seem to achieve one more desiderata of a sound agricultural credit system, namely, efficient and equitable deployment of credit.
- The higher levels of credit deposit ratios of RRBs indicating more resource development within the local areas than mobilised in their areas also proves to be a plus point to these banks
- The proportion of bank personnel employed by RRBs also ascertained to be significant from the point of view of employment opportunities.

It is thus crystal clear from 'the above mentioned achievements, that in terms of the number, area covered and business turnover the Regional Rural Banks as an institution has come to stay. However, in other vital areas they hay not come up to the expectations. The viability of this institution is still not established.

In fact, a majority of Regional Rural Banks were in red and any sick institution cannot be expected to survive long with heavy losses, much less serve any social purpose. Similarly, there is a criticism that credit delivered by Regional Rural Banks is a high cost operation. There is also a demand for merger of RRBs with their respective sponsor banks. It is also contended in certain quarters that they can never become viable. Besides, the RRBs are also suffering from mounting over dues and also becoming politicized to some extent. Therefore, an in depth study should be made to analyse the causes of these problems and also measures to be suggested to improve their viability with a clear cut policy on wages, structure, ownership, control and a more viable resource deployment policy for the RRBs, so that they can become a potent instrument of rural development in the long-run. .

Footnotes

1. "Prime Minister's Speech in Parliament on 21 July, 1969", Quoted in : Journal of Indian Institute of Bankers, Vol.4, No.3, September 1969, p.258.
2. Reserve Bank of India: "Report on Currency and Finance", 1975-76, Economic Review, Vol.I, p.100.
3. Wadhva, Charan, D: *Op.cit.*, p.27.
4. Government of India: "The Gazette of India, Extra-ordinary", New Delhi, 9 February 1976, Part II, Section I, p.149.
5. *Ibid.*
6. Sheker, K.C. : "Banking Theory and Practice (Law & Foreign Exchange)", Vikas Publishing House Pvt., Ltd., New Delhi, 1980, p.206.
7. Subramanian, V.K. : "The Indian Financing System", Abhinav Publications, New Delhi, 1979, pp.206-207.
8. Reserve Bank of India : "Annual Report on Trend and Progress of Banking in India", 1976-77, p.18.
9. *Ibid.*
10. Reserve Bank of India : "Report on Currency and Finance", 1981-82, Economic Review, Vol.I, p.162.
11. NABARD: National Bank for Agricultural and Rural Development, Annual Report, 1982-83, p.95.
12. The Committee laid down that the Regional Rural Banks would be located in such areas where (i) the existing cooperative and commercial banks are weak or providing inadequate coverage to meet large credit gaps, (ii) a substantial majority of people belong to weaker sections of the society and (iii) the potentiality of agricultural development the SC adopted the operational norm of a minimum population per office of 75,000 of the commercial banks in the concerned district.
13. Reserve Bank of India : "Report on Currency and Finance", 1983-84, Economic Review, Vol.I, p.183.
14. Wadhva, Charan D : *Op.cit.*, p.201.
15. Reserve Bank of India " "Annual Report on Trend and Progress of Banking in India", 1977-78, p.40
16. Reserve Bank of India : "Regional Rural Banks : Report of the Review Committee", Bombay, 1978, p.75.
17. "The Dantwala Recommendations", Indian Finance, Vol.CII, No.9, August 1978, Saturday 26, p.174.
18. Reserve Bank of India : "Regional Rural Banks : Report of the Review Committee", *Op.cit.*, p.73.

19. *Ibid.*, p.69.
20. *Ibid.*, pp.75-84.
21. "Report on RRBs", Indian Finance: Vol.CII, NO.5, July 1978, Saturday 29, p.93.
22. *Ibid.*
23. Reserve Bank of India: "Multi-agency Approach in Agricultural Finance: Report of the Working Group".
24. *Ibid.*, p.64
25. *Ibid.*
26. Reserve Bank of India : "Functioning of Public Sector Banks : report of the Committee", Bombay 1978, p.76.
27. Reserve Bank of India : "Annual Report on Trend and Progress of Banking in India", 1980-81, p.36.
28. Reserve Bank of India : "Report on Currency and Finance", 1980-81, Economic Review, Vol.I, pp.150-151.
29. Reserve Bank of India : "Annual Report on Trend and Progress of Banking in India", 1980-81, pp. 36-37.
30. Reserve Bank of India : "Annual Report on Trend and Progress of Banking in India", 1980-81, pp.40-41.
31. *Ibid.*
32. "Regional Rural Banks Role in Rural Development", Bank of Baroda Weekly Review, Vol.20, No.8, 19 February 1982, pp.1-4.
33. NABARD : "National Bank for Agriculture and Rural Development Annual Report", 1982-83, p.82.
34. NABARD : National Bank for Agriculture and Rural Development Annual Report 1983-84", p.20.
35. Sanctioned under the 21 and 24 of NABARD Act respectively.
36. Reserve Bank of India : "Report on Currency and Finance", 1984-85, Economic Review, Vol.I, p.196.
37. NABARD: "National Bank for Agriculture and Rural Development Annual Report", 1982-83, p.95.
38. The Government of India : "Sixth Five Year Plan, 1980-85", p.198.
39. State Bank of Bikaner and Jaipur- 3; State Bank of Hyderabad-4; State Bank of Mysore-2 and State Bank of Saurashtra-3.
40. The Nagaland Rural Bank, Nagaland.
41. The Manipur Rural Bank, Manipur.
42. Including the districts in Union Territories.
43. Reserve Bank of India : "Annual Report on Trend and Progress of Banking in India", 1984-85, p.94.
44. Calculated with the help of the data provided in "Statistics on Regional Rural Banks", NABARD
45. The nine banks having the range between 200 and 150 branches were:
    (1) Shri Visakha Grammena Bank of Andhra Pradesh (168);
    (2) Kasi Kshetriya Grameena Bank of Bihar (164);
    (3) Tungabhadra Grameena Bank of Karnataka (157);
    (4) Malaprabha Grameena Bank of Karnataka (198);
    (5) Prarthana Grameena Bank of Uttar Pradesh (162);

(6) Gorakhpur Kshetriya Grameena Bank of Uttar Pradesh (192);
(7) Samyut Kshetriya Grameena Bank of Uttar Pradesh (154);
(8) Mallabham Grameena Bank of West Bengal (155); and
(9) Vaishali Grameena Bank of Bihar (189).

46. Since year-wise separate division of data on rural artisans, village/ cottage industries, retail trade/small business including self-employment are not available for the early years, they have been dealt with jointly.
47. Belshaw, Horace : "Agricultural Credit in Economically Underdeveloped Countries", FAO, Rome, 965, p.58.
48. Due 'to continued losses 23 RRBs". 5 from West Bengal, 2 from Orissa, one each from Jammu and Kashmir, Karnataka, Maharashtra and Uttar Pradesh had eroded their entire share capital and 27 RRBs. 8 from U.P., 6 from Madhya Pradesh, 5 from Bihar, 2 each in Orissa and Rajasthan and one each from Assam, Jammu and, Kashmir, and Karnataka had eroded more than 50 per cent of their share capital in 1983
49. Sahaya, R and Muninath Sharma: "Functioning of Regional Rural Banks in India", Agricultural Banker, Vol.9, No.2. April-June 1986, PP.14-18.
50. Khan, F.H : "Regional Rural Banks in the Red–A Revamp on the Cards", Indian Cooperative Review, Vol.XXIII, No.1, July 1985, pp.26-35.
51. "Viability of Regional Rural Banks : A Study", Reserve Bank of India Bulletin", *Op.cit.*

5

Growth of Regional Rural Banks in Rayalaseema

"The frequency of famines has increased tremendously in Rayalaseema during 20th century instead of declining in comparison with that of 19th century. While there were only eight famine periods during the previous century, 10 famines have already occurred during the last 61 years of the present century. The average rate of one famine for 12½ years has changed to an average of one famine for 6 years. Thus the incidence of famine in Rayalaseema has doubled in the present century"

D.L. Narayana[1]

Introduction

Andhra Pradesh is the fifth largest state in India, both in terms of population and in terms of area. According to 1981 census[2], it occupies an area of 2.77 lakh sq. kms with a population of 5.37 crores. Of the total population, 77 percent are rural, 5 percent are people belong to Scheduled Castes and Scheduled Tribes and about 42 per cent lives below the poverty line. There are about 27,221 villages and 259 towns.

The average annual rainfall is 896 m.m. The State is predominantly rural[3] and agrarian in its structure broadly resembling that of the country as a whole. About half of the State income comes from agriculture and about 47 per cent of industries are agro based, while about two-thirds of its working force is dependent on agriculture and allied activities. Nearly 60 per cent of the cultivators are small/marginal farmers, 38

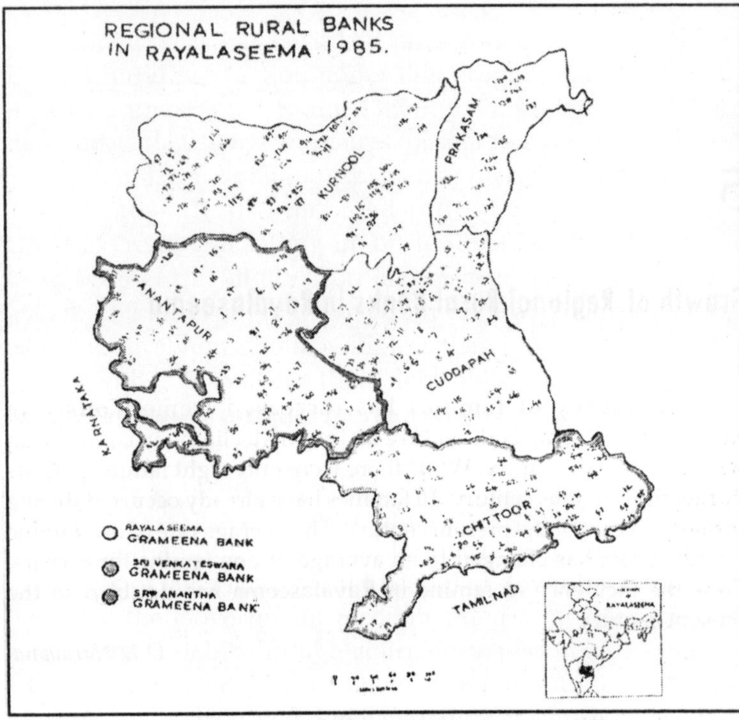

Regional Rural Banks in Rayalaseema 1985

per cent of the work force are agricultural labourers and 35 per cent of the total cultivated area is under irrigation. The State is known as a 'river State' and often called as the 'Granary of South India'.

But in spite of having rich natural resources, economically Andhra Pradesh is not a homogenous State. Even after 29 years of its formation and varying degrees of planning, the State is still considered as backward suffering with the grim problem of regional imbalances. The State has three distinct regions viz., Telangana, Rayalaseema and Coastal Andhra, which have witnessed different levels of economic transformation. Each of these three regions have the broad characteristics required for being treated as distinct physical region in itself. While Coastal Andhra is economically better off by virtue of the fertile soil and greater availability of irrigation facilities the other two regions have lagged behind due to unfavourable economic conditions. To quote the State's Draft Sixth Plan., "The three regions differ considerably from each other in their socio-economic conditions. The Coastal area is dominated by the fertile delta but ending in the north in a backward and a predominantly tribal strip. The Telangana region rich in natural resources has been lagging in economic development due to historical factors. The Rayalaseema region is chronically drought affected area with a very limited potential for agricultural development. The position of Andhra Pradesh is such that in the list of more advanced States, Andhra Pradesh is likely to be at the bottom, while in the list of backward States it is likely to be at the top so that it misses both the present advantage that the former have by their existing level of development and the potential advantage that the latter may have in any scheme of equalization".[4]

If the State has to develop further to reach the standard of developed regions of the Country, it has to correct imbalances in sectoral and area development, since the lack of balance is a contributing factor to backwardness. Also the development of weaker sections would be yet another significant element[5] in removal of social backwardness which also retards development. It the recognition of this fact[6] that the State has been having programmes of accelerated development of backward areas with due regard to the requirement of smaller producers utilising the resources and infrastructural base in larger productive endeavours. Here again, if productive endeavour especially agriculture, small industries and service sectors was to be given a boost, provision of credit, both short and medium was, among other things, an absolute necessity. It was felt that this process would be facilitated by systematic development of banking in the State.

The institutional framework in Andhra Pradesh for extension of rural credit is provided by cooperatives, commercial banks and regional rural banks. The cooperatives had been serving the rural population by providing credit for decades, even through a radical reorganization of the primary societies, amalgamating and regrouping them into viable entities. While there was rapid growth of commercial bank offices in the State after the nationalization of 14 major banks in 1969 there was a significant step up in their lendings during the seventies. By the end of 1981, there were as many as 211 primary agricultural development banks. 663 primary agricultural credit societies and 26 district central cooperative banks in the State, while the rural branches of commercial banks[7] were 1,548.

The establishment of Regional Rural Banks in Andhra Pradesh as a third component in the multi-agency credit system for agriculture and rural development was followed under the Regional Rural Banks act of 1976. Starting with 3 banks[8] in 1976, their number has grown up to 5 in 1981 and 14 at present. These 14 RRBs covered 19 of the total 23 districts in the State, thus constituting 83 per cent of the area. They also made quite a good inroad into the rural areas of the districts in which they were located via vigorous branch expansion. The total number of RRB branches in the State stood at 985 at the end of 1985" thus ranking fourth among the States in Indian Union. Of the 14 RRBs functioning, 9 are sponsored by State Bank of India Group, 3 by Syndicate Bank and 1 by Indian Bank.

In establishing RRBs, preference was given to Telangana, Rayalaseema and non Coastal Andhra as these regions were backward and lacked strong cooperative or commercial structure. By the end of December 1985, the RRBs have covered the whole of Andhra Pradesh excepting the 2 prosperous districts of East Godavari and West Godavari. Thus, there were 8 RRBs in Telangana covering 9 districts viz., Nagarjuna Grameena Bank, Sri Saraswathi Grameena Bank, Sangameswara Grameena Bank, Manjira Grameena Bank. Kakathiya Grameena Bank, Sri Sathavahana Grameena Bank, Golkonda Grameena Bank and Sri Rama Grameena Bank, in Coastal Andhra there were 3 RRBs covering 6 districts namely, Sri Visakha Grameena Bank, Pinakini Grameena Bank, and Chaitanya Grameena Bank, and the whole Rayalaseema region with 4 districts is covered by 3 RRBs viz., Rayalaseema Grameena Bank, Sree Anantha Grameena Bank and Shri Venkateswara Grameena Bank.

All the 14 RRBs have showed a very creditable performance in the State. Either in respect of branches or deposits or advances, Andhra Pradesh is very ahead of all Southern States, while the Southern region's average deposits and advances stand far higher than all India averages. The 14 RRBs together mobilised[9] Rs.111.06 crores of deposits serving 14,79,226 accounts and gave advances to the tune of Rs.177.42 crores in 8,47,428 accounts, by the end of 1985. Economic group-wise, the number of accounts of small/marginal farmers, and landless labourers was 4,45,672 and amount advanced was Rs.I09.79 crores which constituted 62 per cent of total advances and rural artisan and others had 3,05,593 accounts with Rs.47.25 crores.

An attempt is made in this chapter to study the growth of Regional Rural Banks in Rayalaseema region behind the economic background of their respective operating districts and how far they are successful in achieving the objectives on which they were set up in respect of the spread of their offices to the unbanked rural and semi-urban areas deposit mobilisation, credit facilities made available to priority neglected sectors, number of persons provided with employment opportunities and other related matters. As the Rayalaseema region is a chronically drought affected area, the performance of RRBs in the region is thus relevant to assess the effective implementation of rural schemes in the future plans to achieve integrated rural development and also the programmes which ultimately give freedom to the region from its recurring famines.

Since the study deals with three banks of a single region, it is a matter of detailed research and therefore this chapter aims to present only the aggregate aspects rather than aspects from micro point of view. In short, it is a synthesis on growth of Regional Rural Bank's working in Rayalaseema having certain immediate operational significance. The study starts with a note on Rayalaseema region in which the banks are operating.

The Region of Rayalaseema

Rayalasema region comprises Anantapur, Kurnool, Cuddapah and Chittoor districts, besides the two taluks of Giddalur and Markapur included in the newly formed Ongole district. It is situated in the southernmost part of Andhra Pradesh lying between the Northern latitudes 12° 30' and 16° 20' and Eastern longitudes 76° 30' and 80° and mostly at an altitude[10] of 1,000 to 2,000 feet above sea level. The total geographical area[11] extends over 67,400 sq.kms with a population of 96.26 lakhs as per 1981 census, thus accounting 24.2 per cent of the total area and 18 per cent of the total population of the State. The population is predominantly rural with only 20.3 per cent living in urban areas and the population belong to Scheduled Castes/Tribes accounted for 15 per cent. There are about 8,000 villages and 52 towns in the 4 districts. Preponderance of small/marginal farmers and landless labourers in the total workforce is visible throughout the region. Weather remains dry for most of the year, temperature varying from as high as 42°C and to as low as 28°c.

Literally "Rayalaseema" means[12] the land once ruled by the Rayas of Vizianagar empire from 1336 A.D. to 1649 A.D. with Vizianagar as their capital located on the banks of Tungabhadra in Bellary District.[13] It was then an extremely large and thickly populated land with a prosperous agricultural economy having good irrigation facilities and fertile potential. Visiting foreigners during that glorious historical period was fascinated by the way precious pearls were sold in larger quantities in bazaar. Thus, the region of Rayas constituted as unique chapter in the history of Andhra and in grateful memory of the services of those kings to culture and literature, progress and prosperity, the area is referred to as "Rayalaseema" and also as "Rathnalaseema".

That was centuries ago. But all that has changed now. Prosperity yielded place to poverty. For the last hundred years the economic history of Rayalaseema has been the very history of droughts and famines. Today, it came to be called[14] as a "Stalking ground of famines", the Mezzogiorno[15] of Andhra Pradesh", the "famine zone of South India" and "the blackest spot on the famine map of whole India". The entry of the World Bank into this region under its Drought Prone Area Programme (DPAP) perhaps reveals the gravity of the situation as well as the enormity of the problem. The reasons for such a grim state of affairs are two-fold.[16] The region's peculiar physico-natural features described as drought-prone conditions and the special circumstances relating to the formation and the consequent socio-political pulls and pushes in the State.

When the State of Andhra Pradesh was constituted on 1st November 1956 in consequence of the States Re-organisation Act, nine Telangana districts of the erstwhile Hyderabad State were merged with former Andhra State on linguistic basis. But, the new State had to pay a heavy price[17] for this expansion. The merger had made the State to offer certain guarantees to Telangana region and its people. In spite of that, it was regularly embarrassed and periodically threatened with agitations and attendant disturbances by that region for the ensurity of guarantees given. These events were of immense consequence to the Rayalaseema region. Instead of qualifying[18] for unique and undivided attention, it had to share as a minor partner a mere regional allocation with another backward region in the State namely, the Telangana. The physico-natural disadvantages of Rayalaseema region were therefore ignored or, if considered, kept for residual attention.

Regarding the peculiar physiography of the region one can blame the nigardliness of nature: "No high mountain ranges, no thick forests the paucity of perennial rivers, a low rainfall, an enervating climate - these are part of what nature has given to this land and no wonder its material progress is hampered"[19] The two hydrometorologic conditions which cause drought viz., an absence or large deficiency in rainfall and high temperatures are common features of Rayalaseema. As the region lies in the rain shadow of Western Ghats and far away from the coast, the precipitation in the region is very scanty. Even through the region is under the influence of both South-west and North-East monsoons, it cannot derive the full benefit from them since by the time they reach this area, they exhaust[20] a major portion of their potency and it does not get the full force of monsoons. Hence the region is popularly known as one of the important arid zones of India. The normal rainfall in this tract varies from 544 m.m. to 827 m.m. as per the analysis of rainfall data for the years 1901-1950.[21] During 1982-83,[22] the recorded average annual rainfall is 598 m.m. as against 734 m.m. in 1981-82 and 531 m.m. in 1980-81.

An analysis of 77 years rainfall in the Rayalaseema region showed[23] that the occurrence of famine was traceable to the failure of the South-west mansoon in 12 years and to the failure of North-East monsoon in 24 years. Of the 74 taluks identified as chronically drought affected in the State, are in Rayalaseema.

The following tables give an idea about the incidence of famines in Rayalaseema.

Table 1
Famine Calender of Rayalaseema

1901	1907	1908	1909
1920	1921	1922	1923
1924	1931	1932	1934
1935	1937	1938	1941
1942	1943	1945	1946
1951	1952	1953	1954
1962	1963	1965	1966
1972	1973	1976	1980
1981	1983	1984	1985

Source:
1. "Perspective Plan for Rayalaseema Region", Government of Andhra Pradesh. Hyderabad. 1972, Vol. III. pp.577-80.
2. Data Andhra Pradesh: Various issues from 1980-85.

Table 2
Frequency of Famines in Rayalaseema During 1800-1973

District	*1800 to 1900*	*1900 to 1950*	*1950 to 1973*	*Total*
Anantapur	6	7	9	22
Kurnool	6	4	8	18
Cuddpah	6	1	8	15
Chittoor	1	0	8	9

Source:
1. "Perspective Plan for Rayalaseema Region", Government of Andhra Pradesh. Hyderabad. 1972, Vol.III. pp.577-80.
2. "Andhra Pradesh", various issues.

From Table 1, it can be seen that, from 1900 to 1985 as many as 36 years have been marked as famine ridden ones, thus revealing an average of 2.4 years for every famine.

From Table 2, the temporal incidence of famine in various districts of Rayalaseema could be seen. Of the 4 districts in the region, Anantapur was the most vulnerable one topping with 22 years of famine followed by Kurnool with 18 years of drought, Cuddapah with 15 years and Chittoor with 9 years. This is conclusive evidence of backwardness of the region, particularly in comparison with the Coastal region in which very few droughts have occurred during the years under review.

Agriculture forms the mainstay of the States economy and so in Rayalaseema. About 70 per cent of total population depend upon agriculture for their livelihood.

No wonder that the State of agriculture in the region holds the key towards understanding the level of underdevelopment of the region. The net area sown (1979-83) in Rayalaseema is thus 26.84 lakh hectares in comparison to 42.58 lakh hectares in Coastal Andhra and 31.91 lakh hectares in Telangana. However, in relative terms the area sown to total geographical area is higher[24] in Rayalaseema, i.e., about 90 per cent., than the other two regions. This is a matter for alarm for the main problem of the region is the progressive extension of cultivation to marginal and sub- marginal lands. It is indicative of the high pressure on the poor soils of the region.

Soil erosion is another cause responsible for the intensity of famines in Rayalaseema. Though black soils are found in some parts, red soils predominate the region which are said to be highly poor in organic matter and fertility possessing low water holding capacity. In recent years, the soils are found to be not only eroded but also depreciating[25] Further, the undulating terrain of the region is taking[26] its own toll. As against an average slope of 1.5 per cent, the region's slope is said to vary between 2 to 4 per cent, thus promoting a fast run-off rain water. It is estimated[27] that only 10 per cent of the rain water is actually utilised for crop growth. If soil erosion continues in the same way, according to experts, there will be no soil left for cultivation in the next 50 years and the area would get deserted.

In the matter of pattern of land holdings in the region inequalities persist. Two-thirds of the number of holdings in the State account for a little over one-fifth for 5.7 per cent of the area operated. Among the three regions, Coastal Andhra has[28] relatively less uneven holdings with one-third of the area distributed among three-fourths of total holdings of below 2 hectares size group, while in Telangana and Rayalaseema about 17 per cent of the area distributed about 60 per cent of the total holdings of below 2 hectares size group.

Another factor accounting for backwardness of Rayalaseema is its poor irrigation potential. The only major reliable water resource is river Krishna and its tributary Tungabhadra. Though the region is traversed by medium and minor rivers like Pennar, Hagari, Hundri, Papagni, Kunderu, Chitravathi, Gundlakamma, Paler, Avanlar, Kushavathi and swarnamukhi, yet their flows are flashy and vary much from the average. These rivers themselves depend on monsoon and do not have water around the year. There are also good number of tanks, wells, canals and other minor irrigation works existing in this area, but these works are most undependable[29] as these sources often fail due to unseasonal and erratic rainfall.

Less than a quarter of cropped area is irrigated in Rayalaseema in comparison to more than half the sown area irrigated in Coastal area. Area irrigated more than once in Rayalaseema is 33 per cent as against 41 per cent in Telangana.[30] The cropping pattern is very much conditioned by poor irrigational facilities and reveals a marked dispersion, indicating reliance on a variety of crops. Groundnut and jowar are important crops grown. Food crops like rice, bajra, wheat, maize and Ragi and commercial crops like seeds, linseeds, seasamum and sunflower seeds and a variety of vegetables and fruits are grown in different parts of the region. But, the vagaries of monsoons, their timing as well as quantum, limit their effective production. Thus is 1978-79, [31] while coastal area alone contributed more than half (52,75,000 tonnes) of the total food grains production, Telangana (37,07,000 tonnes) and

Rayalaseema (10.09,000 tonnes) have lagged behind. Allied activities to agriculture such as poultry, dairy, pisciculture sericulture, etc., practised in many parts of the region, yet they are still to be developed.

Another distressing feature of Rayalaseema is the inconspicuous size of permanent pastures and other grazing lands which constituted only 2 per cent of total geographical area in comparison to nearly 4 per cent in Telangana and more than 3 per cent in Andhra region. Paradoxically the region has more than its share of livestock population and a hectare of pasture land in the area is burdened with 70 livestocks against half the size in other regions. The Cultivable waste is 6.9 per cent while current fallows are 7.6 per cent and 39.5 per cent is net sown. About 24.6 per cent of total area is under forests which is higher than the State average of 22.3 per cent. However, quite a lot of land classified under 'forests' does not really contribute substantial tree growth, especially in Anantapur district. Nature had endowed abundant mineral wealth - Barytes, Asbestos, Limestone, Steatite Copper, Gold Diamond and Red and Yellow Ochers, but not many industries have been established in the region. There were[32] only 61 industries in Rayalaseema in 1983 as against 183 in Coastal region and 189 in Telangana. As per industrial production the percentage shares of the above three regions are 13, 53 and 34, only 12 per cent of the total factories in the State are in Rayalaseema against 42 per cent in Telangana and 46 per cent in Andhra. 53 per cent of total employees are in Andhra as against 41 per cent in Telangana and 6 per cent in Rayalaseema. The industrial units which have been set up to develop the backward districts also proved to be least in Rayalaseema. 1,109 units with a total investment of 54.39 units were set up in the area. The average investment constituted Rs.0.05 lakh which is very low considering Rs.0.79 lakh and Rs.0.10 lakh for Andhra and Telangana regions respectively.

In respect of development of transport and communications, Rayalaseema, though developed in some ways, lagged behind comparatively with other regions. Both Andhra and Telangana accounted for about 38 per cent each of the total road length of 96, 502 kms[33] in the State leaving for Rayalaseema less than one fifth of the total. In the case of post offices and telephones also the shares of Rayalaseema is at lowest with 23 per cent in both issues, while Andhra has 41 per cent and 51 per cent and Telangana has 36 per cent and 26 per cent respectively.

In social and infrastructural facilities like education, public health, etc., Rayalaseema does not seem to lag behind, as it does in directly productive economic activities.

A scientific study of the regional disparities in Andhra Pradesh by Dr. Haranatha Babu reveals, "Regional disparities in levels of development indicators relating to agricultural sector has been declining, because the less developed regions of Telangana and Rayalaseema have experienced higher absolute increase as well as growth rates, in indicators. In the case of indicators representing manufacturing sector Telangana attains maximum increase in levels and also higher rates of growth. In the case of Rayalaseema both increase in levels and growth rates of indicators have been only marginal. Therefore, the disparity between coastal Andhra and Telangana has been on the decline, while that between the latter and Rayalaseema is on the increase. In levels of indicators of infrastructural sector regional disparities are not significant and have been declining. When all indicators are considered the picture that emerges is that while disparity between Coastal Andhra and Telangana has narrowed, the disparity between Rayalaseema and Telangana has been widening".[34]

So to correct these regional imbalances, the Government of Andhra Pradesh took many steps such as formulation of perspective plans for the three different regions, covering a time period of 15 years, formulation of the six point formula 'under which funds are allocated in the ratio of 5:3:2 among the three regions viz., Telangana, Rayalaseema and Coastal Andhra, etc. Banking was another tool used by the Government to reduce the regional disparities and also to accelerate the development of rural areas through their instrumentality of credit.

Regional Rural Banks in Rayalaseema

There are at present three Regional Rural Banks functioning in Rayalaseema covering the whole region viz., the Rayalaseema Grameena Bank, the Sree Anantha Grameena Bank and the Shri Venkateswara Grameena Bank. The salient features of these banks are the same as every RRB in the country as prescribed under the Regional Rural Banks Act of 1976. As a poor man's bank, each RRB identifies the problems of poverty groups and endeavours to mitigate their difficulties by increasing their income in a phased manner by extending timely credit assistance to further their professions. They lend either directly or through the PACS/ FSSs with simple rules and regulations which are understandable by rural folk. Each of these three banks has an authorised share capital of Rs.1 crore, of which subscribed and paid up capital is Rs.25 lakhs. The share capital is subscribed by Government of India., Government of Andhra Pradesh and the respective sponsor banks in the ratio of 50:15:25, who own fully these banks. Management of each RRB is vested in a 9 member Director Board including the Chairman. Three of the Directors are nominees of Central Government, two are from State Government and three are of sponsor Bank. Use of regional language i.e., Telugu in all business activities is another asset of these banks. All transactions, correspondence with customers, local leaders, etc., are made in Telugu while application forms, loan documents, etc. also translated into easily understandable tongue.

The progress and performance achieved by these three banks against their economic setting is as follows:

The Rayalaseema Grameena Bank

The Rayalaseema Grameena Bank, established on 6th August 1976, was the first Regional Rural Bank to come into existence in Rayalaseema region and second in Andhra Pradesh itself. This is a scheduled bank sponsored by the Syndicate Bank, a premier nationalised bank in the country. The Bank has its headquarters in Cuddapah. The notified area of operation consists of the entire Cuddapah and Kurnool districts, besides four taluks of Prakasam district, namely, Giddalur, Markapur, Yerragondapalem and Bestavaripet. It was Spread[35] over 32,978 sq. kms with a population of around 47.53 lakhs spread over 29 development blocks, 2,039 villages and 31 towns. As per the recent decision of the State Government to introduce Mandals, the area of operation of the Bank covers 117 Mandals (Cuddapah-50, Kurnool-54 and Prakasam-13). Rural population predominates the districts having 78 per cent of total population, while the percentage of Scheduled Castes and Scheduled Tribes constitutes 15 per cent. The average annual rain- fall is 686 m.m. in Cuddapah and 622 m.m. in Kurnool. The features of districts are largely determined by their hill ranges viz., Veligonda, Palakonda, Nallamalais, Lankamalais and Yerramalais. .

Agriculture provides livelihood for more than 70 per cent of the working force. The net cultivable area accounted for 8.50 lakh acres in Cuddapah[36] and the total cultivable area constituted 9.66 lakh hectares in Kurnool. Slack clay, red loans and red clay soils prevail. The major crops grown are paddy, tobacco, ragi, groundnut, cotton, korra, bajra and sugarcane. Added to them, fruit crops like mangoes, oranges, acid limes and various vegetables are also grown extensively in certain taluks. The rural economy of the districts covered by the bank is marked by low level of agricultural development, preponderance of small and marginal farmers and landless agricultural labourers. The livestock of the ryots consists of mainly cattle and buffaloes. Weaker sections maintain sheep and goats while the poorer classes rear pigs, poultry, dairy and fisheries are practiced in different parts of the districts.

There are vast reserves of lime stone, white clay, iron ore, slate stone, manganese ore and copper clay[37]. Especially, Cuddapah district is rich in mineral wealth and construction material. It is a sole producer of high grade asbestos of chrysotile variety in India and also accounts[38] for a major part of its production of barytes. Red sanders are claimed to be the pride of Cuddapah forests. However, there are only 15 large scale industrial units including cement factories, 943 small scale industrial units and 53,784 village and cottage industrial units

Table 3

Year-wise and District-wise Branch Expansion of Rayalaseema Grameena Bank, 1976-85

Year at the End of December	*District*			*Total No. of Branches*	*Year Addition*	*Percentage Increase Over Previous Year*
	Cuddapah	*Kurnool*	*Prakasam*			
1	2	3	4	5	6	7
1976	5	5	-	10	-	-
1977	25	17	3	45	35	350.00
1978	30	29	6	65	20	44.44
1979	31	31	8	70	5	7.69
1980	37	36	10	81	11	15.71
1981	44	44	12	100	19	23.46
1982	44	44	12	100	-	-
1983	45	4S	12	102	2	2.00
1984	51	55	13	119	17	16.67
1985	66	60	15	141	22	18.49

Source :Rayalaseema Grameena Bank:
"Annual Reports".

in Cuddapah. Whereas in Kurnool there are only 11 large and medium industries and 1,430 small scale industries/ tiny units. The important sources of irrigation are canals followed by tanks and wells. River Pennar flows in Cuddapah along with its tributaries viz., Chitravati, Kumudavathi, Papagni, Sagileru, Cheyyeru and Gunjame and river Tungabhadra flows in Kurnool with its 'tributaries namely, Hundri, Krishna, Kunderu and Gandlakamma. But water from these sources are unpredictable in view of the inadequate rainfall. As such, all the taluks are liable to famine. In matters of infrastructural facilities, the districts are well placed with a good number of railway and road links. The number of commercial banks working are 242, whereas the number of PACS and multipurpose cooperative societies including FSSs are 588.

Table 3 shows the year-wise and district-wise branch expansion of Rayalaseema Grameena Bank.

The scheme of setting up of Rayalaseema Grameena Bank was started with 10 branches in 1976. In the very next year their numbers have gone up to 45 recording an increase of 350 percent. Later on their position steadily increased to 65 in 1978, 70 in 1979, 81 in 1980 and 100 in 1981. During the next years 1982 and 1983, just 2 branches have been set up as they were periods for consolidation and to streamline the activities of the Bank. Again in 1984, their numbers increased to 119 and ultimately when the Bank has reached its tenth year of meaningful existence in 1985 their numbers have gone up to 141. The percentage of branch expansion is 44.44 in 1978, 7.69 in 1979, 15.71 in 1980, 23.46 in 1981, 16.67 in 1984 an 18.49 in 1985.

The Bank has opened a branch attached to Head Office under the Head Office Licence during the year 1985. It has thus fulfilled the target allotted by State Government under Branch Expansion Programme and there is no licence pending[39] with the Bank for the plan period 1982-85. Further, it is planning to open all taluk / block headquarters where there is no bank branch of Rayalaseema Grameena Bank during the plan period 1985-90 to solve the problems of the rural branches for liaison and cash remittance. Thus on an average, the RGB

Table 4
Block-wise Branch expansion of Rayalaseema Grameena Bank As At the End of December 1985

Name of the Branch	*Status*	*Block*	*Taluk*
Cuddapah District			
Vallur	Rural	Cuddapah	Cuddapah
Cuddapah	Urban	Cuddapah	Cuddapah
Chintakommadinne	Rural	Cuddapah	Cuddapah
Ramanapalle	Rural	Cuddapah	Cuddapah
Pendlimarri	Rural	Cuddapah	Cuddapah
Thummalur	Rural	Cuddapah	Cuddapah
Kotha Nellore	Rural	Cuddapah	Cuddapah
Tavvaripalli	Rural	Cuddapah	Cuddapah
Veerapanayanipalle	Rural	Kamalapuram	Kamalapuram
Kamalapuram	Semi-Urban	Kamalapuram	Kamalapuram
Chilamukur	Rural	Kamalapuram	Kamalapuram
Uppalur	Rural	Kamalapuram	Kamalapuram
Peddacheppali	Rural	Kamalapuram	Kamalapuram
Veeraballe	Rural	Rayachoti	Rayachoti
Sambepalle	Rural	Rayachoti	Rayachoti
Chinnamandem	Rural	Rayachoti	Rayachoti
Rayavaram	Rural	Rayachoti	Rayachoti
Pincha	Rural	Rayachoti	Rayachoti
Porumamilla	Semi-Urban	Porumamilla	Badvel
Bramhamgarimattam	Rural	Porumamilla	Badvel
Ganugapenta	Rural	Porumamilla	Badvel
Itukalapadu	Rural	Porumamilla	Badvel
Kalasapadu	Rural	Porumamilla	Badvel
Narasapuram	Rural	Porumamilla	Badvel
B. Kodur	Rural	Porumamilla	Badvel
Siddavattam	Semi-Urban	Siddavattam	Siddavattam
Upparapalle	Rural	Siddavattam	Siddavattam
Brahmanapalle	Rural	Siddavattam	Siddavattam
Atlur	Rural	Siddavattam	Siddavattam
Vemula	Rural	Pulivendla	Pulivendla
Vempall!	Rural	Pulivendla	Pulivendla
Lingala	Rural	Pulivendla	Pulivendla
Nallapureddypalle	Rural	Pulivendla	Pulivendla
Thondur	Rural	Pulivendla	Pulivendla
Alavalapadu	Rural	Pulivendla	Pulivendla
Ankalammagutur	Rural	Pulivendla	Pulivendla
Korrapadu	Rural	Proddatur	Proddatur
Kallur	Rural	Proddatur	Proddatur
Kanagudur	Rural	Proddatur	Proddatur
Chinnaguruvalur	Rural	Proddatur	Proddatur
Mydukur	Semi-Urban	Proddatur	Proddatur
Peddapasupula	Rural	Jammalamadugu	Jammalamadugu

Contd.

Name of the Branch	*Status*	*Block*	*Taluk*
Mylavaram	Semi-Urban	Jammalamadugu	Jammalamadugu
Peddamudiyara	Rural	Jammalamadugu	Jammalamadugu
Rajupalem	Rural	Jammalamadugu	Proddatur
Obulavaripalle	Rural	Kodur	Rajampeta
Nagarlpadu	Rural	Kodur	Kodur
Pondalur	Rural	Kodur	Rajampeta
Settigunta	Rural	Kodur	Kodur
Nagavaram	Rural	Kodur	Kodur
Vathalur	Rural	Kodur	Kodur
Anantharajapeta	Rural	Kodur	Kodur
Kondapuram	Rural	Maddanur	Muddanur
Dhodiyam	Rural	Maddanur	Jammalamadugu
Talamanchipatnam	Rural	Maddanur	Jammalamadugu
Galiveedu	Rural	Lakkireddy palle	Lakkireddy palle
Chakrayapeta	Rural	Lakkireddy palle	Lakkireddy palle
Neelakantaraopet	Rural	Lakkireddy palle	Lakkireddy palle
Nooliveedu	Rural	Lakkireddy palle	Lakkireddy palle
Sanipaya	Rural	Lakkireddy palle	Lakkireddy palle
Chittoor	Rural	Lakkireddy palle	Lakkireddy palle
Matli	Rural	Lakkireddy palle	Rayachoty
Nandalur	Semi-Urban	Rajampeta	Rajampeta
Rajampeta	Semi-Urban	Rajampeta	Rajampeta
Tangutur	Rural	Rajampeta	Rajampeta
Akepadu	Rural	Rajampeta	Rajampeta
Kurnool District			
Harivanam	Rural	Adoni	Adoni
Peddathumbalam	Rural	Adoni	Adoni
Halvi	Rural	Adoni	Adoni
Hebbatam	Rural	Adoni	Adoni
Peddakadabur	Rural	Adoni	Adoni
Badinehal	Rural	Adoni	Adoni
Urukunda	Rural	Adoni	Adoni
Nemkal	Rural	Alur	Alur
Alur	Semi-Urban	Alur	Alur
Gulyam	Rural	Alur	Alur
Peddahotur	Rural	Alur	Alur
Deebaguntla	Rural	Allagadda	Allagadda
Gospedu	Rural	Allagadda	Allagadda
Tangutur	Rural	Banaganipalli	Banaganipalli
Nandivargam	Rural	Banaganipalli	Banaganipalli
Betamcherla	Rural	Dhone	Dhone
Garladinne	Rural	Dhone	Dhone
Chityala	Rural	Dhone	Dhone
Veldurthi	Rural	Dhone	Dhone
Jaladurgam	Semi-Urban	Dhone	Dhone
Hussainpuram	Rural	Dhone	Dhone

Contd.

Name of the Branch	*Status*	*Block*	*Taluk*
Krishnagiri	Rural	Dhone	Dhone
Parla	Rural	Kurnool	Kurnool
Kurnool	Rural	Kurnool	Kurnool
Nanoor	Rural	Kurnool	Kurnool
Gargeyapuram	Rural	Kurnool	Kurnool
Hussainpuram	Rural	Kurnool	Kurnool
Krishnanagar	Rural	Kurnool	Kurnool
Uyyalawada	Rural	Koilakuntla	Koilakuntla
Akamalla	Rural	Koilakuntla	Koilakuntla
Kolimigundla	Rural	Koilakuntla	Koilakuntla
Petnikota	Rural	Koilakuntla	Koilakuntla
Nossam	Rural	Koilakuntla	Koilakuntla
Darnipadu	Rural	Koilakuntla	Koilakuntla
Parumanchala	Rural	Nandikotkur	Nandikotkur
Midthur	Rural	Nandikotkur	Nandikotkur
Bannur	Rural	Nandikotkur	Nandikotkur
Gadivemula	Rural	Nandyal	Nandyal
Gajulapalle	Rural	Nandyal	Nandyal
Kanala	Rural	Nandyal	Nandyal
Madduru	Rural	Nandyal	Nandyal
Poluru	Rural	Nandyal	Nandyal
Thimmapuram	Rural	Nandyal	Nandyal
Devanakonda	Rural	Pathikonda	Pathikonda
Ternekal	Rural	Pathikonda	Pathikonda
Peravali	Rural	Pathikonda	Pathikonda
Pathikonda	Semi-Urban	Pathikonda	Pathikonda
Tuggali	Rural	Pathikonda	Pathikonda
Kalruppala	Rural	Pathikonda	Pathikonda
Jonnagiri	Rural	Pathikonda	Pathikonda
Karivena	Rural	Atmakur	Atmakur
Regadagudur	Rural	Atmakur	Atmakur
Sunnipenta	Rural	Atmakur	Atmakur
Nagaladinne	Rural	Yemmiganur	Yemmiganur
Manthralayam	Rural	Yemmiganur	Yemmiganur
Tungabhadra	Rural	Yemmiganur	Yemmiganur
Daivamdinne	Rural	Yemmiganur	Yemmiganur
Kodumur	Semi-Urban	Kodumur	Kurnool
Kothakota	Rural	Kodumur	Kurnool
Polakal	Rural	Kodumur	Kurnool
Prakasam District			
Giddalur	Semi-Urban	Giddalur	Giddalur
Arumalaveedu	Rural	Giddalur	Giddalur
Mokshagundam	Rural	Giddalur	Giddalur
Sangeevaraopet	Rural	Giddalur	Giddalur
Galizerugulla	Rural	Besthavaripet	Besthavaripet
Arthaveedu	Rural	Besthavaripet	Besthavaripet

Contd.

Name of the Branch	*Status*	*Block*	*Taluk*
Ravlpadu	Rural	Besthavaripet	Besthavaripet
Badveeau	Rural	Markapuram	Markapuram
Gajjalakonda	Rural	Markapuram	Markapur
Thippayapalem	Rural	Markapuram	Markapur
Yerragundapalem	Semi-Urban	Yerragundapalem	Yerragundapalem
Pullalacheruvu	Rural	Yerragundapalem	Yerragundapalem
Arrrnanagadipadu	Rural	Yerragundapalem	Yerragundapalem
Naidupalem	Rural	Yerragundapalem	Yerragundapalem
Ramasamudram	Rural	Yerragundapalem	Yerragundapalem

Source: Rayalaseema Grameena Bank: "Annual Reports", 1976-85.

has opened 14 offices per Year during the 1976-85 period. Of the 141 offices opened upto the end of December 1985, 66 are in Cuddapah district, 60 in Kurnool district and 5 in Prakasam district, thus showing the evenness of the spread of branches in these districts during the years.

Regarding the status of these branches the rural predominance is visible. Out of the 141 total offices, 126 were in rural areas, 13 in semi-urban areas and only 2 in urban areas. This reveals the encouraging performance of the Bank in scattering the rural areas. Almost all the taluks of the districts have been judiciously covered. Most of the branches have been opened in unbanked and under banked areas where even sufficient infrastructural facilities are not available. Special care has been taken[40] to ensure that the centres with preponderance of small/marginal farmers and agricultural labourers are selected for branch opening. Thus the Rayalaseema Grameena Bank got 20th place in the field of branch expansion among the 183 RRBs functioning in the country at the end of June 1985 and 3rd place among the 14 RRBs in Andhra Pradesh and the same among the 10 RRBs sponsored by the Syndicate Bank. The particulars of centres opened by the RGB are mentioned in Table 4.

With the opening of branches in the rural areas, concerned efforts were made to mobilize rural savings and to bring large number of rural masses into the banking fold. The year-wise deposit growth of Rayalaseema Grameena Bank and the number of customers it is serving is provided in Table-5.

Table 5
Growth of Deposits of Rayalaseema Grameena Bank. 1976-85

(Amount Rs. in Lakhs)

Year	Total No. of Deposit Accounts	Percentage Growth Over the Year Previous	Total Deposits	Percentage Growth Over the Previous Year	Per Branch Deposit	Percentage Growth Over the Previous Year	Per Capita Deposit (Amount in Rs.)
1	2	3	4	5	6	7	8
1976	4,083	-	14	-	1.40	-	342.88
1977	32,866	704.94	88	600.00	2.18	55.71	298.18
1978	74,174	125.68	200	104.08	3.08	41.28	269.63
1979	1,18,385	59.60	346	73.00	4.94	60.38	292.26
1980	4,46,297	23.57	548	58.38	6.76	36.84	374.58
1981	1,97,962	35.31	760	38.68	7.60	12.42	383.91
1982	2,24,609	13.46	1,063	39.86	10.63	39.86	473.26
1983	2,41,674	7.60	1,298	22.11	12.73	19.76	573.09
1984	2,71,046	12.15	1,633	26.19	13.70	7.62	602.18
1985	2,90,769	7.28	2,031	24.37	14.40	5.11	698.49

Source: Rayalaseema Grameena Bank: "Annual Reports".

From Table-5 it can be seen that the growth of both deposits and number of deposit accounts set an increasing trend, but their percentage growth has been decreasing year after year. Initially, there were total deposits of the orders of Rs. 98 lakhs in 32, 866 accounts in 1977. They have grown steadily to Rs. 346 lakhs in 1,18,385 accounts in 1979, Rs. 760 lakhs in 1,97,962 accounts in 1981, Rs.1,298 lakhs in 2,41,674 accounts in 1983 and Rs. 2031 lakhs in 2,90,769 accounts in 1985. During the same years, the percentage growth of deposits decreased by 600, 73, 39, 22 and 19 while deposit accounts by 710, 60, 35, 8 and 10. Deposit per branch and per capita deposit are also low in absolute and yearly rate of growth. They increased from Rs. 2.18 lakhs and Rs. 298 in 1977 to Rs.14.40 lakhs and Rs. 698 in 1985, showing just a rise of 7 and 2 times.

The reasons for this vulnerable position of deposits are many. As the entire area of operation has been drought prone, deposit accretion proved an uphill task.[41] The total exclusion of the richer sections of the village society from the direct lendings of the Bank, the competition from commercial banks, greater emphasis on internal controls and recoveries, etc., are the other reasons. Despite this, the Bank has been continuously striving to increase its deposit potential with the conscious involvement of all the staff members by offering the full range of usual deposit schemes like the commercial banks at its various branches. Several deposit schemes like Janakalpa i.e., the daily collection deposit, cash certificates and so on have been introduced, which are attracting the small depositors in a big way. The composition of the various kind of deposits mobilised by the Bank are mentioned in Table-6.

More than 70 per cent of deposit accounts of the RGB have been savings accounts during all the years from 1977 to 1985. But their amount in the composition of total deposits though increasing during the years, show a decreasing trend by dropping down from 54 per cent to 33 per cent. Comparatively, the position of cash certificates is better and got first place in the total deposits of the Bank having about 43 per cent share but with only 9 per cent accounts in 1985. The Janakalpa Scheme which was popular among the rural folk has a

Table 6

Comparative Statement Showing Various Deposits of the Rayalaseema Grameena Bank 1977-85

(Amount Rs. in Lakhs)

Category of Deposits	*Amount* 1977	1978	1979	1980	1981	1982	1983	1984	1985
Savings Bank Account	243,94	528,56	850,19	108,544	1,44,578	1,64,584	1,76,444	1,99,390	2,13,759
	(74.22)	(72.30)	(71.82)	(74.55)	(74.11)	(73.28)	(73.01)	(73.56)	(73.51)
Current Account	570	122	151	190	246	344	372	431	454
	(1.73)	(0.17)	(0.13)	(0.13)	(0.13)	(0.15)	(0.15)	(0.16)	(0.16)
Fixed Deposit	16,65	2,,083	2523	2,139	2,558	2,564	2,297	1,897	2,050
	(5.07)	(2.85)	(2.13)	(1.47)	(1.31)	(1.14)	(0.95)	(0.70)	(0.71)
Cumulative Deposit	1,713	3,051	3,493	3,670	5,285	6,593	6,962	8,099	7,977
	(5.21)	(4.18)	(2.95)	(2.52)	(3.71)	(2.94)	(2.88)	(3.00)	(2.74)
Janakalpa deposit	4,203	11,370	18,746	19,036	23,616	26,390	27,216	29,174	33,033
	(12.79)	(15.55)	(15.83)	(13.07)	(12.11)	(11.75)	(11.26)	(10.76)	(11.36)
Cash Certificates	321	2926	7174	10829	16293	21574	23794	24726	25375
	(0.98)	(4.00)	(6.06)	(7.44)	(8.35)	(9.60)	(9.85)	(9.12)	(8.73)
Others	-	697	1279	1139	2500	2560	5689	7329	8121
		(0.95)	(1.08)	(0.82)	(1.28)	(1.14)	(1.90)	(2.70)	(2.79)
Total	32,866	73,105	1,18,305	1,45,597	1,95,076	2,24,609	2,41,674	2,71,046	2,90,769
	(100.00)	(100.00)	(100.00)	(100.00)	(100.00)	(100.00)	(100.00)	(100.00)	(100.00)

Contd.

	Amount 1977	1978	1979	1980	1981	01982	1983	1984	1985
	52.65	102.22	162.91	258.94	313.39	406.16	477.89	561.00	673.19
	(53.82)	(50.89)	(47.12)	(47.20)	(41.24)	(39.18)	(36.80)	(34.35)	(33.14)
	2.78	7.32	5.67	5.97	9.30	10.36	10.82	10.09	15.12

Contd.

	(2.84)	(3.64)	(1.64)	(1.09)	(1.22)	(0.97)	(0.83)	(0.62)	(0.74)
	32.92	37.54	40.05	72.30	83.73	130.68	89.42	105.96	162.51
	(33.65)	(18.69)	(11.58)	(13.18)	(11.02)	(12.28)	(6.78)	(6.49)	(8.00)
	2.07	6.18	10.65	15.67	23.87	30.26	38.78	48.00	59.71
	(2.12)	(3.08)	(3.08)	(2.86)	(3.14)	(2.85)	(2.99)	(2.94)	(2.94)
	5.52	24.72	48.58	59.49	84.16	109.02	141.30	166.97	214.34
	(5.64)	(12.31)	(14.05)	(10.84)	(11.07)	(10.25)	(10.88)	(10.22)	(10.55)
	1.88	20.46	76.58	131.33	237.77	368.36	525.66	715.80	887.78
	(1.92)	(10.19)	(22.15)	(23.94)	(31.29)	(34.63)	(40.48)	(43.84)	(43.72)
	-	2.41	1.33	4.88	7.78	8.94	14.78	25.24	18.66
		(1.20)	(0.38)	(0.89)	(1.02)	(0.84)	(1.14)	(1.55)	(0.92)
	97.82	200.85	345.77	548.58	760.00	1,063.78	1,298.65	1,633.06	2,031.31
	(100.00)	(100.00)	(100.00)	(100.00)	(100.00)	(100.00)	(100.00)	(100.00)	(100.00)

Note: for the year 1984, figures are approximately put as the data in that respective annual report is not correctly given.

Source: Rayalaseema Grameena Bank : "Annual Reports".

consistent share both in accounts and amount of more than 10 per cent. Fixed deposits constitute only 8 percent in 1985 as against 34 per cent in 1977. The bank mobilized minimum number of cumulative deposits.

In the sphere of deposit mobilization, the Rayalaseema Grameena Bank got 15th place among the 183 RRBs in the country, 4th place among the 10 RRBs in the country sponsored by syndicate Bank and 2nd place among the 14 RRBs in Andhra Pradesh as at the end of June 1985.

In the performance of disbursal of credit, the rayalaseema Grameena bank has been working like a development bank for the rural poor. Table-7 illustrates the year-wise picture of advances given and the number of beneficiaries surveyed by the Bank during the 1977-85 period.

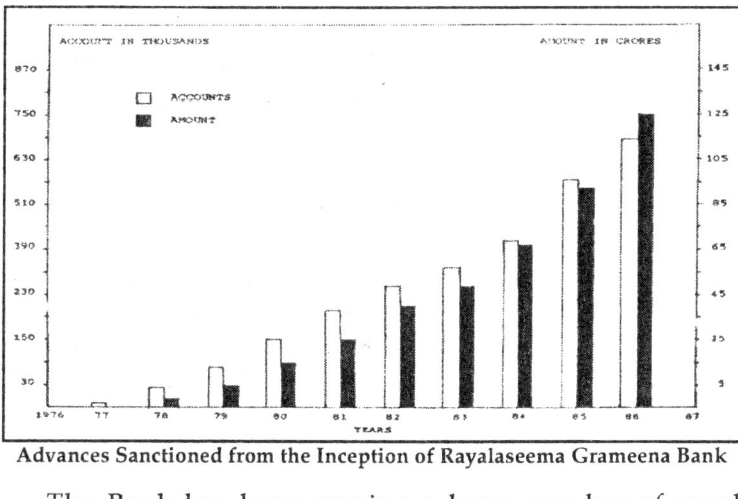

Advances Sanctioned from the Inception of Rayalaseema Grameena Bank

The Bank has been serving a large number of rural borrowers whose number rose from 12,706 in 1977 to 62,703 in 1979, which again went up to 1,19,069 in 1981. There was a set back in the years 1983 and 1984, in which negative growth has been registered. But in 1985, there was an increase in the number which has stabilized at about 1,28,000. This trend has been the same for the amount of advances lent. They reached a peak of Rs. 3,102 lakhs in 1985 as against 1,605 lakhs in 1981, Rs.650 lakhs in 1979 and Rs.78.83 lakhs in 1977. Credit per

Table 7
Growth of Advances of the Rayalaseema Grameena Bank, 1976-85

(*Amount in Lakhs*)

Year	*Number of Accounts*	*Percentage Growth Over the Previous Year*	*Amount of Advance*	*Percentage Growth Over the Previous Year*	*Credit Per Branch*	*Per Account Advance (Amount in Rs.)*
1976	741	-	7.76	-	0.77	1,047
1977	12,706	1,614.70	78,,83	915.85	1.75	620
1978	33,734	165.49	265,,00	236.16	4.08	786
1979	62,703	85.87	650.00	145.28	9.28	1,037
1980	80,.563	28.48	1,026.00	57.84	12.82	1,274
1961	1,19,069	47.79	1,605.00	56.43	16,.05	1,348
1982	1,21,079	1.69	1,853.00	15.45	18.53	1,530
1963	1,13,631	-6.15	1,975.00	6.58	19.36	1,738
1984	1,08,443	-4.57	2,323.00	17.87	19.40	2,142
1985	1,28,575	18.57	3,102.00	33.53	22.00	2,413

Source:
1. Rayalaseema Grameena Bank: "Performance budget", 1977, 1979 and 1980.
2. Rayalaseema Grameena bank: "Annual Reports".

branch increased from Rs 1.75 lakhs to Rs.8.22 lakhs, thus giving a rise of 24 times during the 1977-85 period, whereas per capita rose from Rs.620 to Rs.2,.413 showing an increase of 4 times.

More importantly, of the total advances furnished by RGB, almost all have gone to specified target groups of weaker sections of rural society such as small/marginal farmers, rural artisans, landless labourers and other rural entrepreneurs. The category-wise loans advanced are mentioned in the Table-8.

Over 70 per cent of advances have gone for agricultural purposes. Small farmers are having the highest priority and their position both in accounts and amount have been grown steadily from 35 to 57 per cent and 48 to 59 per cent during the 1977-85 period. Marginal farmers accounted for 13 per cent of advances whose share decreased from 24 per cent in 1977. 10 per cent of advances have gone in favour of small business/ rural artisan group, while others including loans on deposits, jewel loans and indirect finance through cooperatives accounted 18 per cent in 1985 as against 12 per cent in 1977.

The RGB is actively participating in the implementation of various developmental programmes undertaken by the State and Central Governments. During the year 1985, it has financed 3,114 beneficiaries to the extent of Rs.70 lakhs under the IRDP. Under S.C. Action plan for the upliftment of Scheduled Caste families, 612 beneficiaries received Rs.5.14 lakhs. Under Massive Assistance Programme, 408 beneficiaries received Rs.25 lakhs. Under the Twenty Point Programme, 60,168 beneficiaries got Rs. l, 264 lakhs and 989 borrowers received Rs. 8 lakhs under the Differential Interest Rate Scheme.

Another laudable feature of the Bank is its service to the oppressed classes of society viz. the Scheduled Castes, Scheduled Tribes and Backward Classes to eradicate the poverty. Every year during the period of existence, it has been specifically giving financial assistance to these classes for various purposes such as crop production, sheep unit, dairy, piggery and poultry, basket making, shoe weaving, irrigation like wells, pumpsets, agricultural implements, bullock carts and others. Under this classification during the year 1985, the

Table 8

Year-wise and Category-wise Classification of Advances of Rayalaseema Grameena Bank.1976-85

Category	*1976*	*1977*	*1978*	*1979*	*1980*	*1981*	*1982*	*1983*	*1984*	*1985*
Marginal farmers	150 (20)	1,171 (9)	4,03,330 (12)	9,444 (15)	11,979 (15)	11,052 (9)	13,069 (11)	14,710 (14)	15,081 (14)	16,190 (13)
Small Farmers	257 (35)	4,986 (39)	13,029 (39)	20,751 (33)	25,731 (32)	46,888 (39)	47,476 (39)	59,276 (58)	60,916 (56)	73,349 (57)
Landless Labourers	27 (4)	778 (6)	1,222 (4)	2,929 (5)	2,973 (4)	1,039 (1)	904 (1)	747 (1)	703 (1)	630 (-)
Rural Artisans	104 (14)	1,346 (11)	2,546 (8)	4,479 (7)	5,246 (6)	5,563 (5)	6,809 (6)	7,046 (7)	6,898 (6)	6,762 (5)
Small Business	141 (19)	2,965 (23)	6,697 (20)	10,181 (16)	10,583 (13)	11,410 (10)	10,970 (13)	10,594 (14)	14,353 (9)	17,967 (14)
Others (Loans on deposits, jewels and indirect finance)	62 (9)	1,460 (12)	6,210 (18)	14,919 (24)	24,051 (30)	43,117 (36)	41,311 (34)	10,260 (10)	11,771 (11)	13,677 (11)
Total	741 (100.00)	12,706 (100.00)	33,734 (100.00)	62,703 (100.00)	80,563 (100.00)	1,19,069 (100.00)	1,21,079 (100.00)	1,02,613 (100.00)	1,08,443 (100.00)	1,28,575 (100.00)

Contd.

	1976	*1977*	*1978*	*1979*	*1980*	*1981*	*1982*	*1983*	*1984*	*1985*
	12	13	14	15	16	17	18	19	20	21
	1.83	12.62	36.24	116.50	175.63	197.15	264.64	279.09	310.48	402.46
	(24)	(13)	(14)	(19)	(17)	(13)	(14)	(17)	(13)	(13)
	3.70	40.10	124.18	267.37	387.35	641.22	704.94	925.38	1348.25	1838.19
	(48)	(42)	(47)	(41)	(38)	(40)	(38)	(57)	(58)	(59)
	0.08	7.09	8.42	31.55	30.24	2.68	2.64	2.30	2.57	2.51

Contd.

	(1)	(7)	(3)	(5)	(3)	(-)	(-)	(-)	(-)	(-)
	0.47	7.21	9.45	19.41	44.02	32.49	46.36	51.04	51.39	66.82
	(6)	(9)	(4)	(3)	(4)	(2)	(3)	(3)	(3)	(2)
	0.72	13.82	29.43	56.40	68.04	87.56	100.12	105.57	175.12	242.63
	(11)	(9)	(7)	(9)	(7)	(6)	(5)	(7)	(8)	(8)
	0.97	14.08	57.12	159.05	321.55	644.21	733.84	261.81	435.53	550.48
	(12)	(15)	(21)	(24)	(31)	(40)	(40)	(16)	(19)	(18)
	7.77	94.92	264.84	650.29	1026.83	1605.10	1852.52	1625.19	2323.35	3102.09
	(100.00)	(100.00)	(100.00)	(100.00)	(100.00)	(100.00)	(100.00)	(100.00)	(100.00)	(100.00)

Note:

1) Figures in brackets are percentages to total.
2) As the separate break ups for small formers. Marginal farmers and landless labourers are not available from 1980-85 Reports, agricultural term loans with allied activities. Short-term crop lcans and consumption loans have been put in their respective columns.

Source:

1. Rayalaseema Grameena bank : "Annual Reports".
2. Rayalaseema Grameena Bank : "Performance Budgets".

Bank has provided Rs_625.77 lakhs to Scheduled Castes, Rs.116.27 lakhs to Scheduled Tribes and Rs.2,054.94 lakhs to backward classes. The details of credit assistance rendered to these sections for the three years 1979, 1982 and 1985 is furnished in the Table-9.

Thus the placement of Rayalaseema Grameena Bank in advances among the 183 RRSs in the country is 12th one, while both among the 10 RRBs sponsored by Syndicate Bank and the 14 RRBs in Andhra Pradesh it acquired 3rd place at the end of June 1985.

A further classification of Bank deposits and advances is furnished in Table-10.

Cuddapah district is ahead of other districts and it mobilized 53 per cent of total deposits and lent 47 per cent of total advances at the end of 1985. In comparison, Kurnool mobilised 38 per cent and lent 45 per cent" and Prakasam mobilized 9 per cent and lent 8 per cent. The credit-deposit ratios are 136, 180 and 130 for the respective districts. For the Bank as a whole the C-D ratios were erratic during the years. in accordance with changes in deposits such as 80.4 in 1977, 187.9 in 1979, 211.2 in 1981 and 152.7 in 1985. The drought prone conditions prevailing in the area are responsible for hindering the Bank's Progress. The recovery rate thus showed a declining trend by falling from 70 per cent in 1978 to 61 per cent in 1980, which again went down to 46 per cent in 1983 and 43 per cent in 1985. The productivity, on the other hand, increased from Rs.l.13 lakhs in 1978 to Rs 8.28 lakhs in 1981 and to Rs. 7 .89 lakhs in 1985, thus showing an increase of 7 times during the 1978-85 period.

The Bank is getting refinance from institutions such as NABARD, IDBI, and Syndicate Bank which have strengthened the resources position of the Bank from time to time. To this extent it availed Rs.384 lakhs and Rs.81.29 lakhs under general and systematic landings of NABARD during 1985 and the out standings against them are Rs.1,045.35 lakhs and Rs.187.28 lakhs by the end of 1985. Similarly it availed Rs.485 lakhs and Rs.7.67 lakhs under general and DRI landings of Syndicate Bank and the outstandings against them are Rs.499.58 lakhs

Table 9
Assistance given to Scheduled Castes / Scheduled Tribes and Backward Classes by Rayalaseema Grameena Bank

Purpose	1979		1982		1985	
	No. of Accounts	Amount Rs. in 000's	No. of Accounts	Amount Rs. in 000's	No. of Accounts	Amount Rs. in 000's
Scheduled Casts						
Crop Production	2,523	1,748	7,389	8,153	19,520	22,311
Sheep units	163	469	980	3,827	2,002	7,768
Dairy	1,332	1,427	2,035	2,830	3,840	6,314
Piggery & Poultry	36	65	176	267	144	791
Basket weaving	160	87	283	208		
Shoe making	980	391	2135	1706	5,547	5,190
Consumption loans	158	41	325	169	574	160
Others (bullocks, petty trade, artisans)	1,014	1,135	2,804	3,335	14,994	20,221
Total	7,566	5,364	16,127	20,496	46,621	62,755
Scheduled Tribes						
Crop Production	432	463	702	968	2,640	3,092
Sheep units	88	247	355	1,209	791	2,945
Dairy	122	155	169	262	251	419
Piggery & Poultry	101	199	168	232	123	279
Basket weaving	211	121	535	481	1958	1,818
Shoe making	15	5	10	10		
Consumption loans	3	7	62	207	21	7
Others (bullocks, petty trade, artisans)	160	91	589	2,063	2,127	3,067
Total	1,132	1,281	2,590	5,433	7,911	11,627

Contd.

Purpose	1979		1982		1985	
	No. of Accounts	Amount Rs. in 000's	No. of Accounts	Amount Rs. in 000's	No. of Accounts	Amount Rs. in 000's
Backward Classes						
Crop Production	8,717	7,553	22,714	29,420	85,618	1,24,924
Sheep units	809	2,050	2,538	8,542	4,050	14,235
Dairy	1,570	1,751	2,045	2,397	3,799	5,527
Piggery & Poultry	51	120	120	278	101	839
Basket weaving	292	171	763	535	10,913	11,146
Shoe making	125	70	579	1010		
Consumption loans	374	214	69	574	1,131	378
Others (bullocks, petty trade, artisans)	6,814	455	10,300	11,391	38,620	48,445
Total	18,752	16,335	39,936	54,549	1,44,232	2,05,494

Source: Rayalaseema Grameena Bank, "Annual Reports".

and Rs.10.55 lakhs. It availed Rs. 1 lakh from IDBI and the outstanding against is Rs.1.45 lakhs. In addition, the Bank submitted claims to OICGC for Rs.52.44 lakhs over 5,143 accounts and settled for Rs.42.86 lakhs over 4,602 accounts upto 31.12.1985.

Table 10
Distrit-wise Operations of Rayalaseema Grameena Bank
(As at the End of December 1985)

District	*Deposits*	*Advances*	*C-D Ratio*
Cuddapah	1,068.69 (53)	1,454.81 (47)	136.1
Kurnool	773.11 (58)	1,407.39 (45)	181.0
Prakasam	189.51 (9)	239.89 (8)	130.2
Total	2,031.31 (100)	3,102.09 (100)	152.7

Note: Figures in brackets are percentages to total.
Source: Rayalaseema Grameena bank: "Annual Report; 1985".

The RGB had sponsored eight Farmers' Service Co-operative Societies, four in Cuddapah and another four in Kurnool during the years 1977 and 1978" These societies are successfully functioning under the sponsored guidance of the Bank making headway in achieving their main objectives of providing not only integrated credit service but also inputs, technological know-how and other services to the weaker sections particularly the small marginal farmer, agricultural labourer and artisan groups. By the end of 1985, these eight societies have a member-ship of 15,655 and share capital to the tune of Rs.30.47 lakhs. The outstanding loans and public deposits of the societies were Rs. 275.78 lakhs and Rs. 31. 50 lakhs respectively. The details are provided in Table-11.

Further the Bank has actively participating in the District Annual Plans and so far successfully achieved the targets and accepted the revised targets Under the strategy of area development approach the Bank has also adopted Villages totaling to 1,210 by the end of 1982. With the object of achieving the integrated rural development in the adopted villages and to make rural families economically better off and self-sufficient a special scheme known as (Intensive Integrated Rural Development Programme has been launched.[42] The scheme envisages all round development of the selected villages by providing full employment and better standard of living to rural people through productive programmes to benefit the identified target groups. The family would be treated as a unit for this purpose.

Table 11
Progress of Farmers Service Cooperative Societies Sponsored by Rayalaseema Grameena Bank (As at the End of 1985)

(Rs. in lakhs)

Name of the Society	*Membership*	*Share Capital*	*Loans Outstanding*	*Public Deposit*
Cuddapah District				
Devuni Cuddapah	3,306	5.59	67.67	13.09
Lingapuram	2,078	3.93	21.89	2.17
Thalla Proddatur	2,112	3.81	30.42	2.74
Thiumasamudram	1.086	2.66	28.73	0.80
Kurnool District				
Harivanam	1,857	3.39	33.04	1.91
Yerraguntla	1,666	3.20	24.45	2.42
Ramadurgam	1,438	4.62	39.94	2.91
Pamulapadu	2,112	3.27	29.64	5.46
Total	15655	30.47	275.78	31.50

Source: Rayalaseema Grameena Bank: "Annual Report, 1985".

The RGB is attempting to solve the phenomenon of unemployment by providing job opportunities. At the end of 1985, the bank's personnel consisted of 650 members, of which 223 are officers including field supervisors and 427 are workmen. 98 per cent of the total staff are trained ones and about 12 per cent are people belong to Scheduled Castes/ Tribes. The year wise and cadre-wise staff strength of the Bank is furnished in Table-12.

Table 12

Cadre wise and Year-wise Staff Strength of the Rayalaseema Grameena Bank, 1977-85

Category	*1977*	*1978*	*1979*	*1980*	*1981*	*1982*	*1983*	*1984*	*1985*
Officer(Branch Manager)	37	66	85	89	128	117		223	223
Officer (Field Supervisor)	10	10	70	62	75	88			
Senior-Clerk-cum- Cashier	40	82	9	8	55	34		344	426
Junior-Clerk-cum- Cashier	69	96	124	144	188	194			
Driver-cum- Messenger	-	-	-	2	2	2		1	1
Total	156	254	288	305	448	436	443	568	650
Percentage increase over previous year	-	62.82	13.38	5.90	46.88	-2.68	1.61	28.44	14.44

Source: "Annual Reports".

Generally, the employees of the bank are trained at Staff Training Centre in Ananthapur and a few selected upper cadre staff like branch managers at College of Agricultural Banking, Pune. Along with, the bank conducts internal promotional tests. There is an inspection department in the Bank which carries regular inspection and one short inspection of each branch at odd interval. In the year 1985, regular inspections were conducted in respect of 79 branches and short inspection/ visits were done in respect of 55 branches.

The operating Results of the Rayalaseema Grameena Bank is provided in Table-13.

Table 13
Operating Results of the Rayalaseema Grameena Bank 1977-85

(Rs.in Lakhs)

Year	*Income*	*Expenditure*	*Profit/Loss.*
1977	6.51	9.89	-3.38
1978	22.15	29.14	-6.99
1979	62.90	64.07	-1.17
1980	106.29	95.47	10.82
1981	171.13	161.29	9.84
1982	230.90	224.43	6.47
1983	249.98	245.23	4.75
1984	270.33	277.30	-6.97
1985	342.35	376.56	-34.21

Source: "Annual Reports".

The bank's total income rose from Rs. 6.51 lakhs in 1977 to Rs. 22.15 lakhs in 1978 and gain to Rs 62.90 lakhs in 1979. But it is disheartening to note that total expenditure of the Bank also set an increasing trend over taxing the income level by Rs.9.89 lakhs, Rs.29.14 lakhs and Rs.64.07 lakhs during 1977, 1978 and 1979. This had resulted into net losses of Rs.3.38 lakhs, Rs.6.99 lakhs and Rs.1.17 lakhs. But, the Bank was able to control its expenditure and consolidate its economic strength and earned net profits amounted to Rs.10.82 lakhs, Rs. 9.84 lakhs and Rs 6.47 lakhs and Rs.4.75 lakhs in the years 1980, 1981, 1982 and 1983. However for the latest years 1984 and 1985, again the expenditure overtook the income resulting into net losses amounted to Rs.6.97 lakhs and Rs 34.21 lakhs. This is a matter of serious concern for the bank.

The Sree Anantha Grameena Bank

The Sree Anantha Grameena Bank (SAGS) is the second Regional Rural Bank functioning in Rayalaseema region covering the single district of Anantapur. It. was established on 1st November 1979 The Bank is sponsored by the Syndicate Bank, the lead bank in the district. Having been completed six years of dedicated service to the weaker sections of rural society by providing credit and other facilities, the Bank continues to endeavour to bring about social transformation in the backward district of Anantapur.

Anantapur has a total geographical area of 19,130 sq kms with a population of 25.48 lakhs which spread over 964 villages, 3 revenue divisions and 63 mandals.[43] More than 80 per cent of total population are rural and around 17 percent of the people are belong to Scheduled Castes and Scheduled Tribes. Important soils are red and black cotton which constitute 71.4 per cent and 28.6 per cent of the total area. It is the second most chronic drought prone district in the country. As it lies in the hinterland and rain shadow, it has a highly erratic uneven and undependable and low rainfall of 544 mm. annually which is 355 mm. less than the State average. Within the district, the scanty rainfall is ill-distributed, resulting in frequent famines and droughts.

Anantapur consists[44] of predominantly people with smaller land holdings to an extent of 80 per cent concentrated with small farmers and agricultural labourers. There are 3.52 lakh land holders, cultivating an area of 11.40 lakh acres. Out of which, 1.82 lakh acres belong to marginal farmers and 0.92 lakh acres to small farmers. The percentage of area sown more than once to the net area sown constitutes only 3.5 per cent. This speaks of the lack of intensive cropping pattern existing in the area. Paddy groundnut and oil seeds are the major crops grown in the district. Sugarcane is also grown in some parts. There are three major rivers viz., Pennar, Chitravathi and Chinna Hagari besides small rivers and streams like Kushavathi, Swarnamukhi. Tadakaleru and Maddaleru. But all these rivers are rainfed and remain dry for most of the year. Thus, out of 9.57 lakh hectares of total cropped area only 8.3

per cent is irrigated. Canal water is the main source of irrigation. There is one major irrigation project - Tungabhadra High Level Canal System. Also there were 1,245 tanks and 56,830 wells. But there is no water in most of these irrigation sources. In recent times, this dry district is subjected to severe droughts and even drinking water is denied for its people and livestock as the open wells and the bore wells have gone dry and the water table has gone down 50 metres below deep. Ser1culture is an important occupation conceived successfully in Anantapur offering tremendous scope to improve the lot of small and marginal farmers and providing employment to the rural youth. At present, the Mulberry cultivation is in about 53,000 acres spreading in all the 16 blocks. There are also 20,301 local looms, of which 20 are in cooperative field. The district is industrially backward and it has only 11 large and medium scale industries, and 2,442 small scale industries. In addition, there are number of rural artisan complexes and clusters in the district financed under IRDP and District Industries Centre for providing guidance to the perspective entrepreneurs. The district is famous for places like Lepakshi, Ramagiri and Vajrakarur. There are 17 financial institutions having a network of 202 branches. Of them 2 are cooperative banks with 22 branches and 7 are Nationalised banks with 61 branches. Sree Anantha Grameena Bank is functioning with 67 operating branches.

Table-14 shows Year-wise Branch Expansion of Sree Anantha Grameena Bank.

Table 14
Year-wise branch Expansion of Sree Anantha Grameena Bank

Year at the End of December	*Number of Branches*	*Year Addition*	*Percentage Increase Over Previous Year*
1979	1	-	-
1980	10	9	900.00
1981	32	22	200.00
1982	46	14	43.75
1983	50	4	8.70
1984	54	4	8.00
1985	67	13	24.07

Source: Sree Anantha Grameena bank: "Annual Reports" – 1979-85.

Starting with one single branch in 1979, the Bank had opened 9 more branches in 1980. 1981 was a 'year of planned expansion' as for the corporate objective of the Bank. Pursuant to this 22 branches were opened by May 1981 at the rate of one branch per one week commencing from 1st January 1981. The corporative objective for the year 1982 being consolidation with limited expansion, 14 more branches were opened in various parts of the district. 4 new branches were opened both in 1983 and 1984 and 13 more were added in 1985 thus totaling the number of branches to 67.

Out of the total 67 branches, 54 are in rural areas and 13 in semi-urban areas. Most of the rural branches are located in un banked centres. The Bank has covered 749 of the total 936 Villages. The particulars of branches opened by Sree Anantha Grameena Bank are furnished in Table-15.

The performance of SAGS in the sphere of deposit mobilisation is quite impressive considering the drought prone conditions prevailing in the district. Table-16 presents the data relating to the growth of deposits of Sree Anantha Grameena Bank.

Table 15
Mandal Wise Branch Expansion of Sree Anantha Grameena Bank as at the End of December 1985

Name of the Branch	*Status*	*Name of the Mandal*
Anantapur	Rural	Anantapur
Bandameedapalli	Rural	Anantapur
Gandlaparthi	Rural	Raptadu
Gandladinne	Rural	Gandladinne
Kudair	Rural	Kudair
Tarimela	Rural	Singanamala
Gugudu	Rural	Narpala
B. Pappuru	Rural	Narpala
Chimalavagupalli	Rural	Tadipatri
Rayalacheruvu	Rural	Yadiki
Peddapapur	Semi Urban	Peddapappur
Muchukota	Rural	Peddapappur
Putlur	Rural	Putlur
P.K. Cheruvu	Rural	Guntakal
Nagasamudram	Rural	Guntakal

Contd

Name of the Branch	*Status*	*Name of the Mandal*
Pamidi	Semi Urban	Pamidi
Eddulapalli	Rural	Pamidi
Raketla	Rural	Uravakonda
Ragulapadu	Rural	Vajrakurur
Palturu	Rural	Vidupanakal
Bathalapalli	Semi Urban	Bathalapalli
D. Cherlopalli	Rural	Bathalapalli
Kanumukkala	Rural	Chinnekothapalli
Kanaganipalli	Rural	Kanaganipalli
Peruru	Rural	Ramagiri
Dadithota	Rural	Tadimarri
Kuntimaddi	Rural	Raagiri
Kalyandurg	Semi Urban	Kalyanadurg
Muddlnayanipalli	Rural	Kalyandurg
Duradakunta	Rural	Kalyandurg
Tagguparti	Rural	Beluguppa
Thimmapuram	Rural	Kambadur
Nuthimadugu	Rural	Kambadur
Dharmavaram	Semi Urban	Dharmavaram
Setturu	Rural	Setturu
Rayadurg	Semi Urban	Rayadurg
D.Hirehal	Rural	D.Hirehal
Somalapuram	Rural	D.Hirehal
Gumagatta	Semi Urban	Gumagatta
Bhupasamudram	Rural	Gummagatta
Udhehal	Rural	Boanahal
Peddamanturu	Rural	Roddam
Puttaparti	Semi Urban	Puttaparti
Pedaballi	Rural	Puttaparti
Kothapalli	Rural	Kothacheruvu
Talamarla	Rural	Kothacheruvu
Marala	Rural	Bukkapatnam
Pamadurthi	Rural	Bukkapatnam
Madakasira	Semi Urban	Madakasira
Neelakuntapuram	Rural	Madakasira
Heavathi	Rural	Amarapuram
Rolla	Rural	Rolla
Lepakshi	Rural	Lepakshi
Kodikonda	Rural	Chilamathur
Gorantla	Semi Urban	Gorantla
Gownivaripalli	Rural	Gorantla
Badhili	Rural	Gorantla
Kadiri	Semi Urban	Kadiri
Kalasamudranm	Rural	Kadiri
Nallamada	Rural	Nallamala

Contd

Name of the Branch	*Status*	*Name of the Mandal*
N.Pulakunta	Rural	Nambulipulakunta
Talupula	Rural	Talupula
Nallacheruvu	Rural	Nallacheruvu
O.D.Cheruvu	Rural	O.D.Cheruvu
Nallaguntapalli	Rural	Tanakal
Amdegur	Rural	Aadagur
Gandlapenta	Rural	Gandlapenta

Source: Lead bank Scheme: "Annual Action Plan", Ananthapur District.

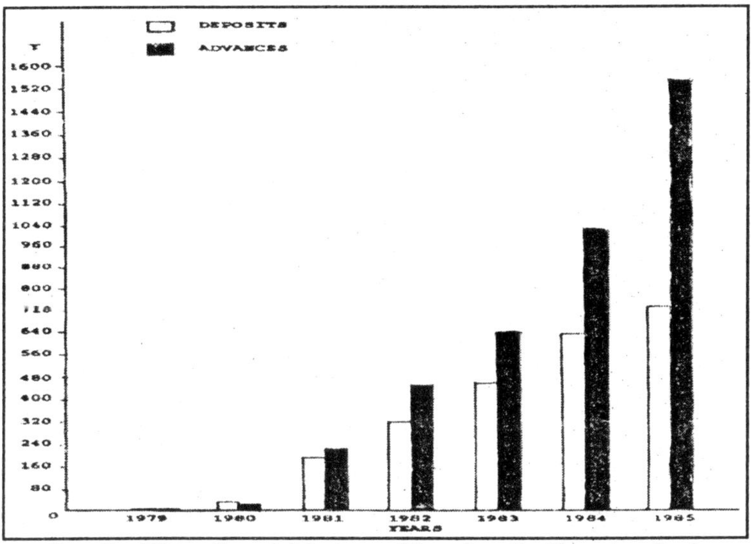

Growth of Deposits and Advances of Sree Anantha Grameena Bank

The total deposits mobilised by the Bank was Rs. 31 54 lakhs in 1980. They increased to Rs.195.43 lakhs in 1981 with a growth of 520 per cent. During the years 1982, 1983, 1984, and 1985 they rose up considerably to Rs.320.75 lakhs Rs.450.50 lakhs Rs. 633.52 lakhs and Rs.733.05 lakhs but the percentage growth showed a decreasing trend as 64.13, 42.95, 25.63 and 15.91. Likewise, the number of depositors had increased to 1,36,536 in 1985 as against 68,051 in 1982 and a mere 287 in 1979. But the percentage growth has been dropping down year after year. The average deposit per branch which rose from 3.15 lakhs in 1980 to Rs 6.97 lakhs in 1982 and to Rs.10.94 lakhs in 1985, showed an increase of just 3.5 times whereas the per

Table 16

Growth of Deposits of Sree Anantha Grameena Bank, 1976-85

(Rs. in Lakhs)

Year	*Total Deposits*	*Growth in Percentage Over the Previous Year*	*No. of Deposit Accounts*	*Growth in Percentage Over the Previous Year*	*Average Deposit Per Branch*	*Growth in Percentage Over the Previous Year*	*Per Capita Deposits (Amount in Rupees)*
1	2	3	4	5	6	7	8
1979	0.72	-	287	-	0.72	-	251
1980	31.54	4, 280.56	4,403	1,434.15	3.15	337.50	716
1981	195.43	519.63	40,838	827.50	6.10	93.65	479
1982	320.75	64.13	68,051	66.64	6.97	14.26	471
1983	458.50	42.95	89,698	31.81	9.17	31.56	511
1984	633.52	27.63	1,12,742	25.69	11.73	27.92	562
1985	733.05	15.71	1,36,536	21.10	10.94	6.73	537

Source: Sree Anantha Grameena Bank: "Annual Reports" 1979-85.

capita deposit had fallen down from Rs.716 in 1980 to Rs.471 in 1982. Again in 1985 it slowly went up to Rs.537.

The absolute increase achieved in the amount of deposits in the early years was the result of the Banks hard effort which it did by devising various saving schemes to suit the multifarious needs of people and thereby tapping the petty amounts saved by them. Particularly the rural branch staff have been kept good rapport with the village elders, by conducting themselves in a pleasing way and proved themselves as the real friends of villagers. If the deposits of the Bank have slowed down in recent years, it is the environmental drawbacks that mostly account for it. The recurring droughts[45] year after year have left the majority of rural people with low incomes and thereby hampering their drive for deposit mobilisation. So the semi-Urban branches have borne the brunt of mobilising substantial deposits.

In spite of all these setbacks, the Bank has been endeavouring to mobilise greater levels of rural deposits. It has introduced various novel deposit schemes to suit the needs and habits of rural masses, so as to inculcate the saving habit amongst them. A few worth mentioning deposit schemes are Abhyudaya Deposit Scheme (collection of daily savings), monthly savings Fixed Deposit Scheme and Cash Certificates. For a few years a new deposit scheme called 'Swasakthi Deposit' was introduced for the rural peasants to mobilise an equal amount to their investment over a period of 5 years so as to make them self-sufficient in the same period. Table-17 shows the comparative position of different deposit accounts of Sree Anantha Grameena Bank.

Most of the deposit account have been the savings bank account. Their percentage share remained high at more than 73 per cent on all years from 1981 to 1995 in the case of accounts, while in the case of amount it as 48 per cent both in 1981 and 1985. Cash certificates share increased from 11 to 34 per cent during 1979-85 period though it has got very less number of depositors. The Abhyudaya Scheme got the third place with 11 per cent of accounts and 14 per cent of amount in 1985. Lack of fixed deposits and a very minimum number of current

Table 17

Comparative Statement Showing of Various Deposits of the Sree Anantha Grameena Bank 1979-85

(Rs. in Lakhs)

	Account						
Type of Activity	*1979*	*1980*	*1981*	*1982*	*1983*	*1984*	*1985*
Savings bank Account	188	2,832	29,718	49,749	67,246	84,936	1,03,975
	(65.51)	(64.32)	(72.77)	(73.11)	(74.97)	(75.38)	(76.15)
Current Account.	-	24	62	78	87	121	134
		(0.54)	(0.15)	(0.11)	(0.10)	(0.11)	(0.10)
Fixed Deposit	4	55	10,890	651	923	890	-
	(1.39)	(1.25)	(26.67)	(0.96)	(1.03)	(0.79)	-
Monthly Savings Deposit	13	56	-	1,328	1,856	2,110	2,377
	(4.53)	(1.27)	-	(1.95)	(2.07)	(1.87)	(1.74)
Abhudaya Deposit	77	1375	-	10,845	12,058	13,882	15,433
	(26.83)	(31.23)	()	(15.94)	(13.44)	(12.31)	(11.30)
Cash Certificate	3	39	-	3,761	5,176	7,683	10,910
	(1.07)	0.89)		(5.53)	(5.77)	(6.82)	(7.99)
Swasakthi Deposit	-	-	-	1242	-	-	-
	-	-	-	(1.82)	-	-	-
Others	2	22	168	397	2352	3070	3707
	(0.70)	(0.50)		(0.58)	(2.62)	(2.72)	(2.72)
Total	287	4,403	40,838	68,051	89,698	1,12,742	1,36,536
	(100.00)	(100.00)	(100.00)	(100.00)	(100.00)	(100.00)	(100.00)

Contd.

Amount						
1979	1980	1981	1982	1983	1984	1985
0.49	4.94	92.82	143.54	271.94	324.31	352.40
(68.05)	(15.66)	(47.50)	(44.75)	(59.31)	(51.20)	(48.07)

Contd.

-	0.46	2.39	3.32	2.69	2.95	2.14
-	(1.46)	(1.22)	(1.03)	(0.59)	(0.47)	(0.29)
0.12	21.13	97.02	83.17	44.38	72.37	-
(16.67)	(66.99)	(49.64)	(25.93)	(9.68)	(11.43)	-
-	0.11	-	4.88	8.80	14.10	19.96
-	(0.35)	-	(1.52)	(1.92)	(2.23)	(2.72)
0.02	3.40	-	46.86	54.20	77.31	101.34
(2.78)	(10.78)	-	(14.61)	(11.82)	(12.21)	(13.82)
0.08	1.04	-	32.32	67.75	127.99	245.27
(11.11)	(3.30)	-	(10.08)	(47.78)	(20.20)	(33.46)
-	-	-	1.48	-	-	-
-	-	-	(0.46)	-	-	-
0.01	0.46	3.20	5.18	8.74	14.30	11.94
(1.39)	(1.46)	(1.64)	(1.62)	(1.90)	(2.26)	(1.63)
0.72	31.54	195.43	320.75	458.50	643.33	733.05
(100.00)	(100.00)	(100.00)	(100.00)	(100.00)	(100.00)	(100.00)

Note: Figures in Parentheses are percentages to total. For the year 1981, deposits break-up for monthly savings, abhyudaya and cash certificates are not available. The total sum of all these three are included in fixed deposits.

Source: Sree Anantha Grameena Bank: "Annual Reports".

accounts are the noticeable problems faced by the Bank in mobilising deposits. The Swasakthi Deposit introduced only for one year i.e. for 1982.

Thus the SAGB attained 50th place in the sphere of deposit mobilisation among the 188 RRBs in the country at the end of 1985.

In the field of credit deployment, faster expansion was made by the Sree Anantha Grameena Bank aiming to uplift the down-trodden and to fulfill the ideals enshrined in the Twenty-Point formula. The growth of advances of the Bank is shown in Table-18.

Accordingly, about 1,690 borrowers received an amount of Rs.22.25 lakhs in 1980. In 1981, about 18,773 borrowers got Rs.225.81 lakhs recording an increase of 915 per cent over 1980. The following years, both 1982 and 1983 being the years of consolidation with limited expansion, vigorous credit disbursal took place. Rs.448.53 lakhs to 28,174 borrowers and Rs.640.88 lakhs to 36,665 borrowers were provided in the respective years. 1984 constitutes "The year of reaching break-even point", Rs.1,035.77 lakhs were extended to 47,958 borrowers. Again in 1985, which was "The year of profitability with productivity" the total advances reached to a peak of Rs.1,552.00 lakhs in 53,808 accounts. The percentage growth in advances was 99,43,62 and 50 during the above said respective years. In the six-year period 1980-85, the per branch credit has grown from Rs.2.25 lakhs to Rs.23.16 lakhs, thus showing an increase of 10.4 times, Whereas the per capita credit rose from Rs.l,156 to Rs.2,884 or by 2.5 times.

Table-19 provides the sector-wise and purpose wise classification of advances.

The sectoral classification of outstanding advances of Sree Anantha Grameena Bank reveals that the priority sector lending has a dominating share of 95 per cent at the end of 1985 which increased from 92 per cent in 1983, from 77 per cent in 1981 and from 27 per cent in 1979. The position has been the same in the case of accounts of the priority sector agriculture and its allied activities contributing to the small/ marginal farmer and agricultural labourer share was highest

Table 18

Growth of Outstanding Advances of Sree Anantha Grameena Bank, 1979-85

(Amount in Rs. Lakhs)

Year	*Total Advances*	*Percentage Growth Over the Previous Year*	*No. of Accounts*	*Percentage Growth Over the Previous Year*	*Per Branch Credit*	*Per Capita Credit (Amount in Rs.)*
1979	0.15	-	21	-	0.15	714
1980	22.25	14,733.33	1,690	7,947.62	2.23	1,156
1981	225.81	914.88	18,773	1,010.83	7.06	1,203
1982	448.53	98.63	28,174	50.08	9.75	1,592
1983	640.88	42.88	36,665	30.14	12.82	1,748
1984	1,035.77	61.62	47,958	30.80	19.18	2,160
1985	1,552.00	49.84	59,482	24.03	23.16	3,609

Source: Sree Anantha Grameena bank: "Annual Reports".

Table 19

Sector-wise and Purpose-wise Classification of Outstanding Advances of Sree Anantha Grameena Bank

(Amount Rs. in Lakhs)

	Account						
Purpose	*1979*	*1980*	*1981*	*1982*	*1983*	*1984*	*1985*
Priority Sector							
Agriculture	2 (9)	430 (21)	6,506 (38)	13,920 (49)	18,497 (50)	25,214 (53)	33,113 (56)
Allied Activities	-	92 (4)	1,719 (10)	3,123 (11)	3,422 (9)	3,436 (7)	3,652 (6)
Rural Artisans	5 (24)	20 (1)	1,105 (7)	2,524 (10)	2,330 (12)	5,857 (12)	6,388 (11)
Small business men	- -	169 (8)	1,416 (8)	3,253 (11)	5,181 (14)	7,439 (16)	9,170 (15)
Total of Priority Sector	7 (33)	711 (34)	10,746 (63)	22,820 (81)	31,430 (86)	41,946 (87)	52,323 (88)
Non Priority Sector							
Consumption Loans	- -	- -	26	25 -	50 -	88 -	168 -
Others (including jewel loans and loans on deposits)	14 (67)	1,352 (66)	6,167 (36)	5,329 (19)	5,185 (14)	5,924 (12)	6,991 (12)
Total of Non-Priority Sector	14 (67)	1,352 (66)	6,193 (37)	5,354 (19)	5,235 (14)	6,012 (13)	7,159 (12)

Contd.

Amount						
1979	*1980*	*1981*	*1982*	*1983*	*1984*	*1985*
0.02 (13)	4.71 (21)	103.75 (46)	256.42 (57)	379.39 (59)	667.81 (65)	934.17 (60)

Contd.

	-	2.82	42.07	72.20	79.06	90.48	242.29
		(12)	(19)	(16)	(12)	(9)	(16)
	0.02	0.18	11.32	22.05	46.20	68.39	80.43
	(13)	(1)	(5)	(5)	(7)	(7)	(5)
	-	1.78	16.39	46.60	88.24	151.75	217.99
	()	(8)	(7)	(10)	(14)	(15)	(14)
	0.04	9.56	173.53	398.23	592.81	978.43	1,474.88
	(27)	(43)	(77)	(89)	(92)	95()	(95)
	-	-	0.06	0.15	0.69	1.51	5.56
	-	-	-	-	-	-	-
	0.11	12.71	52.22	50.15	47.38	53.69	71.34
	(73)	(57)	(23)	(11)	(7)	(5)	(5)
	0.11	12.71	52.28	50.30	48.07	55.20	76.90
	(73)	(57)	(23)	(11)	(8)	(5)	(5)

Note: Figures in parentheses are percentages to total.
Source: Sree Anantha Grameena Bank: "Annual Reports".

at 76 per cent of the total advances which were 71, 65, 13 per cent in 1983, 1981 and 1979. Small business accounted for 14 Per cent and rural artisan about 5 per cent. The non-priority sector has a minimum share of consumption loans and others including jewel loans and loans on deposits.

The SAGB has been helping the backward classes since its inception. It has financed about 1,900 Scheduled Caste families to the tune of Rs.50 lakhs and about 67 Scheduled Tribal beneficiaries to the tune of Rs.0.59 lakhs in 1985. Further, the Bank has been maintaining its predominant position in implementation of various government sponsored programmes. Under IRDP it has financed 493 beneficiaries to the extent of Rs.10 lakhs and is instrumental in getting subsidy to them to the extent of Rs.3.60 lakhs during the year 1985. Under Massive Assistance Programme, it extended Rs.18.0 lakhs to about 167 beneficiaries. Under DRI, it financed 60 beneficiaries to the tune of Rs.0.74 lakhs. The SAGB thus got 26th place among the 188 RRBs in the country in the field of credit disbursal.

Furthermore the Bank has made attempts for the all round development of the villages. It has established 3 poultry complexes and 14artisan complexes which are reported to have run satisfactorily. It offered pledge loans to farmers so that they do not go in for distress sales and can wait to favourable prices. It pursued[46] the policy of educating the farmers in the latest new technology in different farming practices by conducting various extension programmes like Expert lecture, Crop Demonstration, Vanamahotsavam, etc. Special emphasis on Harijans and artisans was brought about by organising Harijana Samkshema Week and "Artisan Days". Different branches have organised "Future Farmer's Club, "Farm Information Exchange Clubs" as a means of establishing better rapport with the Clientele and for better understanding their problems. For speedy sanction of advances. "Credit Camp Approach" was followed. The village Karanam, DRDA authorities and the Banker participate in the programme to finalise the identification of the farmer as well as the loan then and there. In view of quick disposal involved, this approach was very much appreciated by the farmer society. Further, a micro pilot project[47] sponsored by Vikas Volunteer Vahini under the aegis of NABARD was implemented at Chennamanayanikota village through Anantapur branch.

Refinance from NABARD, sponsor bank and Industrial Development Bank of India are the other sources of finances for the Bank. It has drawn refinance to the tune of Rs.65.1 lakhs and Rs. 257.47 lakhs from NABARD under General and Schematic Lending during the year 1985. The out standings against them are Rs.133.68 lakhs and Rs.562.67 lakhs at the end of the year. Similarly, Rs.200.00 lakhs and Rs.0.85 lakhs were drawn from the sponsor bank under General and DRI lendings and the out standings against them are Rs.425.00 lakhs and Rs.2.85 lakhs. Further, the Bank has settled 98 out of 169 claims invoked in the DICGC amounting to Rs.1.01 lakhs during the same year. Also of the 104 loan accounts filed in court, 24 accounts amounting to Rs.0.56 lakhs were given decrees.

The credit-deposit ratio showed an increasing trend. It rose from 20.8 in 1979 to 115.6 in 1981, then again to 139.8 in 1983 and 211.7 in 1985. The productivity of the Bank went up from Rs.2.29 lakhs in 1981 to Rs.8.19 lakhs in 1985, showing an increase of 3.6 times. The recovery level was falling down from 65 per cent in 1981 to 42 per cent in 1985, thus giving rise to overdues.

The staff strength of Sree Anantha Grameena Bank is given in Table-20.

The total staff strength of the Bank had grown from 121 in 1980 to 184 in 1981 and again to 200 in 1982, to 231 in 1983, to 234 in 1984 and to 259 in 1985. The overall growth rate in 1985 over 1980 is 131. The number of staff on deputation from sponsor bank has been reduced from 7 to 4 (of the total 279 staff members in 1985, the number of branch managers are 58, the number of field supervisors are 64 and the workmen accounted for 157. About 98 per cent of total staff are trained and 19 per cent are selected from Scheduled Castes/Tribes.

Immense importance was given to personnel training in various procedures like orientation, reorientation, project formulation, industrial relations and workshops on specified

Table 20
Cadre-Wise and Year-wise Staff Position of Sree Anantha Grameena Bank, 1979-85

Category	*1979*	*1980*	*1981*	*1982*	*1983*	*1984*	*1985*
Officer (Branch Manager)	-	35	49	47	51	65	58
Officer(Field Supervisor)	-	35	48	44	46	58	64
Senior Clrk-Cum-Cashier	-	11	14	21	17	21	21
Junior Clrk-Cum-Cashier	-	40	73	88	112	85	135
Driver- Cum-Messenger	-	-	-	-	-	1	1
Total	-	121	184	200	231	234	279
Number of Staff of Deputation from Sponsor bank	7[@]	5	5	5	5	4	4

[@] Including 3 of them deputed from Rayalaseema Grameena Bank.
Source: Sree Anantha Grameena Bank: "Annual Reports".

subjects. The Banks Inspection Department works attentively apart from doing investigation of frauds, complaints etc. In 1985, 25 branches had internal audit and Inspection. Further, 7 short inspections were also conducted

Table 21
Profit and Loss Position of Sree Anantha Grameena Bank

(Rs. in Lakhs)

Year	*Income*	*Expenditure*	*Profit/Loss*
1979	0.19	0.17	0.02
1980	4.16	4.60	-0.44
1981	18.35	25.40	-7.05
1982	43.70	51.87	-8.17
1983	65.74	79.25	-13.51
1984	98.95	108.39	-9.44
1985	155.84	173.36	-17.52

Source: "Annual Reports".

The operating results of Sree Anantha Grameena Bank is provided in Table-21.

Except in the year of inauguration of the Bank, all the years from 1980 to 1985 were showing the negative performance in the economic viability of the institution. When the income was Rs.0.19 lakhs in 1979, the expenditure amounted Rs.0.17 lakhs, thereby showing a net profit of Rs.2,000. But when the total earning rose to Rs.4.16 lakhs in 1980, total expenditure too increased to Rs.4.60 lakhs, thus showing a net loss of Rs.0.44 lakhs. This trend was followed in the latter years 1981, 1982, 1983, 1984 and 1985 in which expenditure overtook income, thus giving rise to heavy net losses amounted to Rs.7.05 lakhs, Rs.8.17 lakhs, Rs.13.51 lakhs, Rs.9.44 lakhs and Rs.17.62 lakhs.

The Shri Venkateswara Grameena Bank

The third Regional Rural Bank working in the Rayalaseema area covering the single district of Chittoor is the Shri Venkateswara Grameena Bank (SVGB). It was established on 22nd March 1981 by naming it after the presiding Deity of the area Lord Venkateswara of Tirumala. It was the fifth Grameena Bank in the State of Andhra Pradesh and first of its kind to be sponsored by the Indian Bank, the lead bank of the district. The Bank has its head- Quarters at Chittoor.

According to 1981 census, Chittoor district has a population of 27.47 lakhs spread[48] over 15,152 sq.kms of area, which comprises, of 15 taluks, 20 panchayat samithis and 1,889 inhabited villages. The natural corollary to the backwardness of the district is the preponderant, rural population which constitute 83.2 per cent of total population. About 77 per cent of total population have agriculture as their main occupation. There are about 0.94 lakh small farmers, 1.73 lakh marginal farmers and 3.98 lakh agricultural labourers while the people belong to Scheduled Castes/Tribes are 5.58 lakhs. Chittoor has a climate which is not so favourable for the farming community. Dry and salubrious weather prevails. The average annual rainfall is 828 m.m. However the incidence of rainfall is not uniform in all parts of the district. 8 blocks in the western parts are liable to drought and three blocks in the eastern parts are vulnerable to severe cyclone. These frequent occurrence of drought and cyclone in successive seasons in one area or other of the district caused great damage to the economic pursuits of a total population dependent on agricultural operations.

Of the total area, 33.5 per cent or 5.07 lakh hectares comprises the net sown area. Out of the total cultivated area only 36.4 per cent has irrigation facilities. Lack of perennial rivers and drying up of existing ones due to the scanty and erratic precipitation resulted in dearth of major irrigation projects. The district has, however, 9 medium irrigation projects and 8,515 minor irrigation tanks. Different types of soils such as black, red, alluvial and gravel sand are found in different parts. Red loamy and red sandy soils together account for 57 per cent and 34 per cent of the total area respectively. Paddy, sugarcane, groundnut, ragi, bajra and jowar are the major crops grown. An area of 15.62 lakh acres has been divided into 3,63,246 land holdings.[49] Of them, farmers who have holdings below 1 acre predominate with 1.11 lakhs, while only 33 thousand farmers have above 10 acres. Bamboo, sandalwood, timber, soapnut, myrobalan, honey and custard apple are some of the important forest products. But the mineral wealth of the district is not significant, though low-grade steatite; iron-ore and granite metal are found in some parts. Allied agricultural activities such as dairy, poultry, sheep rearing, sericulture, fisheries, etc., are gaining momentum in the area providing additional income to the small and marginal farmers and landless labourers. Industrially, the district is very backward with only large and medium scale industries and about 800 registered small scale industries. The raw materials required to support industrialization are lacking in the area in a big way. However, there are several artisan complexes such as rope making complex, mat weaving complex and leather goods manufacturing complex all over the district. There are well connected road and railway facilities.[50] in the area to the principal, commercial, administrative and industrial centers of the country. The commercial banks are having a network of 90 rural offices at the end of 1962, while the number of credit cooperatives including the multipurpose societies accounted for 348.

The year-wise branch expansion of Shri Venkateswara Grameena Bank is provided in Table-22.

Table 22
Year-Wise Branch Expansion of Shri Venkateswara Grameena Bank 1981-85

Year at the End of December	*Number of Branches*	*Year Addition*	*Percentage Increase Over Previous Year*
1981	7	-	-
1982	19	12	171.43
1983	36	17	89.47
1984	53	17	47.22
1985	66	13	24.53

Source: Shri Venkateswara Grameena Bank: 'Fifth Annual Report, 1985'.

Since its inception, the SVGB had been vigorously expanding by setting up of branches in every nook and corner of the district. Starting with 7 offices in 1981 the total number of bank offices went up to 19 in 1982, 36 in 1983, 53 in 1984 and 66 in, 1985. The percentage growth registered had been 171,89,45 and 25. Thus on an average 13 offices were opened every year. This is a praiseworthy fact considering the short span of about 5 years time the Bank has existed.

Most of the branches have been rural. Due care was taken to establish branches in unbanked and underbanked centers. By the end of 1985, the Bank has covered almost all the blocks of the district. The centre-wise particulars of branches are provided in Table-23.

Table 23
Branch Expansion of Shri Venkateswara Grameena Bank As at the End of December 1985

Name of the Branch	*Status*	*Name of the Block*	*Date of Opening*
Chittoor	Rural	Chittoor	22.03.81
189, Kothapalli	Rural	Chittoor	12.06.81
Kothapallemitta	Rural	Karvetinagar	11.07.81
Thugundru	Rural	Gangadhara Nellore	11.11.81
Narasingarayani peta	Rural	Chittoor	21.11.81
Kanipakkam	Rural	Bangarupalem	09.12.81
Mogili	Rural	Bangarupalem	28.12.81
Vanamaladinne	Rural	Punganur	26.06.82
Nanjampeta	Rural	Chowdepalli	09.07.82
Yerravaripalem	Rural	Chinnagottigallu	15.07.82
Mahal	Rural	Vayalpadu	17.07.82
Marripadu	Rural	Vayalpadu	17.07.82
Chembakur	Rural	Punganur	17.07.82
Kolamasanapalli	Rural	Palamaner	14.08.82
Muduvedu	Rural	Madanapalle	17.08.82
Kandur	Rural	Chowdepalli	14.10.82
Vijalapuram	Rural	Kuppam	16.10.82
A.Rangampeta	Rural	Chandragiri	20.10.82
Kuppambahadur	Rural	Puttur	03.11.82
Vijayapuram	Rural	Pitchatur	06.04.83
Palasamudram	Rural	Karvetinagar	09.04.83
Palamangalam	Rural	Nagari	16.04.83
Ugranampalli	Rural	Gangadhara Nellore	22.04.83
Talapula	Rural	Chinnagottigallu	28.04.83
Pallam	Rural	Srikalahasti	24.05.83
K.V.B.Puram	Rural	Thottambedu	24.05.83
Thumbakuppam	Rural	Bangarupalem	06.06.83
Chowdasamudram	Rural	Thaballapalle	10.06.83
Kandukur	Rural	Thaballapalle	10.06.83
Gudupalle	Rural	Kuppam	25.06.83

Contd.

Name of the Branch	*Status*	*Name of the Block*	*Date of Opening*
B.N.Kandriga	Rural	Thottambedu	28.06.83
Santhavellore	Rural	Sathyavedu	29.09.83
S.R.Puram	Rural	Karvetinagar	26.10.83
T.P.Kota	Rural	Sathyavedu	02.11.83
Veligullu	Rural	Thamballapalle	01.12.83
Nendragunta	Rural	Pulicherla	08.12.83
Nudaramdoddi	Rural	Kuppam	25.04.84
Komapalle	Rural	Puttur	27.01.84
Santhipuram	Rural	Kuppam	10.05.84
197, Ramapuram	Rural	Chittoor	15.06.84
Munagalareddipalle	Rural	Thottambedu	25.06.84
Muthyalareddipalle	Rural	Chandrairi	27.06.84
Akkurthi	Rural	Srikalahasti	26.07.84
Eguvaveedi	Rural	Thottambedu	14.11.84
Bangarupalem	Rural	Bangarupalem	24.11.84
Piler	Rural	Chinnagottigallu	24.11.84
Vengalathur	Rural	Pichatur	28.11.84
Peddakanili	Rural	Srikalahasti	12.12.84
M.Bandapalle	Rural	Gangadhara Nellore	24.12.84
Yellampalle Santhagate	Rural	Bangarupalem	24.12.84
Kona	Rural	Vayalpadu	26.12.84
Peddamandyam	Rural	Thamballapalle	26.12.84
Tarigonda	Rural	Vayalpadu	28.12.84
Nindra	Rural	Pichatur	28.01.85
Karani	Rural	Sathyavedu	28.01.85
Sathyavedu	Rural	Sathyavedu	28.01.85
Kasiralla	Rural	Chittoor	31.01.85
Sankararayala peta	Rural	Punganur	31.01.85
Thottambedu	Rural	Thottambedu	11.03.85
Puttur	Rural	Puttur	11.03.85
Reddivaripalle	Rural	Madanapalle	11.03.85
Bodevandlapalli	Rural	Chinnagottigallu	11.03.85
Theertham	Rural	Palaaner	11.03.85
Gajulapalli	Rural	Bangarupalem	25.03.85
Buga Agraharam	Rural	Nagari	26.03.85
Kommireddigari palli	Rural	Pulicherla	26.03.85

Source: Shri Venkateswara Grameena Bank: "Annual Reports, 1985".

In the field of deposit mobilisation, the Bank has registered stupendous growth. Various attractive saving schemes have been offered to suit the saving habits of rural masses and intensive canvassing has been undertaken by the branches. The growth of total deposits of Shri Venkateswara Grameena Bank and the statement showing composition of various deposit schemes are furnished in Table-24 and Table-25.

As could be seen from T'able-24, the total deposits of the Bank were Rs.20.20 lakhs from 1,992 accounts in 1981. They rose up to Rs.135.38 lakhs in 13,082 accounts in 1982. In 1983, they further went up to Rs.271.05 lakhs in 42,319 accounts. In the next two years followed 1984 and 1985, they further grew up to Rs. 448.18 lakhs in 75,740 account and Rs.834.04 lakhs in 1,09,628 accounts. Thus the percentage growth recorded during the years were 570, 100, 65 and 86 in amounts and 557, 223, 79 and 45 in accounts. Within a short span of about 5 years, the SVGB has succeeded in achieving its objective of 'mass banking' by cultivating the saving habit among the rural and downtrodden population in Chittoor district. The fact that the Bank was able to gather a large number of rural deposits and stood first[51] amongst the 14 RRBs in Andhra Pradesh for the year 1985 is a praiseworthy achievement considering the severe drought winds blowing in the district during that particular year.

Table-25 illustrates that most of the deposits[52] of the Bank were from Savings Bank Account on all the years from 1981 to 1995 followed by Term Deposits. The composition of Fixed Deposits was minimum and that of Current and Recurring Deposits had been negligible. Thus, by the end of 1985, of the total deposits of Rs.834.05 lakhs, Rs.462.67 lakhs were constituted Savings Bank Account, Rs.273.28 lakhs in Special Term Deposit, Rs.53.22 lakhs in Fixed Deposit, Rs.24.16 lakhs in Current Account and Rs.20.72 lakhs in Recurring Deposit Account. Thus, in the field of deposit mobilisation the SVGB got 56th place among the 188 RRB s in the Country.

Substantial progress has been achieved by the Bank in the sphere of credit disbursal. As a poor-man's bank, it is extending timely credit to the weaker sections of rural society. The total advances outstanding of Sri Venkateswara Grameena Bank are furnished in Table-26.

In 1981, Rs.9.15 1akhs were advanced to 776 borrowers. By 1982 they increased to Rs.60.62 1akhs to 4,629 borrowers registering an increase of 562 per cent and 496 per cent. By

Table 24
Growth of Deposits of Shri Venkateswara Grameena Bank

(*Rs. in Lakhs*)

Year	*Total Deposits*	*Growth in Percentage Over the Previous Year*	*No. of Deposit Accounts*	*Growth in Percentage Over the Previous Year*	*Per Branch Deposit*	*Growth in Percentage Over the Previous Year*	*Per Capita Deposits (Amount in Rs.)*
1	2	3	4	5	6	7	8
1981	20.20	-	1,992	-	2.89	-	1,014.06
1982	135.38	570.20	13,082	556.73	7.13	146.71	1,034.86
1983	271.05	100.21	42,319	223.49	7.53	5.61	640.49
1984	448.18	65.35	75,740	78.97	8.46	12.35	591.73
1985	834.04	86.09	1,09,628	44.74	12.64	49.41	760.80

Source: Shri Venkateswara Grameena Bank: "Annual Reports".

Table 25

Statement Showing Composition of Various Deposits of Shri Venkateswara Grameena Bank

(Amount in lakhs of Rupees)

Type of Deposits	*1981*	*1982*	*1983*	*1984*	*1985*
Fixed Deposit	0.31	43.56	10.91	26.75	53.22
	(1.53)	(32.18)	(4.03)	(5.97)	(6.38)
Savings Bank Account	12.10	68.36	185.71	267.68	462.67
	(59.90)	(50.49)	(68.51)	(59.73)	(55.47)
Recurring Deposit	0.26	1.26	5.25	10.65	20.72
	(1.29)	(0.93)	(1.94)	(2.37)	(2.48)
Special Term Deposit (Re-investment Deposits)	5.60	18.59	55.65	132.21	273.28
	(27.72)	(13.73)	(20.53)	(29.50)	(32.77)
Current Account	1.93	3.61	13.53	10.89	24.16
	(9.58)	(2.67)	(4.99)	(2.43)	(2.90)
Total	20.20	135.38	271.05	448.18	834.05
	(100.00)	(100.00)	(100.00)	(100.00)	(100.00)

Note: Figures in brackets are percentages to total.
Source: Shri Venkateswara Grameena Bank: "Annual Reports".

Table 26

Year-wise Advances of Shri Venkateswara Grameena Bank, 1981-85

(Amount in Rs. Lakhs)

Year	Total Advances	Percentage Growth Over the Previous Year	No. of Accounts	Percentage Growth Over the Previous Year	Credit Per Branch	Per Capita Credit (Amount in Rs.)
1981	9.15	-	776	-	1.31	1.179
1982	60.62	562.51	4.629	496.52	3.19	1.310
1983	261.57	331.49	14.162	249.15	7.27	1.618
1984	775.88	196.62	37.630	132.83	14.64	2.062
1985	1,275.84	64.44	53.808	42.99	19.33	2.371

Source: Shri Venkateswara Grameena Bank : "Annual Reports".

1983, again the advances and beneficiaries rose up to Rs.261.57 lakhs and 16,162 with an increase of 331 per cent and 249 per cent. This increasing trend has been followed in the next two years 1984 and 1985 in which Rs.771.88 lakhs lent to 37,630 borrowers and Rs. 1, 275.84 lakhs to 53,808 borrowers. Credit per branch reached to Rs.19.33 lakhs in 1985 as against Rs.1.31 lakhs in 1981, thus showing an increase of 15 times. The per capita credit rose up from Rs.1, 179 to Rs.2,371, with an increase of 2 times during the 1981-85 period.

Table-27 depicts the purpose-wise classification of outstanding advances.

Agriculture and its allied activities account for most of the advances of the Bank in all the years from 1981 to 1985. Further, almost all the advances disbursed under agricultural sector have gone to the small marginal farmer and agricultural labourer category in consonance with the objectives of RRBs. Thus in 1985, 66 per cent of advances were given for short term crop loans, 12 per cent for agricultural investments and 10 per cent for allied agricultural activities. The small business including self-employment category got 5 per cent whereas rural artisan classes availed 3 per cent.

Apart from this, the Bank has been keenly involved in financing specified target groups i.e., people belong to Scheduled Castes and Scheduled Tribes. It extended Rs.25.31 lakhs to about 1,962 Scheduled Case/ Scheduled Tribe families in 1983 as against Rs.5.01 lakhs to 563 families in 1982 and also against Rs.0.73 lakhs to 92 families in 1981. The details of the financial assistance given to this category is provided in Table 28.

Further more, the Bank has been actively participating in financing special schemes implemented by the Government of India like the IRDP, DRI and others. Under the IRDP, the Bank has extended[53] Rs.56.14 lakh to about 3,946 beneficiaries in 1985 as against Rs.49.23 lakhs to 3,557 beneficiaries in 1984. Under DRI it provided Rs.0.40 lakhs to 25 beneficiaries in 1984. Under other programmes, it extended Rs.823.47 lakhs in 32,165 accounts in 1985.

Table 27
Out Standing Advances of Shri Venkateswara Grameena Bank: Purpose-wise (Account in '000') (Amount in Rs. Lakhs)

Type of Activity	Number of Accounts				
	1981	1982	1983	1984	1985
Short-term crop loans	685 (88)	2901 (63)	10133 (63)	21956 (58)	29037 (54)
Term Loans					
a) Agricultural investments	3 (-)	62 (1)	314 (10)	2705 (7)	5288 (10)
b) Allied Activities	3 (-)	174 (4)	1398 (9)	2953 (8)	4243 (8)
Rural Artisan, Village and Cottage Industries	- (9)	421 (7)	1087 (7)	2480 (8)	4312
Retail Trade Small business and Self employment	54 (7)	885 (19)	2737 (17)	6045 (16)	8462 (16)
Other purposes	31 (4)	186 (4)	493 (3)	1491 (4)	2465 (5)
Total	776	4629	16162	37630	53807

Contd.

Amount				
1981	1982	1983@	1984	1985
8	9	10	11	12
8.11	43.92	186.30	488.08	805.13
(88)	(71)	(71)	(66)	(66)
0.20	1.30	8.98	84.64	149.79
(2)	(2)	(3)	(11)	(12)

Contd.

	0.08	3.61	26.98	76.98	117.46
	(1)	(6)	(10)	(10)	(10)
	-	3.10	10.58	24.40	79.07
	(5)	(4)	(3)	(3)	
	0.39	7.30	20.59	46.66	66.83
	(4)	(12)	(8)	(6)	(5)
	0.39	2.35	8.27	23.39	45.52
	(4)	(4)	(3)	(3)	(4)
	9.17	61.58	261.57	744.15	1223.84

Note: For the yeas 1984 and 1985, data is given without accrued interest. @ Data relating to June 1983.

Source:

1. Shri Venkateswara Grameena Bank: "Annual Reports".
2. NABARD: "Statistics on Regional Rural Banks", December 1985.

Table 28

Financial Assistance Given to Scheduled Castes/ Scheduled Trbes by Shri Venkateswara Grameena Bank.

(Amount in Rs. Lakhs)

	Number of Accounts			*Amount*		
Type of Activity	*1981*	*1982*	*1983*	*1981*	*1982*	*1983*
Agricultural Short-term Production loans	66	274	862	0.59	2.45	7.77
Agricultureal Term loans	1	4	62	0.003	0.06	1.31
Allied Agricultural Term Loans	-	63	320	-	1.04	6.32
Village and Cottage Industries	18[*]	62	403	0.11	0.41	7.64[**]
Rural Artisans	-	71	-	-	0.20	-
Small Business	-	58	223	-	0.66	1.78
Self-Employed	-	26	92	-	0.12	0.39
Others	7	5	-	0.03	0.07	-
Total	92	563	1962	0.73	5.04	25.21

[*] Total of other priority sector advances.

[**] Includes total of rural artisans.

Source: Shri Venkateswara Grameena Bank: "Annual Reports".

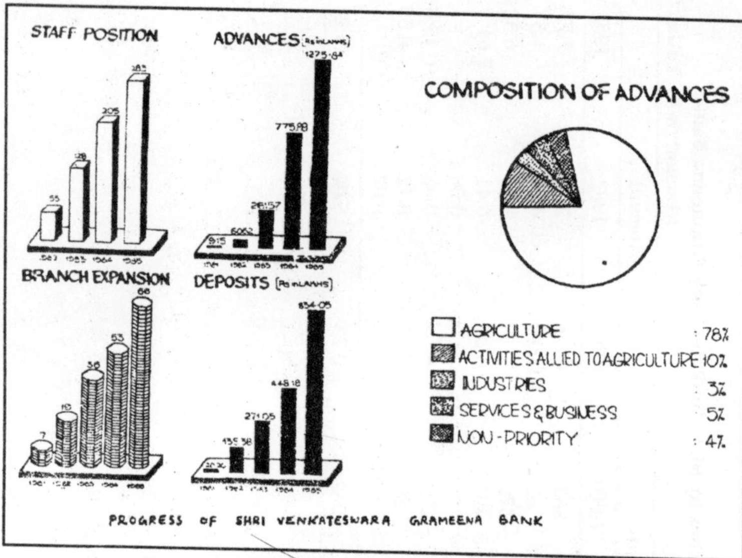

Progress of Shri Venkateswara Grameena Bank

Shri Venkateswara Grameena Bank was adjudged[54] as the "Best Bank" in the district for 2 successive years 1983-84 and 1984-85 in the implementation of IRDP. It has also got a Rolling Cup from the District Rural Development Authority and another one from the District Scheduled caste Cooperative Society for performing well in the district in the implementation of their programmes for the year 1984-85. Thus, the SVGB acquired 39th place among the 188 RRBs in the country in the field of credit disbursal.

The bank has been enthusiastically undertaking schemes like crop Insurance Scheme, opening of Fair prices shops and other land-based schemes already in vogue. Special emphasis is being given for financing non-agricultural schemes such as artisan complexes which generate employment potential as well as additional productivity in rural areas.

The Bank drew during the year 1984, a sum of Rs.234.46 lakhs under refinance from the NABARD against the figure Rs.87.16 lakhs in 1993. It also availed a sum of Rs. 195.00 lakhs as re finance from the Sponsor Bank.

The credit.-deposit ratio of the Bank was low in the initial two years at 41.7 and 44.8 in 1981 and 1982. Later on, it slowly went up to 96.5, 173.1 and 153.0 during the years 1993. 1984 and 1985 indicating that balance between advances given and deposits mobilised has been restored. Per employee business which is another important growth indicator grew Up from Rs.3.36 lakhs in 1982 to Rs.7.46 lakhs in 1985 thus showing an increase of 122 per cent. The percentage of recovery to total advances was 71 in 1983 and 69 in 1984. In the year 1985 the Bank has collected Rs.305.46 lakhs against a demand amount of Rs.529.36 lakhs. thus showing 58 per cent recovery compared favourably with the All India average performance of 55 per cent of all RRBs in India.

The personnel position of the Shri Venkateswara Grameena Bank is illustrated in Table-29.

The staff on deputation from sponsor hank which were 17 in 1981 had been slowly reduced to 8 in 1983 and 6 in 1985 while that of Bank's own staff had gone up gradually as the Bank made rapid strides in many areas, from 17 in 1981 to 83 in 1982, again to 136 in 1983, to 211 in 1984 and to 289 in 1985. Of the aggregate 289 staff members 71 are branch managers. 89 are field supervisors 115 are junior clerk-cum-cashiers and 8 are messengers including a driver. Of the total staff, 35 per cent employees are trained ones while 17 per cent are from people belong to Scheduled Castes/ Tribes and there are about 20 women employees.

Utmost importance has been given to training of the employees. Different levels of staff are getting training facilities at various centres such as Bankers Institute for Rural Development, Lucknow, College of Agricultural Banking, Pune and Regional Training Centre of NABARD at Mangalore. Sponsor Bank also provides induction training to the employees, particularly of lower cadres. During 1985, 32 field supervisors and 28 junior clerks got training at sponsor bank while 20 officers went vigorous training at different centres. An Inspection cell was situated at head office with a view to strengthen the control mechanism. All the 66 branches of the Bank were covered by either snap inspection or full inspection during 1985.

Table 29
Strength of the Staff of the Shri Venkateswara Grameena Bank, 1981-85

Category	*1981*	*1982*	*1983*	*1984*	*1985*
1. On deputation from sponsor bank					
i) Officers	9	27	8	6	6
ii) Clerks	8	1	-	-	-
Total of 1	17	28	8	6	6
2. Bank's own staff					
i) Officers (Branch Managers)	-	27	45	58	71
ii) Field Supervisors	-	-	30	61	89
iii) Junior Clerk-Cum Cashiers (JCCS)	-	28	53	86	115
iv) Messengers	-	-	-	-	8
Total of 2	-	55	128	205	283
3. Grand Total (1+2)	17	83	136	211	289
4. Percentage growth over the previous year.	-	388.24	63.86	55.15	36.97

Source: Shri Venkateswara Grameena Bank: "Annual Reports".

Like the RRBs in other parts of Andhra Pradesh and all over India, the Shri Venkateswara Grameena Bank was suffering from heavy net losses in its budget year after year, as a consequence of its high expenditures followed by low incomes. The year-wise working results of the Bank is given in Table-30.

Table 30
Working Results of Shri Venkateswara Grameena Bank 1981-85
(Amount in lakhs in Rupees)

Year	*Income*	*Expenditure*	*Profit/Loss (Accumulated)*
1981	3.72	3.58	0.14
1982	13.54	14.74	-1.20
1983	31.62	40.47	-10.05
1984	67.86	79.16	-21.35
1985	138.38	153.32	-36.29

Source: Shri Venkateswara Grameena Bank: "Annual Reports".

Initially in 1981, income of the Bank was Rs.3.72 lakhs and the expenditure Rs.3.58 lakhs. This had resulted into a net profit of Rs. 0.14 lakhs. Later on, during the years 1982, 1983, 1984 and 1985, though total income rose up, the total expenditure overtook it, thereby resulting heavy net losses. Thus, the break-even planned in the corporate plan for 1985 did not materialise.

Conclusion

Rayalaseema, consisting of Cuddapah, Kurnool Anantapur, Chittoor and parts of Prakasam districts is not only a backward area but also a stalking ground of famines. Predominance of Rural population, underdeveloped agrarian operations inferior soils, limited area under cultivation, lack of irrigation potential, uncertain and unpredictable rainfall, very little industrialization and existence of a large agricultural proletariat who find themselves impoverished by recurring droughts are the common characteristics of the region. Successive and frequent failure of monsoons leading to severe droughts and consequent starvation and malnutrition of larger section of small/marginal farmers and agricultural labourers are the real problems in Rayalaseema.

Banking is one of the many instruments which was used by the Government to correct the regional imbalances and sectoral variations in the process of development planning. In recent times mass banking was introduced through "the institution of Regional Rural Banks" under the Regional Rural Banks Act of 1976 to serve the poorest of the poor and also to fill up the credit gaps left off by the co-operatives and commercial banks in rural areas. The essence of the, Regional Rural banking is the purpose orientation rather than security-orientation. In Rayalaseema region three such banks were opened Viz., The Rayalaseema Grameena Bank, the Sree Anantha Grameena Bank and the Shri Venkateswara Grameena Bank.

The Rayalaseema Grameena Bank has now a history of 9½ years. By covering the three districts of Cuddapah, Kurnool and parts of Prakasam, it was able to make an inroad into rural unbanked and under banked areas by establishing 141 branches. By cultivating saving habit among the rural folk, it has succeeded in mobilising rural deposits considerably. By fulfilling the objective of meeting the financial needs of people of small means, it has enabled to lessen the influence of moneylenders in its jurisdiction. The average deposit (Rs.14.04 lakhs) and the average credit (Rs,22.00 lakhs) showed-'n impressive trend. With the assistance of devoted staff members it is successfully financing special programmes implemented by the Government. In spite of the drought prone conditions prevailing in the districts much has been achieved by the Bank.

The Sree Anantha Grameena Bank covering the dry district of Anantapur is of 7 years old. Set with certain corporate objectives, it was striving hard to achieve rural development linked with credit in the second 'hard core' area of the country. It has established about 67 branches in every nook and corner of the area undeterred by the fact that many of the locations have not even basic amenities. By supplying cheaper credit at the right time and right place, the Bank has involved itself into the uplift of weaker, vulnerable and downtrodden sections of population. Though its deposit strength has been hampered due "to un-favourable droughts and unseasonal crop failures, the Bank's rural branch staff, by steering clear of village factions and developing good rapport with village folks, are campaigning for larger amount of deposits. The Bank's per branch deposit is Rs.10.94 lakhs and per branch credit is Rs.23.16 lakhs. It is well set to march ahead on the path of service and success.

The 4½, years old Shri Venkateswara Grameena Bank working in 'the district of Chittoor. Though young in age, spectacular growth has been achieved by the Bank on all its fronts. Over 66 branches have been set up by the Bank, most of them being in unbanked and under-banked rural centres. Despite having an unhelpful topography and an unenterprising social conditions in the district, it was able to tap massive amounts of rural deposits and stood first amongst the 14 RRBs in Andhra Pradesh during 1985. Similarly, in the field of credit expansion, the performance of the Bank is quite laudable. It has been serving the poorer sections by giving timely credit assistance and helping to monetise the rural economy of the area. The average deposit (Rs. 12.64 lakhs) and the average credit (Rs.19.33 lakhs) of the Bank look quite impressive. With the help of efficient and devoted staff the Bank has progressed well and set the record of being the "Best Bank" in the district for two successive years.

But all the three RRBs in Rayalaseema are suffering from one single disease i.e., incurring recurring losses.

Footnotes

1. Narayana, D.L : "Rayalaseema : A Famine Spot of India", The Asian Economic Review, Vol. IV, No.3, May 1962, p.341.
2. "Andhra Pradesh Statistical Abstract", 1983, Government of Andhra Pradesh, Hyderabad, Table 1.1.
3. "Andhra Pradesh Impressive Growth", Commerce, Vol, 149, No.3820, 18 August 1984, p.227.
4. "Andhra Pradesh Sixth Five Year Plan, 1980-85", Vol. I Government of Andhra Pradesh, Hyderabad, pp.1-2.
5. "Development of Banking-, Andhra Pradesh, Vol. XXII, No.6, April 1978, p.11.
6. *Ibid.*
7. Andhra Pradesh Sixth Five Year Plan 1980-85", *Op.cit.*, p.214.
8. "Banking Trends in Andhra Pradesh-, Data Andhra Pradesh Vol.3, No.9, May 1-15, 1980, p.838.

9. NABARD: "Statistics on Regional Rural Banks", 1985.
10. "Techno-Economic Survey of Andhra Pradesh-, National Council of Applied Economic Research, New Delhi, 1962, p.22.
11. Andhra Pradesh Statistical Abstract", 1983, *Op.cit.*, Table 1.3.
12. Narayana, D.L : *Op.cit.*, p.341.
13. Originally Bellary district was in Rayalaseema region. Consequent on the reorganization of the States, it had gone to Karnataka State.
14. "Techno-Economic Survey of Andhra Pradesh" *Op.cit.*, p.7
15. In Italy "Mezzogiorno" was used to refer an extreme case of regional disparity. In recent development literature any hard core area of a country came to be referred as the Mezzogiorno.
16. Subbaramaiah, A and Nageswara Rao, K : "Economic Development of Rayalaseema Region", "Indian Economic Development and Policy, Essays in Honour of Prof. De 'Souza", P.R. Brahmananda, D. Anjundappa. and B.K. Narayana (Ed.), Vikas Publishing House Pvt. Ltd., New Delhi, 1979,pp. 306-20.
17. *Ibid.*
18. *Ibid.*
19. "Planning and Development of Backward Regions, A Case Study of Rayalaseema", "Phisiography, Vol.1, Resource Inventory, Government of Andhra Pradesh, Hyderabad, 1970, p.113.
20. Narayana, D.L. : *Op.cit.*, p.344.
21. Venkatanarayana, B: "An Outline Proposal for Improving Irrigated Agriculture in the Rayalaseema Districts", "Planning and Development of Backward Regions", *Op.cit.*, p.310.
22. "Andhra Pradesh Statistical Abstract", 1983, *Op.cit.*, Table 3.3.
23. "Note on Development of Rayalaseema", Y. Pitchi Reddy's Report, Planning and Development of Backward Areas", *Op.cit.*, p.71.
24. Appa Rao, B. "Regional Imbalances in Andhra Pradesh: Study of Trends over Three Decades", Southern Economist, Vol.22, No.1. November 1-15, 1983. pp.15-18.
25. According to an stimate, the soil of Anantapur is said to be deficient in zinc, while an area of land in under cultivation in Cuddapah loses 5 lbs. of Nitrogen and 25 lbs. of Phosphorous Phentoxide.
26. Krishna Murthy, C.H. : "Improved Agricultural Production in Rainfed Areas, Prospects and Problems", "Planning and Development of Backward Areas, *Op. cit.*, p.241.
27. *Ibid.*, p.188.
28. "Comparative Andhra Pradesh-2 (Regional Variations)" Data Andhra Pradesh, Vol.1, No.2, January 15-31, 1978, pp.3-4., p.188.
29. Planning and Development of Backward Areas", "Irrigation *Op.cit.*, p. 287.
30. Subbaramaiah, S and Nageswara Rao, K. : *Op.cit.*
31. Appa Rao, B: *Op.cit.*
32. "Andhra Pradesh Year Book", 1984, Government of Andhra Pradesh, Hyderabad
33. *Ibid.*

34. Haranatha Babu D.: "Regional Disparities in Andhra Pradesh: An Emperical Study", Ph.D. Thesis, Andhra university, 1980, pp.97-98.
35. Andhra Pradesh Statistical Abstract, 1993, *Op.cit.*, Table - 1.3.
36. "Lead Bank Scheme-Annual Action Plan 1985, Cuddapah District", Syndicate Bankl Cuddapah, p.1.
37. "Cuddapah, the Heart of Rayalaseema", Andhra Pradesh, Vol. XXII, No. 10, August 1974, pp. 40-41.
38. "Integrated Rural Development Programme, Cuddapah District (A.P). Annual Plan 1983-84", District Rural Development Agency, Cuddapah p.4.
39. Rayalaseema Grameena Bank: "Annual Report, 1985".
40. "Performance Report - 1980 & Performance Budget 1981 Rayalaseema Grameena Bank, Cuddapah, p.2.
41. Rayalaseema Grameena Bank: "Perspective Plan 1983-85 and Performance Plan 1983", p.4.
42. Rayalaseema Grameena Bank: "Annual Report, 1980", P.5.
43. Lead Bank Scheme, Annual Action Plan 1986, Anantapur District', Syndicate Bank, Anantapur.
44. Lead Bank Scheme, Annual Action Plan 1985, Anantapur District', Syndicate Bank, Anantapur.
45. The year 1980 was partially drought affected, while 1981 was slightly better and 1982 was severely affected with drought. The years 1984 and 1985 were even harder for the farming community in which the rainfall received was very low at 548.7 m.m. and 349.1 m.m. During the year 1985, crops failed in a large scale and even grass is being transported from other districts.
46. Sree Anantha Grameena Bank: "Annual Report, 1981", p.4.
47. It has bagged third prize at All-India level in 1985 for working efficiently.
48. Indian Bank: District Credit Plan 1983-85 and Annual Action Plan 1983 for Chittoor District
49. *Ibid.*
50. *Ibid.*
51. Shri Venkateswara Grameena Bank: "Annual Report, 1985".
52. Data relating to the number of accounts of various deposit schemes are not available from the respective Annual Reports of the Bank.
53. NABARD: Statistics on Regional Rural Banks, December 1985.
54. Shri Venkateswara Grameena Bank: "Annual Report" 1985.

6

Comparative Banking Efficiency of the Three Regional Rural Banks in Rayalaseema

"Where the objective of the type of financial institutions (RRBs) is socio-economic, an initial period of financial loss may well be a price worth paying for the achievement of the larger social objective of widening the area of credit coverage".

Working Group on Rural Banks[1]

Introduction

The main objective of this chapter is to make a comparative study of the three Regional Rural Banks which are functioning in Rayalaseema region in accordance with their relative banking efficiency. This is in an attempt to highlight the comparative importance of factors which help or hinder the management of programmes of these banks for achieving their objectives. By setting together the performance of each bank against the other, it is endeavoured to ascertain some of their accomplishments as well as their failures. As the three banks are situated in a single contiguous territory, this analysis would not only provide the total picture of Regional Rural Bank movement as a whole in the region, but also enable to understand which particular bank is marching ahead in which certain field and also its relative backwardness in different spheres in comparison to other banks. Comparative case studies of this kind would ultimately expect to help the policy makers in formulating the future programmes of these banks and guide them in improving their efficiency.

The three Regional Rural Banks in Rayalaseema, namely, the Rayalaseema Grameena Bank, the Sree Anantha Grameena Bank and the Shri Venkateswara Grameena Bank were set up on different dates and years. The Rayalaseema Grameena Bank was the first one to come into existence on 6th August 1976 covering the districts of Cuddapah, Kurnool and parts of Prakasam and sponsored by the Syndicate Bank. The Sree Anantha Grameena Bank was the second Regional Rural Bank in the region opened on 1st November 1979 covering the Anantapur district. This bank was also sponsored by the Syndicate Bank. The Shri Venkateswara Grameena Bank was the third Regional Rural Bank, established on 3rd March 1981 covering the district of Chittoor and sponsored by the Indian Bank. As the 3 banks were of different age groups, i.e., 9½ years in the case of Rayalaseema Grameena Bank, 6 years of Sree Anantha Grameena Bank and about 5 years of Shri Venkateswara Grameena Bank, it is difficult to make comparison of them on all years. It is, therefore, natural to expect that the first established bank might be in a better position than the latter ones. Further, the Rayalaseema Grameena Bank, which was not only a case of early set up one nearing its first decade of existence in the region but also had a jurisdiction of 2½ districts under its coverage unlike the single district jurisdiction as in the case of Sree Anantha and Shri Venkateswara. So, it is mostly possible that the performance of Rayalaseema Grameena Bank might be better than the other two. Hence, the assessment of comparative performance of 3 Grameena Banks is attempted here during their first five years of operation on one side and their last 5 years on the other, irrespective of their establishment years and dates. As time plays an important role in the development of any institution, this study would enable us to comprehend the comparative trend[2] of the progress of the banks and also to predict their future tendencies.

However, there appears certain limitations even to this method of comparative study. Firstly, out of the 3 RRBs studied, only one bank i.e., the Rayalaseema Grameena Bank has got full quota of first five and last five years while for the other two, both the years were remained almost the same. Secondly, when the RRBs were initially launched in the country there were certain doubts about their continuation just after 2 years of their arrival in the country. So, the Rayalaseema Grameena Bank, which was a case of early start on, might have suffered some limitations due to lack of experience and established procedures. The Sree Anantha Grameena Bank and the Shri Venkateswara Grameena Bank, on the other hand, were started in early eighties in which the RRB movement in the country touched its peak. Hence the progress of these banks might be better than the former one in many ways. Considering all these constraints, the current chapter aims to evaluate the performance of the selected RRBs during their first five and last five years of operation, apart from giving information on all years and their latest position.

The study covers important factors about the branch expansion and staffing pattern of the RRBs selected. For the purpose of assessment of efficiency, performance indicators such as (i) Mobilization of deposits, (ii) Advances, (iii) Credit-deposit ratio, (iv) Recoveries and (v) Financial viability are identified and needed statistical data also presented. As for comparison, growth rates, both linear and compound, are worked out. While the linear growth rate shows a constant absolute amount of change from year to year, the compound growth rate gives a constant rate of change.

The formulas used for the purpose are as follows:

Linear Growth Rate

A linear relationship between two variables Y and T is given by

$$Y_i = a + bt_i + \varepsilon_i ; i = 1,2, \ldots\ldots\ldots\ldots n$$

Where

Y = Index number of deposits/ advances/ income/ expenditure

t = Time periods

ε = Error term

n = Number of observations on each variable

Here a and b are unknown constants (parameters) to be estimated by using the following formula :

$$\hat{b} = \left[\frac{\sum ty - \frac{(\sum t)\ (\sum Y)}{n}}{\sum t^2 - \frac{(\sum t)^2}{n}} \right]$$

$$\hat{a} = \bar{Y} - b\bar{t}$$

Where

$$\bar{Y} = \frac{\sum Y}{n} \text{ and } \bar{t} = \frac{\sum t}{n}$$

Here $\hat{a}$ and $\hat{b}$ are called least squares estimates of a and b respectively.

The Linear Growth Rate (L.G.R.) is given by

$$\text{L.G.R.} = \left[\frac{\hat{b}}{\bar{Y}} \right] 100$$

To test the significance of b, we use the Student's t-test statistic, which is given by

$$t = \left[\frac{\hat{b} \sqrt{\sum t^2 - \frac{(\sum t)^2}{n}}}{\hat{\sigma}} \right]$$

Where

$$\hat{\sigma} = \sqrt{\frac{\sum y^2 - \frac{(\sum Y)^2}{n} - b\left[\sum tY - \frac{(\sum t)\ (\sum Y)}{n}\right]}{n-2}}.$$

Compare the calculated value of t with the critical value of t for (n-2) degrees of freedom at 5% or 1% level of significance and draw inference accordingly.

Compound Growth Rate

An exponential relationship between two variables Y and t is given by

$$Y_i = a\,b^{t_i} e^{i};\ i = 1, 2, \ldots.\ n$$

Taking logarithms on both sides of the relationship, we get

$$\text{Log } Y_i = \log a + (\log b)\, t_i + \log e)_i$$

$$\text{Or } V_i = A + Bt_i + u_i,\ i = 1,2,\ldots\ n$$

Where

$V = \log Y$

$A = \log a$

$B = \log b$

u = Error term.

The least squares estimates of A and B are given by

$$\hat{B} = \left[\frac{\sum tV - \frac{(\sum t)\ (\sum V)}{n}}{\sum t^2 - \frac{(\sum t)^2}{n}}\right]$$

$$\hat{A} = \bar{V} - \hat{B}\ \bar{t}$$

Where

$$\bar{V} = \frac{\sum V}{n} \text{ and } \bar{t} = \frac{\sum t}{n}$$

Here $\hat{a}$ and $\hat{b}$ are estimates of A and B respectively.

Now, the least squares estimates of a and b are given by

$$\hat{a} = \text{Anti log}\,(\hat{A})$$

$$\hat{b} = \text{Anti log}\,(\hat{B})$$

The Compound Growth Rate (C.G.R) is given by

$$\text{C.G.R.} = (\hat{b} - 1)\,100$$

To test the significance of B, we use Student's t-test statistic, which is given by

$$t = \left[\frac{\hat{B}\sqrt{\sum t^2 - \frac{(\sum t)^2}{n}}}{\hat{\sigma}} \right]$$

Where

$$\hat{\sigma} = \sqrt{\frac{\sum V^2 - \frac{(\sum V)^2}{n} - \hat{B}\left[\sum tV - \frac{(\sum t)\ (\sum V)}{n}\right]}{n-2}}$$

Compare the calculated value of t with the critical value of t for (n-2) degree of freedom at 5% or 1% level of significance and draw inference accordingly.

To make consistent comparisons, the abbreviations of the names of the banks viz., Rayalaseema, Sree Anantha and Shri Venkateswara are used in the place of Rayalaseema Grameena

Bank, Sree Anantha Grameena Bank and Shri Venkateswara Grameena Bank for convenience. For Sree Anantha Grameena Bank, in computing growth rates, the year 1981 has been taken as its first year of operation to make the calculations easier.

Branch Expansion

One of the important indicators for highlighting any bank's efficiency is the extent of its branch expansion. The setting up of largest network of branches enables the banking sector to cater the financial and developmental needs of all sections of people including the rural, semi-urban, urban and metropolitan. The systematic spread of branches also helps progressive reduction of regional disparities in the provision of banking facilities. Further, the intensive geographical expansion of branches facilitates the extension of credit assistance to the right people at the proper places and at the right time.

Spreading of banking facilities to forlorn corners of rural areas particularly to unbanked and under banked centres is the main objective of Regional Rural Banking. This was aimed with a view to create new vistas for financial sources to be invested in rural areas so that the standard of living of its population can be increased via enhanced employment opportunities. In Rayalaseema region, the total number of RRB branches has grown steadily during the decade 1976-85. They went up from a mere 10 offices in 1976 to 65 in 1978, which further increased to 91 in 1980, to 165 in 1982, to 226 in 1984 and to 274 in 1985. The share of Rayalaseema at the end of 1985, thus constitutes 28 per cent of aggregate RRB branches in Andhra Pradesh and 2.2 per cent of all RRBs in Indian Union. Out of the total 274 branches in the region, 141 branches were opened by Rayalaseema Grameena Bank[3] in the districts of Cuddapah (66), Kurnool (60) and Prakasam (15); 67 branches were opened by Sree Anantha Grameena Bank in the district of Anantapur; and 66 by Shri Venkateswara Grameena Bank in the Chittoor district.

The comparative statement showing the branch expansion of Regional Rural Banks in Rayalaseema is provided in Table-1.

Table 1
Comparative Statement Showing Branch Expansion of RRBs in Rayalaseema Region 1976-85

Year at the End of December	*Rayala-seema*	*Sree Anantha*	*Shri Venka-teswara*	*Rayala-seema Region*	*Andhra Pradesh*	*India*
1976	10	-	-	10 (18.7)	53	503
1977	45	-	-	45 (28.1)	160	1187
1978	65	-	-	65 (28.1)	231	1762
1979	70	1	-	71 (28.1)	253	2420
1980	81	10	-	91 (29.4)	309	3279
1981	100	32	7	139 (37.3)	373	4795
1982	100	46	19	165 (37.8)	436	6191
1983	102	50	36	188 (32.5)	578	7795
1984	119	54	53	226 (27.7)	816	10245
1985	141	67	66	274 (27.8)	985	12606

Note: Figures in brackets are percentages to State

Source:

1. "Annual Reports of Rayalaseema, Sree Anantha and Shri Venkateswara Grameena Banks"
2. "Data Andhra Pradesh", Various Issues.
3. Reserve Bank of India : "Report on Currency and Finance", Statistical Statements 1976-77 to 1984-85.

The progress achieved in the sphere of branch expansion of RRBs in Rayalaseema is faster in the last 5 years of their operation rather than in their first 5 years. The number of RRB offices, which were only 91 in 1976-80. Period, were almost doubled to 183 in 1981-85 period, thus totaling to 274 at the end of 1985. The reason for this development is easy to guess. Initially, there was only 1 RRB viz., the Rayalaseema Grameena Bank in the region, which was functioning during the 1976-79 period. The second bank i.e., the Sree Anantha Grameena Bank was started on the last quarter of 1979, while the Shri Venkateswara Grameena Bank, the third one has joined only in 1981. So it is natural that the number of RRB branches was vigorously expanded in the latter half of its decade in which 3 RRBs were functioning covering the whole region as against 1 RRB covering 2½ districts in its first 5 years. Thus the total number of branches of Rayalaseema Bank increased from 10 to 141 during the 1976-85 period, whereas for Sree Anantha, they rose up from 10 to 67 during the 1980-85 period and for Shri Venkateswara from 7 to 66 during the 1981-85 period.

Apart from the increase in aggregate numbers, more impressive has been the coverage of rural areas by selected RRBs. The rural orientation of Regional Rural Banking in Rayalaseema can be verified from Table 2.

Table 2
Centre-wise Distribution of Bank Branches by Selected RRBs as at the End of 1985

Centre	*Rayalaseema*	*Sree Anantha*	*Shri Venkateswara*	*Rayalaseema Region*
Rural	126(89.4)	54(80.6)	61(92.4)	241(88.0)
Semi-urban	13(9.2)	12(17.9)	4(6.1)	29(10.9)
Urban	2(1.4)	1(1.5)	1(1.5)	4(1.1)
Total	141(100.0)	67(100.0)	66(100.0)	274(100.0)

Note: Figures in brackets are percentages to total.
Source: "Annual Reports".

Of the total 274 RRB branches in Rayalaseema as much as 88 per cent are in rural areas, while 10.9 per cent are in semi-urban areas and a negligible 1.1 per cent in urban areas. Shri Venkateswara had highest number of rural branches at 92.4 per cent followed by Rayalaseema at 89.4 per cent and Sree Anantha at 80.6 per cent. Reflectively, Shri Venkateswara got third place in the semi-urban branches at 6.1 per cent. Rayalaseema and Sree Anantha appeared second and first at 9.2 per cent and 17.9 per cent respectively. In the case of urban centres, Rayalaseema had 2 branches, while 1 each for Sree Anantha and Shri Venkateswara. Thus the rural orientation of RRBs in Rayalaseema in expanding offices at every nook and corner of the drought-ridden areas looks successful and satisfactory.

Another striking feature of the branch expansion of selected RRBs which appears almost revolutionary is the coverage of unbanked centres. Almost all rural branches opened were in unbanked centres. This helped the rural folk to avail of banking facilities and also cultivate the habit of banking where organized banking facilities were totally lacking. The progress achieved by the RRBs in Rayalaseema in covering unbanked centres is illustrated in Table-3.

Of the total 274 RRB offices at the end of 1985 in Rayalaseema, as many as 234 or 87.2 per cent are located in unbanked centres while a minimum of 40 or 12.8 per cent are found in banked areas. This is really a commendable fact considering many of the branches are located in areas which have no basic amenities and lack of infrastructural facilities like roads, bus routes, post offices, accommodation for housing the branches, etc. A further scrutiny into the above table reveals that the Shri Venkateswara, as in case of rural branches, accounts for greater coverage of unbanked centres at 90.9 per cent of total followed by Rayalaseema and Sree Anantha at 85.8 per cent and 79.0 per cent respectively.

Table 3
Unbanked Centres Covered by Selected RRBs as at the end of 1985

Name of the Bank	*Total No. of Branches*	*Number of Branches Opened at*		*Percentage of Col.4 to Col.3*
Rayalaseema	141	121	20	85.8
Sree Anantha	67	53	14	79.0
Shri Venkateswara	66	60	6	90.9
Rayalaseema Region	274	234	40	87.2

Source: "Annual Reports".

Another yardstick for measuring the efficacy of branch expansion is the average population per branch served. Table-4 provides the population served by each RRB in Rayalaseema during the 1976-85 period.

It is heartening to note that the region's average population per RRB office which was 10,05,000 in 1976, progressively declined to 155,000 in 1978 and further to 110,000 in 1980; to 61,000 in 1982; to 44,000 in 1984; and to 37,000 in 1985. This is a remarkable achievement considering the higher state and national averages, which stood at 55,000 and 54,000 by the end of 1985. The population per bank branch for Rayalaseema has been reduced from 475,000 in 1976 to 34,000 in 1985. In the case of Sree Anantha, it declined from 225, 000 in 1980 to 38,000 in 1985. For Shri Venkateswara it went down from 392,000 in 1981 to 42,000 in 1985. This rapid decline in averages clearly shows that each of the selected RRBs has been reaching more and more people every year and directly participating in their welfare.

Table 4
Population Per Bank Office

('000)

Year	*Rayala-seema*	*Sree Anantha*	*Shri Venka-teswara*	*Rayala-seema Region*	*Andhra Pradesh*	*India*
1976	475	-	-	1005	1013	1362
1977	106	-	-	223	336	577
1978	73	-	-	155	232	389
1979	68	-	-	142	212	283
1980	59	255	-	110	174	209
1981	48	80	392	72	144	143
1982	48	55	145	61	123	111
1983	47	51	76	53	93	88
1984	40	47	52	44	66	67
1985	34	38	42	37	55	54

Note: In the calculation of population served, 1981 census figures are taken for all years.

Source: "Annual Reports"

Another and perhaps the more crucial test of performance in branch expansion is the number of offices opened in relation to the number each was expected to open within a prescribed period and also the comparative test of each RRB in its first five and last five years of existence as per the aim of research study. Though there does not appear to be any uniform directive from the Government on the number of offices to be opened, the understanding was that each RRB would open 20 branches within the first year of its operation and another 20-30 branches in the second year. Applying this norm, it is found that only 1 of the 3 selected RRBs, namely, the Rayalaseema Bank, succeeded in achieving the prescribed target with 45 branches in its first 2 years of operation. Both Sree Anantha and Shri Venkateswara were unable to achieve the target. However, this is not considered a serious omission in view of the numerous teething troubles faced by them. Even for Rayalaseema Bank, the target become possible because of its greater jurisdiction than the other two. So, its accomplishment in this respect does not prove significant.

As for the comparative performance of 3 RRBs in Rayalaseema during their first five and last five years of operation in the field of branch expansion, the same observation can be maintained. The details of new offices opened by the selected RRBs are presented in Table-5.

Table 5
New Branches Opened by Selected RRBs

Year	*Rayala-seema*	*Sree Anantha*	*Shri Venka-teswara*	*Rayala-seema*	*Andhra Pradesh*	*India*
1976	10	-	-	10	53	503
1977	35	-	-	35	107	684
1978	20	-	-	20	71	575
1979	5	1	-	6	22	658
1980	11	9	-	20	56	859
1981	19	22	7	48	64	1516
1982	-	14	12	26	63	1396
1983	2	4	17	23	142	1604
1984	17	4	17	38	238	2450
1985	22	13	13	48	169	2361

Source: "Annual Reports"

The Rayalaseema Grameena Bank set up 81 branches in its first five years in the order of 10, 35, 20, 5 and 11 in successive years while its last five years in opened 60 branches, in the order of 19, nil, 2, 17 and 22. Thus by 1985, its total branches stood at 141 and the average member of branches opened per year was 14.1. Sree Anantha, on the other hand, opened 67 branches in its six years at the rate of 9, 22, 14, 4, 4 and 13 annually. The average per year was 11.2 branches. In the case of Shri Venkateswara, 66 branches were opened with an average of 13.2 and in the annual order of 7, 12, 17, 17 and 13. Though Rayalaseema appears to have opened greater number of branches in contrast to Sree Anantha and Shri Venkateswara, its progress is only a narrow one considering its larger jurisdiction. Further, if we look at the latest figures on district-wise coverage of RRB branches in the region, i.e., Cuddapah

66, Kurnool 60, Anantapur 67, Chittoor 66, and Prakasam 15, it is clear to understand that the principle of equi-marginal distribution was followed by the RBI in giving licences to the branches opened in Rayalaseema. Thus, the RRB offices were evenly spread in all the drought-ridden districts and on all the blocks of the respective districts of the region. This is the outstanding feature of the branch expansion of RRBs in Rayalaseema.

The reasons for this successful story of branch expansion in the region are: (a) the favourable licencing policy of the RBI, (b) the sincerely planned efforts of sponsor banks, both Syndicate Bank and Indian Bank and (c) the basic thrust of Regional Rural banking to cover the hitherto unbanked centres.

Staffing Pattern

Another special feature of Regional Rural Bank Scheme is that RRBs were to be economically staffed. By recruiting staff from the local area (which may be the same village or the same district or a nearby district of the same state) on a much lower salary structure that is consistent with rural areas, it was expected to stimulate greater involvement of the staff in the development of that area. It was also provided[4] that during the first 5 years of operation of a RRB, the sponsor Bank, on request from the RRB, may depute its officers and other staff as required by RRB. The RRB was expected to become self-sufficient in this matter overtime. Further, a typical branch[5] of the RRB was generally manned by a permanent staff of three persons, the branch manager, the field officer and the accountant.

The three Regional Rural Banks heavily depended for the staff on deputation from their sponsor banks in the initial years. But, as years went by, substantial progress were made by them towards the recruitment of their own manpower and reducing the number of staff on deputation from their respective sponsor banks.

The details of comparative staff strength of the 3 RRBs in Rayalaseema is shown in the following table.

Table 6
Staff Strength of RRBs Selected

As at the End of Year	*Rayala-seema*	*Sri Anantha*	*Shri Venka-teswara*	*Rayala-seema Region*	*India*
1977	156	-	-	156	3441
1978	254	-	-	254	6454
1979	288	-	-	288	8761
1980	305	121	-	426	12393
1981	448	184	-	632	NA
1982	436	200	55	691	NA
1983	443	231	128	802	28581
1984	568	234	205	1007	36610
1985	650 (98)	279(98)	283(36)	1212(83)	44605(74)

Note:
1. Figures in brackets are percentages of trained staff to total staff.
2. NA : Not Applicable

Source:
1. "Annual Reports".
2. RBI : "Statistical Tables Relating into Banks in India".

Out of the total 44,605 RRB employees in India by December 1985, 1,212 or 3 per cent of them are in Rayalaseema. Of the total RRB employees in Rayalaseema, the Rayalaseema Bank recruited greater number of employees at 650 (54 per cent of total), which increased from 156 in 1977. The Sree Anantha reinforced 279 (23 per cent of total) employees in 1985 as against 121 in 1980. The Shri Venkateswara restored 283 (23 per cent of total) employees in 1985 as against 55 in 1982. The percentage growth rates over the initial years were 317, 131 and 415 for the respective banks.

Simultaneously, the strength of the staff on deputation from sponsor banks had been reduced in all 3 RRBs. In Rayalaseema Bank, the staff on deputation from sponsor bank thus reduced from 21 to 3 during the 1976-85 period; in Sree Anantha it decreased from 7 to 4 during the 1979-85 period and in Shri Venkateswara from 17 to 6 during the 1981-85 period.

All RRBs gave allotment to recruitment of persons belonged to Scheduled Castes and Scheduled Tribes in their staffing pattern. At the end of 1985, 12 per cent of total staff in

Rayalaseema Bank, 19 per cent in Sree Anantha and 17 per cent in Shri Venkateswara were constituted with persons from Scheduled Castes/ Scheduled Tribes. This is a scoring point in favour of RRBs in Rayalaseema as they are not only serving poorer sections by extending credit but by employing the hitherto neglected classes.

Utmost importance has been given to training of the personnel in all the 3 RRBs. Separate training facilities were provided for employees of different cadres. Specific training was allowed in various procedures like orientation, reorientation, project formulation, industrial relations and workshops on specified subjects. The Staff Training Centre at Anantapur serves both Rayalaseema Bank and Sree Anantha in providing training to staff of lower cadre like clearks, whereas Shri Venkateswara largely depends on it sponsor bank, viz., the Indian Bank in this matter. For upper cadre such as branch managers and field surveyors, the RRBs get training facilities from various institutions like College of Agricultural Banking, pune; Bankers Institute for Rural Development, Lucknow; and Regional Training Centre of NABARD, Mangalore. Thus, at the end of 1985, 98 per cent of total staff were trained both in Rayalaseema Bank and in Sree Anantha, while in Shri Venkateswara only 35 per cent were trained. The reason for having less trained staff in Shri Venkateswara largely lies in the training rules of its sponsor bank and also its younger age which was certainly lower than the other two.

Syndicate Bank, the sponsor bank of both Rayalaseema Bank and Sree Anantha, has been playing an important role in the speedy progress of both these banks, like the Indian Bank in the case of Shri Venkateswara. Both the sponsor banks are apart from giving sufficient staff strength and financial assistance in their initial years of infancy, also rendering useful service in establishing their image by advising them in various policy matters and in suggesting them to conduct various novel programmes for the welfare of the poorer sections.

The Chairmen of the 3 RRBs have been playing a pivotal role in the development of these banks. Each of bank, particularly in the liaison, planning and coordinating functions.

Each of the 3 RRBs has had 2 chairmen so far. These chairmen seemed to have tried hard to bring harmony between the head office of the RRB and the sponsor bank on one hand and the head offices and their respective branches on the other. They also appeared to have maintained personal approach and good rapport with their staff. Besides this, the chairmen were also conducting frequent visits to their branches in their office Jeeps and exhort their staff in enhancing their efficiency.

Each of the 3 RRBs has installed an Inspection Department in its bank, which carries both regular and short inspection of their branches at odd intervals. It also conducts investigation of frauds and complaints.

Even though the RRB Act does not provide for the formation of Trade Unions, each of the 3 selected RRBs has its own association for discussing and negotiating its personnel policy with the management. As at the All-India level, there was discontent among the staff of these RRBs about their low pay scale. They have been demanding for higher wages on par with salary scales of comparable staff in the State Government as they perform the similar kind of work as an employee of a rural branch of a commercial bank. This is an issue for discussion which may be settled in the long run.

All in all it can be said that, in the matter of staffing, all the 3 RRBs in Rayalaseema were adequately staffed who were appreciably trained. They also very much appeared to be capable of performing the tasks expected of them. Apart from that, the 3 RRBs have succeeded to a considerable extent in ensuring rural orientation and local touch in the appointment of their staff with a salary structure consistently lower at all levels than the ones prevalent in commercial banks. This is a significant achievement of RRBs in Rayalaseema.

Mobilisation of Deposits

One of the important measures to determine the success or failure of any credit institution is the extent to which it is able to mobilize the savings of the community in the form of deposits. Deposits constitute the single largest source of bank funds. It is a pre-requisite for deployment of credit and fulfillment of other obligations of the banking system. Apart from that, banks through deposit mobilization can inculcate a habit of thrift among the people and initiate banking consciousness in their minds. More importantly, in rural areas, in which a small segment of barter system still prevails and where people are more accustomed to conspicuous consumption, the deposit accretion role of banks proves crucial. By collecting surplus funds from such areas banks can channelise them into socially purposeful lines which otherwise would go into less important form of assets like gold, silver, etc. Hence the successful performance of any bank can be decided in their capacity to mobilize deposits.

A wider spread of branches coupled with vigorous efforts of bankers led to a significant creation of deposits by the 3 selected RRBs in Rayalaseema. The comparative picture showing year-wise deposits and depositors of these banks are provided in Table–7.

The aggregate deposits of RRBs in the region which were Rs.14 lakhs in 1976 moved up to Rs.200 lakhs in 1978. Again they increased to Rs. 579.84 lakhs in 1982 and to Rs.1,519.13 lakhs in 1984 and Rs.3,598.09 lakhs in 1985. The percentage share of Rayalaseema in the total RRB deposits of Andhra Pradesh thus increased consistently from 9.4 per cent in 1976 to 17.5 per cent in 1978, to 22.9 per cent in 1980, to 29.3 per cent in 1982, to 31.7 per cent in 1984 and to 32.4 per cent in 1985. Thus it can be drawn from the above analysis that the total RRB deposits in Rayalaseema though exceeded slowly in the initial years when there was only Rayalaseema Bank, they improved further, when the other two joined in due course of time. A similar story holds in terms of growth of deposit accounts whose share for the region stood at 36.3 per cent in 1985 of all RRBs in Andhra Pradesh as against 23.1 per cent in 1980 and 12.8 per cent in 1976.

In the same way, the deposit per branch and the per capita deposit for RRBs in Rayalaseema set an increasing trend, even much higher in some years against the State figure. Thus the Per branch deposit for RRBs in Rayalaseema which was Rs.1.40 lakhs in 1976, went up to Rs.6.37 lakhs in 1980, which again has gone up to Rs. 13.13 lakhs in 1985. The State figures for the same years were Rs. 2.80 lakhs, Rs. 8.56 lakhs and Rs.11.27 lakhs. This reveals that initial years in comparison to State, improved well in the latter years and ultimately gone up higher than the State figure. On the other hand, the per capita deposit also increased considerably to Rs. 670 in 1985 as against Rs.488 in 1980 and Rs.343 in 1976. The State figures for the same years were Rs.751, Rs. 414 and Rs. 465.

As for the comparative efficiency of the 3 RRBs selected, the picture looks different. Even though no specific directive was issued, the Government's expectation was that each RRB would collect deposits of about Rs.1 crore in its first year of operation. Considering from this yardstick the performance of the RRBs selected does not look that satisfactory, and they were unable to reach the prescribed target at that time. However, this cannot be taken as a serious omission in view of the drought prone conditions prevailing in the districts in which the respective banks are operating and the numerous teething troubles they faced in establishing branches in hitherto unbanked centres. Further, the RRBs completed this target and more by the end of second year of their operation.

The performance of both Sree Anantha and Shri Venkateswara Grameena Banks on the front of deposits appears impressive in comparison to the big bank Rayalaseema during their first five years of operation. While Sree Anantha had mobilized total deposits to the tune of Rs. 31.54 lakhs in its first year, Shri Venkateswara had mobilized Rs.20.20 lakhs and Rayalaseema Rs.14 lakhs. The capacity of Sree Anantha in mobilizing deposits seemed higher than the other 2 banks during the next 3 years in which total deposits of the Bank rose up in the order of Rs.195.43 lakhs, Rs. 320.75 lakhs and Rs.458.50 lakhs in comparison to Rs.135.38 lakhs, Rs. 271.05 lakhs, Rs. 448.18 lakhs of Shri Venkateswara and Rs.98.0 lakhs, Rs.200.0 lakhs, Rs.346.0 lakhs and Rs.548.0 lakhs of Rayalaseema. However, during the fifth year Sree Anantha lagged behind Shri Venkateswara with total deposits amounting to Rs.633.52 lakhs as against Rs.834.04 lakhs while Rayalaseema got only Rs. 548.0 lakhs.

Table 7
Comparative Statement Showing Deposits and Depositors of RRBs in Rayalaseema Region 1976-85

	As at the End of Year									
Parameter	*1976*	*1977*	*1978*	*1979*	*1980*	*1981*	*1982*	*1983*	*1984*	*1985*
Total Deposits (Amount Rs. in lakhs)										
Rayalaseema	14.00	98.00	200.00	346.00	548.00	760.00	1063.00	1298.00	1633.0	2031.00
Sree Anantha	-	-	-	0.72	31.54	195.43	320.75	458.50	633.52	733.05
Shri Venkateswara	-	-	-	-	-	20.20	135.38	271.05	448.18	834.05
Rayalaseema	14.00	98.00	200.00	346.72	579.54	975.63	1519.13	2027.55	2714.70	3598.09
Region	(9.4)	(17.4)	(17.5)	(22.2)	(21.9)	(27.5)	(29.3)	(31.2)	(31.7)	(32.4)
Andhra Pradesh	148.4	561.9	114.37	1560.0	2645.9	3548.4	5187.2	6489.5	8566.1	11105.9
Total No. of Depositors										
Rayalaseema	4083	32,866	74,174	118385	116297	197962	224609	241674	271046	290769
Sree Anantha	-	-	-	287	4403	40838	68051	89698	112742	136536
Shri Venkateswara	-	-	-	-	-	1992	13082	42319	75740	109628
Rayalaseema	4.011	32866	74174	118572	118700	240792	305742	373691	459528	536933
Region	(12.8)	(24.0)	(24.2)	(30.8)	(23.1)	(34.0)	(37.1)	(38.2)	(38.9)	(36.3)
Andhra Pradesh	31935	136727	305924	385487	514926	708087	824566	977270	1181688	1479226
Deposit per Branch (Amount Rs. in lakhs)										
Rayalaseema	1.40	2.18	3.08	4.94	6.76	7.60	10.63	12.73	13.70	14.40
Sree Anantha	-	-	-	0.72	3.15	6.10	6.97	9.17	11.73	10.94
Shri Venkateswara	-	-	-	-	-	2.89	7.13	7.53	8.46	12.64
Rayalaseema Region	1.40	2.18	3.08	4.88	6.37	7.02	9.21	10.78	12.01	13.13
Andhra Pradesh	2.80	3.51	4.95	6.17	8.56	9.5	11.90	11.23	10.50	11.27

Contd.

Parameter	As at the End of Year									
	1976	1977	1978	1979	1980	1981	1982	1983	1984	1985
Per Capital Deposit (Amount in Rs.)										
Rayalaseema	343	298	270	292	375	384	473	573	602	698
Sree Anantha	-	-	-	251	716	479	471	511	562	537
Shri Venkateswara	-	-	-	-	-	1014	1035	640	592	761
Rayalaseema Region	343	298	270	292	488	405	497	543	591	670
Andhra Pradesh	465	411	374	405	414	501	629	664	725	751

Note: Figures in parentheses are percentages to Andhra Pradesh , Source: "Annual Reports"

A comparison of deposits of the RRBs during their last 5 years, on the other hand, naturally puts the Rayalaseema into broader light because of its higher age and being in existence for about a decade. The aggregate deposits of Rayalaseema thus rose up to at the rate of Rs.760 lakhs, Rs.1,063 lakhs, Rs.1298 lakhs, Rs.1633 lakhs and Rs.2031 lakhs during its last 5 years from 1981-85. The comparative performance of Shri Venkateswara and Sree Anantha in their last 5 years remains the same as in their first 5 years because of their late arrival on the scene. The total deposits of Sree Anantha, however, enhanced to Rs.733.05 lakhs during its final year of last 5 years.

In the matter of deposit accounts, both Sree Anantha and Rayalaseema had larger numbers, while Shri Venkateswara had smaller ones in relative terms. For Rayalaseema, the total number of depositors increased from 4,083 to 116297 in its first 5 years. For Sree Anantha the numbers went up from 4,403 to 136536 and for Shri Venkateswara from 1,992 to 109628. In the matter of indicators like per branch deposit and per capita deposit, Shri Venkateswara exceeds other 2 RRBs. During its 5 years of operation, it enlarged its per branch deposit from Rs.2.89 lakhs to 12.64 lakhs while Sree Anantha and Rayalaseema increased from Rs.3.15 lakhs to Rs.11.73 lakhs and from Rs.1.40 lakhs to Rs.6.76 lakhs respectively. However, during the last 5 years, Rayalaseema was able to enhance its figure from Rs.7.60 lakhs to Rs.14.4 lakhs and Sree Anantha to Rs.10.94 lakhs in its final year. Similarly the per capita deposit of Shri Venkateswara stood very high at the end of its fifth year at Rs.760 in comparison to Rs.562 of Sree Anantha and Rs.375 of Rayalaseema. Though Rayalaseema was able to achieve a per capita deposit of Rs. 698 during its tenth year of operation, yet it appears poor in comparison to other RRBs as they achieved this much in their first 5 years itself. This indicates that Rayalaseema needs to work hard to enhance its deposit potential, so that it can serve better the people in its area.

In order to understand how far the RRBs in Rayalaseema were successful in mobilizing deposits from its rural folk, growth rates, both linear and compound are worked out. They are provided in Table-8.

Table 8

Distribution of Percentage Growth Rates of Deposits and Depositors of RRBs in Rayalaseema

Item	*Years*	*Linear Growth Rate*					*Compound Growth Rate*				
		Rayala-seema	*Sree Anantha*	*Shri Venka-teswara*	*Rayala-seema*	*Andhra Pradesh*	*Rayala-seema*	*Sree Anantha*	*Shri Venka-teswara*	*Rayala-seema*	*Andhra Pradesh*
Total Deposits	First 5 years	54.56**	29.64**	56.76**	55.68**	49.45**	122.55*	34.99*	122.55*	122.55 ^{NS}	82.21 ^{NS}
	Last 5 years	22.93**	29.64**	56.76**	29.72**	26.50**	22.14 ^{NS}	34.99*	122.55*	34.99*	22.14 ^{NS}
	All years	27.87**	38.59**	56.76**	31.94**	28.58**	58.50**	162.29*	122.55*	70.46**	52.84**
Total No.of Depositors	First 5 years	49.21**	26.35**	57.24**	45.19**	44.17**	122.55 ^{NS}	22.14 ^{NS}	145.96 ^{NS}	122.55*	82.21 ^{NS}
	Last 5 years	9.46**	26.35**	57.24**	19.46**	18.37**	-	22.14 ^{NS}	145.96 ^{NS}	22.14**	10.52 ^{NS}
	All years	20.64**	37.24**	57.24**	26.66**	23.34**	43.86**	144.21*	145.96 ^{NS}	56.59**	42.12**
Deposit per Branch	First 5 years	35.40*	15.59*	25.87*	33.50**	26.93**	34.99 ^{NS}	10.52 ^{NS}	34.99 ^{NS}	34.99 ^{NS}	22.14 ^{NS}
	Last 5 years	13.55*	15.59*	25.87*	14.38**	1.84 ^{NS}	10.52 ^{NS}	10.52 ^{NS}	34.99 ^{NS}	10.52 ^{NS}	-
	All years	20.51**	25.62*	25.87*	19.55**	13.12**	28.99*	48.12*	34.99 ^{NS}	27.43"	17.07**
Per Capital Deposit	First 5 years	1.484 ^{NS}	4.04 ^{NS}	-11.74 ^{NS}	8.40 ^{NS}	-2.60 ^{NS}	-	-	-9.52 ^{NS}	-	-
	Last 5 years	13.86**	4.04 ^{NS}	-11.74 ^{NS}	11.53**	9.11**	10.52 ^{NS}	-	-9.52 ^{NS}	10.52 ^{NS}	-
	All years	10.40**	4.13 ^{NS}	-11.74 ^{NS}	9.50**	7.92*	10.18*	3.64 ^{NS}	-9.52 ^{NS}	8.86**	7.54*

Note:

1.* : Significant at 5 per cent level

**: Significant at 1 per cent level

NS : Not Significant

2. Growth rates are calculated.

The RRBs had succeeded in achieving highly significant growth rates during all their years in all indicators in the field of deposit mobilization. This is an important accomplishment of RRBs in Rayalaseema. All the 3 banks, during their first 5 years and in their last 5 years and also in all years had mostly achieved highly significant linear growth rates at 1 per cent level and significant compound growth rates at 5 per cent level. As all RRBS were having growth rates of considerable importance, there is only limited scope to make comparison among them. All the same, a closer scrutiny of the table provides the information that, while the region's growth rates as whole were greater than the State rates, Shri Venkateswara Bank leads ahead of other two RRBs in having higher growth rates in all indicators in all years. A look at the table also reveals that in the case of Rayalaseema, the growth rates are considerably better in their first 5 years rather than in their last 5 years. And Sree Anantha has impressive rates, which were just behind the rates of Shri Venkateswara. The composition of various types of deposits and their respective growth rates are provided in Table-9 and Table-10.

All types of deposits viz., savings bank account, current account, fixed and recurring deposits, cash certificate and others had increased in the 3 selected RRBs between 1977-85 period. Most of the deposits have been savings bank accounts for all the banks on all the years surveyed. Fixed and recurring deposits, though got second place in the first few years, cash certificates overtook them in latter years. Particularly fixed deposits diminished so low in all the banks. And the current accounts look insignificant.

Thus in 1985, Rayalaseema, Sree Anantha and Shri Venkateswara had their savings accounts in the order of 33 per cent, 48 per cent and 55 per cent of their total deposits, while cash certificates, consisted of 44 per cent, 33 per cent and 33 per cent and the fixed and recurring deposits in the order of 11 per cent, 3per cent 9 per cent. The linear and compound growth rates tell the same story.

Table 9

Comparative Statement Showing Composition of Various Deposits of Selected RRBs

(Amount in Rs lakhs)

	1977	1978	1979	1980	1981	1982	1983	1984	1985
Savings Bank Account									
Rayalaseema	52.65(54)	102.22(51)	162.91(47)	258.94(47)	313.39(41)	406.16(38)	477.89(37)	561.00(34)	673.10(33)
Sree Anantha	-	-	0.49(18)	4.94(16)	92.82(47)	143.54(45)	271.94(59)	324.91(51)	352.40(48)
Shri Venkateswara	-	-	-	-	12.10(60)	68.36(50)	185.71(69)	267.68(60)	462.67(55)
Current Account									
Rayalaseema	2.78(3)	7.32(6)	5.67(2)	5.97(1)	9.30(1)	10.36(1)	10.82(1)	10.09(1)	15.12(1)
Sree Anantha	-	-	-	0.46(1)	2.39(1)	3.32(1)	2.69(1)	2.95(1)	2.14(-)
Shri Venkateswara	-	-	-	-	1.93(10)	3.61(3)	13.53(5)	10.89(2)	24.16(3)
Fixed and Recurring Deposits									
Rayalaseema	34.99(36)	43.72(22)	50.70(16)	87.97(16)	107.60(14)	160.94(15)	128.20(10)	153.96(9)	222.22(11)
Sree Anantha	-	-	0.12(17)	21.24(67)	97.02(50)	88.05(27)	53.18(12)	86.47(14)	19.96(3)
Shri Venkateswara	-	-	-	-	0.57(3)	44.82(33)	16.16(6)	37.40(8)	73.94(9)
Cash Certificate									
Rayalaseema	1.88(10)	20.46(10)	76.58(22)	131.33(24)	237.77(31)	368.36(35)	525.66(4)	715.80(44)	887.78(44)
Sree Anantha	-	-	0.08(11)	1.04(3)	-	32.32(10)	67.75(15)	127.99(20)	245.27(33)
Shri Venkateswara	-	-	-	-	5.60(27)	18.59(14)	55.65(14)	132.21(29)	273.28(33)
Others									
Rayalaseema	5.52(6)	27.13(14)	49.91(14)	64.37(12)	91.94(12)	117.96(11)	156.08(12)	192.21(12)	233.00(11)
Sree Anantha	-	-	0.03(4)	3.86(12)	3.20	53.52(17)	62.94(14)	91.61(14)	113.28(115)
Shri Venkateswara	-	-	-	-	-	-	-	-	-

Contd.

	1977	1978	1979	1980	1981	1982	1983	1984	1985
Total Deposits									
Rayalaseema	14.00(100)	98.00	200.00	346.00(100)	548.00(100)	760.00(100)	1063.00(100)	1298.00(100)	1633.00(100)
Sree Anantha	-	-	-	0.72(100)	31.54(100)	195.43(100)	320.75(100)	458.50(100)	633.352(100)
Shri Venkateswara	-	-	-	-	-	20.29(100)	135.38(100)	371.05(100)	448.18(100)

Note: Figures in parentheses are percentages to total
Source: "Annual Reports"

Table 10

Distribution of Growth Rates of Different Deposits of RRBs in Rayalaseema 1976-85

Type of Deposit	Years	Linear Growth Rate			Compound Growth Rate		
		Raya-laseema	*Sree Anantha*	*Shri Venka-teswara*	*Raya-laseema*	*Sree Anantha*	*Shri Venka-teswara*
Savings Bank Account	Last 5 years	17.97**	29.52**	55.19**	10.52 ^{NS}	34.99 ^{NS}	122.55*
	All years	23.11**	39.33**	55.19**	32.75**	181.71**	122.55*
Current Account	Last 5 years	9.88 ^{NS}	-	57.35*	-	-	82.21*
	All years	13.95**	9.83 ^{NS}	57.35*	16.18**	25.68 ^{NS}	82.21*
Fixed and Recurring Deposits	Last 5 years	14.36 ^{NS}	-43.36 ^{NS}	40.20 ^{NS}	10.52 ^{NS}	-25.92 ^{NS}	145.96 ^{NS}
	All years	19.80**	9.97 ^{NS}	40.20 ^{NS}	24.19**	83.52 ^{NS}	145.96 ^{NS}
Cash Certificate	Last 5 years	30.11**	61.90*	66.76*	34.99*	716.62 ^{NS}	145.96*
	All years	34.21**	55.69**	66.76*	94.77**	348.17*	145.96*
Others	Last 5 years	22.50**	39.75**	-	22.14 ^{NS}	101.38 ^{NS}	-
	All years	26.72**	43.69**	-	46.72**	236.79**	-

Note:
1. * : Significant at 5 per cent level
   ** : Significant at 1 per cent level
NS : Not Significant
2. Growth rates are calculated

Thus, from the above analysis it can be said that the 3 RRBs in Rayalaseema were successful in mobilizing deposits of considerable importance and thereby in spreading the banking habits among the rural folk. The personnel of these banks who coupled with local touch and rural familiarity were largely responsible for this success. They maintained good rapport with rural population. The excellent customer service provided by them also served as an asset to these banks. The offer of extra 0.5 per cent interest on their deposits also proved beneficial in mobilizing more deposits.

However, if we look at the inner differences in each bank and the factors responsible for slower growth of deposits in Rayalaseema and Shree Anantha in comparison to that of Shri Venkateswara the drought prone topography of the operating districts stood ahead. The recurring droughts year after year in these districts were weakening the saving potentiality of the poor proletariat day by day. Secondly, the total exclusion of rich farmers and wealthy traders in this sphere is also proving as a great disadvantage to these banks. Thirdly, the competition from the early started commercial bank branches are also having negative effects on the efficacy of these banks. If Shri Venkateswara has succeeded largely in this field, it is only due to its slightly favourable economic conditions prevailing in its operating district in comparison to others. So, it is necessary to notice that steps should be taken by both Sree Anantha and Rayalaseema to raise their deposit strength in their respective jurisdiction. As deposits alone facilitate the banks to have better earnings which it turn help in giving loans and advances, more of its mobilization would enable the efficient functioning of these banks.

Advances

As a case of mass banking, the success or failure of Grameena Banks largely depends upon the extent of credit they purveyed to the poorer sections of rural society, which were neglected by the banking industry so far. Shifting from the traditional credit worthiness principle, the RRBs were supposed to bestow emphasis on the purpose of investment rather than on security.

They were also expected to give credit to weaker sections at cheaper costs and preferences in lending to backward areas so as to set right regional imbalances and more attention to small and marginal farmer, agricultural labourer, rural artisan and other neglected groups.

The three RRBs as a whole in Rayalaseema had put together a very creditable performance in providing credit to weak sections. This can be verified from Table-11.

The aggregate advances given by all RRBs in Rayalaseema which were Rs.7.76 lakhs in 1976, had gone up to Rs.265.00 lakhs in 1978; which further increased to Rs.1,048.25 lakhs in 1980. Later on in 1982 the amount rose to Rs.2,363.15 lakhs, in 1984 to Rs.4,134.65 lakhs and in 1985 to Rs.5,929.84 lakhs. The share of Rayalaseema in the total RRB advances of Andhra Pradesh thus stood at 33.4 per cent in 1985 as against 32.8 per cent 1n 1984, 30,5 per cent in 1982, 22.2 per cent in 1980, 8.1 per cent in 1978 and 5.6 per cent in 1976. This analysis reveals that advances in magnitude rose more between 1981-85 period than between 1976-80 period. Similarly the total number of borrowers served by these banks increased from 741 to 82,253 during 1976-80 period and from 1,38,618 to 2,41,865 during 1981-85 period.

In terms of per branch credit and per capita credit, the position of Rayalaseema looks better and even more for some years in comparison to figures related to Andhra Pradesh. Thus the per branch credit of RRBs in Rayalaseema rose up from Rs.0.77 lakhs in 1976 to Rs.9.16 1akhs in 1979, which again went up to Rs.14.32 lakhs in 1982 and to Rs.21.64 lakhs in 1985. The figures for same years for Andhra Pradesh stood at Rs.2.61 lakhs, Rs.14.51 lakh, Rs.17.75 lakhs and Rs.18.01 lakhs respectively. The per capita credit, on the other hand, stood at Rs.2,452 in 1985 as against Rs.1,274 in 1980 and Rs.1,047 in 1976. For Andhra Pradesh, the figures for the same years were Rs.2,094, Rs.1,298 and Rs.1,091.

As for the lending rules, the general assumption set by the Government was that a RRB should disburse credit to the tune of Rs.5 crores in its first year of operation. It can be observed from the above table that none of the 3 banks have

Table 11

Comparative Statement Showing Year-wise Advances Given by RRBs in Rayalaseema Region 1976-85

Item	As at the End of Year									
	1976	1977	1978	1979	1980	1981	1982	1983	1984	1985
Total Advances (Amount Rs. in lakhs)										
Rayalaseema	7.76	78.83	265.00	650.00	1026.00	1605.00	1853.00	1975.00	2323.00	3102.00
Sree Anantha	-	-	-	0.15	22.25	225.81	448.53	640.88	1035.77	1552.00
Shri Venkateswara	-	-	-	-	-	9.15	60.62	261.57	775.88	1275.84
Rayalaseema Region	7.76	78.83	265.00	650.15	1048.25	1839.96	2362.15	2877.45	4134.65	5929.84
	(5.6)	(7.9)	(8.1)	(17.7)	(22.2)	(27.3)	(30.5)	(31.7)	(32.8)	(33.4)
Andhra Pradesh	138.2	993.4	3276.3	3671.1	4766.2	6747.2	7737.5	9089.9	12604.7	17741.6
Total No. of Borrowers										
Rayalaseema	741	12706	33734	62703	80563	119069	121979	113631	108443	128575
Sree Anantha	-	-	-	21	1690	18773	28174	36665	47958	59482
Shri Venkateswara	-	-	-	-	-	776	4629	16162	37630	53808
Rayalaseema Region	741	12706	33734	62724	82253	138610	153882	166458	194031	241865
	(5.8)	(13.3)	(13.5)	(18.5)	(13.5)	(26.5)	(29.4)	(29.9)	(28.7)	(28.5)
Andhra Pradesh	12665	95420	250683	338583	375748	522578	523790	556658	676858	847428
Per Branch Credit (Amount Rs. in lakhs)										
Rayalaseema	0.77	1.75	4.08	9.28	12.82	16.05	18.53	19.36	19.40	22.00
Sree Anantha	-	-	-	0.15	2.23	7.06	9.75	12.82	19.18	23.16
Shri Venkateswara	-	-	-	-	-	1.31	3.19	7.27	14.64	19.33
Rayalaseema Region	20.77	1.75	4.08	9.16	11.52	13.24	14.32	15.31	18.29	21.64
Andhra Pradesh	2.61	6.21	14.18	14.58	15.42	18.09	17.75	15.73	15.45	18.01

Contd.

Item	*As at the End of Year*									
	1976	*1977*	*1978*	*1979*	*1980*	*1981*	*1982*	*1983*	*1984*	*1985*
Per Capita Credit (Amount in Rs.)										
Rayalaseema	1047	620	786	1037	1274	1348	1530	1738	1599	2413
Sree Anantha	-	-	-	714	1156	1203	1592	1748	2160	2609
Shri Venkateswara	-	-	-	-	-	1179	1139	1618	2062	2371
Rayalaseema Region	1047	620	786	1037	1274	1327	1535	1729	2131	2452
Andhra Pradesh	1091	1041	1307	1084	1268	1291	1477	1633	1862	2094

Note: Figures in parentheses are percentages to Andhra Pradesh.
Soure: "Annual Reports"

been able to meet the target. As the banks were forced to lend only to the target segments of borrowers, this was not considered a serious omission as the identification of suitable borrowers poses a general problem.

It is evident from Table-11, that all RRBs have performed impressively 1n the field of advancing credit and they were reaching out more and more people every year. Singularly, the execution of Sree Anantha and Shri Venkateswara looks better in comparison to Rayalaseema during the first 5 years. Thus the advances outstanding of Sree Anantha were Rs.22.25 lakhs in its first year in comparison to Rs.7.76 lakhs of Rayalaseema and Rs.9.15 lakhs of Shri Venkateswara. In the second year they were increased to Rs. 225.81 lakhs for Sree Anantha, to Rs.78.83 lakhs for Rayalaseema and to Rs.60.62 lakhs for Shri Venkateswara. For the next 3 years, the total, advances had grown among the 3 banks almost balancingly. Thus they rose up in the order of Rs.448.53 lakhs,

Rs. 640.88 lakhs and Rs.1,035.77 lakhs in the third, fourth and fifth years for Sree Anantha, while for Rayalaseema they increased to Rs.265.00 lakhs. Rs.650.00 lakhs and Rs.1,026.00 lakhs and for Shri Venkateswara Rs.261.57 lakhs. Rs.775.88 lakhs and Rs.1,275.84 lakhs respectively.

The last 5 years picture, however puts Rayalaseema on a bright side. The total advances during this period went up at the rate of Rs.1,605.00 lakhs, Rs.1,853.00 lakhs, Rs.1,975.00 lakhs, Rs.2,.323.00 lakhs and Rs.3,102.00 lakhs for the big bank, whereas for the other two the figures were the same as in their first 5 years. For Sree Anantha, the total advances went up to Rs.1,552.00 lakhs in its sixth year.

Rayalaseema leads ahead of other 2 RRBs in the matter of borrowal accounts because of its larger jurisdiction. The total number of borrowers served by it thus went up from 741 to 80,563 in its first 5 years and from 1,19,069 to 1,28,575 in its last 5 years. For Sree Anantha, the number rose from 1,690 to 59,482 during in its six year period, while for Shri Venkateswara from 776 to 53,808 during in its 5 years.

In the matter of indicators like per branch credit and per capita credit, Sree Anantha and Shri Venkateswara were ahead of Rayalaseema. During its 5 years of operation, the per branch credit of Shri Venkateswara thus rose up from Rs.1.31 laKhs to Rs.19.33 lakhs while for Sree Anantha and Rayalaseema they increased from Rs.2.23 lakhs to Rs.19.18 lakhs and from Rs.0.77 lakhs to Rs.12.82 lakhs. During the last 5 years, however, Rayalaseema has improvised it from Rs.16.05 lakhs to Rs.22.00 lakhs and Sree Anantha to Rs.23.16 lakhs in its sixth year. In the same way, the per capita credit of Shri Venkateswara, Sree Anantha and Rayalaseema were stood at Rs.2,371, Rs.2,160 and Rs.1,274 at the and of their first 5 years. Though Rayalaseema was able to achieve a per capita credit of Rs.2,413 during in its tenth year of operation, in comparison to other 2 RRBs, its performance looks poor as they achieved this much in their first 5 years itself. Therefore, there is a need for Rayalaseema to improvise its lending capacity.

Table-12 gives the growth rates achieved by 3 RRBs in Rayalaseema in the field of advances given.

The RRBs, as in case of deposits, succeeded in achieving highly significant growth rates during all their years in all indicators in the field of advances. This is a commendable fact about the success of these RRBs. All the 3 banks, during their first 5 years, and in their last 5 years and also in all years were mostly achieved highly significant linear growth rates at 1 per cent level and significant compound growth rates at 5 per cent level. This limits the scope to make internal comparisons among the 3 RBBs. However" a deeper look into the above table reveals that while the region's growth rates as a whole were greater than the State rates, Shri Venkateswara were having higher growth rates than the other two. Between Rayalaseema and Sree Anantha, the former appears good in its first 5 years, while Sree Anantha in total years. Rayalaseema's growth rates were considerably lower in their last 5 years in comparison to their first 5 years.

The purpose-wise classification of advances outstanding of 3 RRBs selected and their respective growth rates are shown in Table-13 and Table-14.

Agriculture and allied activities got highest share of total advances in all banks for all years followed by retail trade/

Table 12

Distribution of Percentage Growth Rates of Advances and Borrowers in Regional Rural Banks

Item	Years	Linear Growth Rate					Compound Growth Rate				
		Rayala-seema	Sree Anantha	Shri Venka-teswara	Rayala-seema Region	Andhra Pradesh	Rayala-seema	Sree Anantha	Shri Venka-teswara	Rayala-seema Region	Andhra Pradesh
Total Advances	First 5 years	64.29**	41.49**	68.15*	64.68**	46.45**	200.42*	49.18 NS	232.01*	200.42*	122.55 NS
	Last 5 years	15.95 NS	41.49**	68.15*	29.02**	24.90*	10.52 NS	49.18 NS	232.01*	22.14 NS	22.14 NS
	All years	26.48**	45.20**	68.15*	31.79**	25.68**	72.54**	261.72*	232.01*	85.55**	51.00**
Total No. of Borrowers	First 5 years	55.03**	26.48**	61.50**	55.42**	45.16**	171.83 NS	22.14 NS	171.83*	200.42**	122.55*
	Last 5 years	0.53 NS	26.48**	61.50**	13.78**	12.83*	-	22.14 NS	171.83*	10.52 NS	10.52 NS
	All years	18.88**	37.46**	61.50**	24.71**	19.93**	51.00**	202.57*	171.83*	64.37**	40.41**
Per Branch Credit	First 5 years	54.01*	28.48**	51.38**	51.32**	31.17*	101.38**	34.99**	82.21 NS	101.38**	49.18 NS
	Last 5 years	6.29*	28.48**	51.38**	12.08*	-1.18 NS	-	34.99**	82.21 NS	10.52 NS	-
	All years	20.62**	36.31**	51.38**	20.70**	9.75**	40.41**	104.27**	82.21 NS	38.72**	15.66*
Per Capita Credit	First 5 years	9.14 NS	18.15**	18.36**	9.15 NS	3.43 NS	-	10.52 NS	10.52 NS	-	-
	Last 5 years	12.74 NS	18.15**	18.36**	15.51**	11.91**	10.52 NS	10.52 NS	10.52 NS	10.52 NS	10.52 NS
	All years	11.54**	18.42**	18.36**	12.82**	7.54**	11.53**	19.55**	10.52	12.89**	6.25**

Note:

1. * : Significant at 5 per cent level

** : Significant at 1 per cent level

NS : Not Significant

Table 13
Comparative Statement Showing Purpose-wise Classification of Advances of Selected RRBs

(Amount in Rs. Lakhs)

Parameter	As at the End of Year									
	1976	*1977*	*1978*	*1979*	*1980*	*1981*	*1982*	*1983*	*1984*	*1985*
Agriculture and Allied Activities										
Rayalaseema	5.61(73)	53.81(62)	168.84(64)	415.42(68)	562.98(55)	838.36(52)	969.58(52)	1204.47(74)	1658.73(71)	2240.65(72)
Sree Anantha	-	-	-	0.02(13)	7 58(34)	145.82(65)	329.62(73)	458.37(71)	758.29(74)	1176.45(76)
Shri Venkateswara	-	-	-	-	-	8.39(91)	48.83(79)	222.13(84)	649.70(87)	1072.38(88)
Rural Artisan, village & Cottage Industries										
Rayalaseema	0.47(6)	7.21(9)	9.45(4)	19.41(3)	44.02(4)	32.49(2)	46.36(3)	51.04(3)	51.39(2)	66.82(2)
Sree Anantha	-	-	-	0.02(13)	0.18(1)	11.32(5)	22.01(5)	46.20(7)	68.39(7)	80.43(5)
Shri Venkateswara	-	-	-	-	-	-	3.10(5)	10.58(4)	24.40(3)	39.07(3)
Retail Trade/ Small Business & Self-employment, etc.										
Rayalaseema	0.72(9)	3.73(14)	29.43(11)	56.40(9)	68.04(7)	87.56(6)	100.12(5)	102.57(7)	175.13(8)	241.63(8)
Sree Anantha	-	-	-	-	1.78(8)	16.39(7)	46.60(10)	88.24(14)	151.75(15)	217.99(14)
Shri Venkateswara	-	-	-	-	-	0.39(4)	7.30(12)	20.59(8)	46.66(6)	66.83(5)
Other Purposes										
Rayalaseema	0.96(12)	14.08(15)	57.12(21)	159.05(24)	351.79(34)	646.89(40)	736.48(40)	264.11(16)	438.10(19)	552.99(18)
Sree Anantha	-	-	-	-	12.71(57)	52.28(23)	50.30(11)	48.07(7)	55.20(5)	76.90(5)
Shri Venkateswara	-	-	-	-	-	0.39(4)	2.35(4)	8.27(3)	23.39(3)	45.52(4)
Total Advances										
Rayalaseema	7.76(100)	78.83(100)	265.00(100)	650.00(100)	1026.00(100)	1605(100)	1853.00(100)	1975.00(100)	2323.00(100)	3102.00(100)
Sree Anantha	-	-	-	0.15(100)	22.25(100)	225.81(100)	448.53(100)	640.88(100)	1035.77(100)	1552.00(100)
Shri Venkateswara	-	-	-	-	-	9.15(100)	60.62(100)	261.53(100)	775.88(100)	1275.84(100)

Note: Figures in brackets are percentage to total advances.
Source: "Annual Reports".

Table 14
Purpose-wise Distribution of Percentage Growth Rates of Advances of RRBs in Rayalaseema

Purpose of Advance Given	Years	Linear Growth Rate			Compound Growth Rate		
		Rayalaseema	Sree Anantha	Shri Venkateswara	Rayalaseema	Sree Anantha	Shri Venkateswara
Agriculture and Allied Activities	First 5 years	61.16**	43.38**	68.15*	200.42*	64.87**	232.01*
	Last 5 years	25.27**	43.38**	68.15*	22.14 NS	64.87**	232.01*
	All years	28.71**	46.44**	68.15*	72.54**	364.46*	232.01*
Rural Artisan, Village and Cottage Industries	First 5 years	61.44*	40.29**	64.15**	171.83*	64.87**	504.96 NS
	Last 5 years	14.71*	40.29**	64.15**	10.52 NS	64.87**	504.96 NS
	All years	21.80**	45.07**	64.15**	51.00**	288.51**	504.96NS
Retail Trade/ Small Business and Self-employment	First 5 years	59.06**	48.76**	60.66**	200.42*	82.21*	232.01*
	Last 5 years	27.09*	48.76 **	60.66**	22.14 NS	82.21*	232.01*
	All years	27.20**	50.11**	60.66**	68.41**	135.64*	232.01*
Other Purposes	First 5 years	72.56*	9.55 NS	69.44*	305.52*	-	200.42*
	Last 5 years	-9.21 NS	9.55 NS	69.44*	-	-	200.42*
	All years	20.69*	26.30**	69.44*	76.77**	119.40 NS	200.42*

Note:
1. * : Significant at 5 per cent level
** : Significant at 1 per cent level
NS : Not Significant

small business and self-employment, rural artisan and village/cottage industries and other purposes. For the year ending 1985, the percentage shares of Rayalaseema, Sree Anantha and Shri Venkateswara were 72, 76 and 88 for agriculture and allied activities; 8, 14, and 5 for retail trade groups: 2, 5 and 3 for rural artisan and Village industries and 18, 5 and 4 for others.

Highly significant growth rates can be seen from Table-14 for the purpose-wise classification of advances on all years. Thus the success of regional rural banking in Rayalaseema is quite noteworthy.

All the three RRBs were extending both Short-term and medium-term loans. Of the total agricultural loans given by them 60 per cent were allotted to small farmers, 20 per cent for marginal farmers and another 20 per cent for agricultural labourers in most of the cases. As the region was under the clutches of severe droughts for many successive years, the need for development of irrigation was very much appreciated by these banks. They ear marked 20 per cent of advances to tap the underground water and granted loans for construction of wells/bore wells and installation pumpsets. Credit assistance was also provided by these banks for land development purposes such as control of erosion, soil conservation, graded bunding etc. Farm mechanisation was also popularised by the RRBs in their respective districts. They gave loans to purchase power-tillers, tractors and so on, as the operational holdings are very small and scattered thereby limiting the scope of large sized mechanization.

As the poor farmers of the region often suffer from untimely rains, the activities allied to agriculture supplement the insufficient income earned by them. In view of this all the three RRBs are encouraging a variety of allied agricultural activities such as dairy, poultry, piggary, bullock-carts, sheep breeding, sericulture, horticulture and pisciculture. While dairy, bullock-carts, sheep breeding schemes got top priority in the total allied agricultural advances of Rayalaseema sericulture was specially popularised by Sree Anantha as the climate was favourable for mulbery cultivation in the area. Shri Venkateswara, on the other hand, is disbursing loans to horticulture i.e., plantation crops like mango, orange, coconut, etc. Substantial provisions were made in all banks for financing of bio-gas plants to fulfill the policy of nation.

The Banks earmarked 30 per cent of loans to rural artisans, another 30 per cent to small business, and about 40 per cent to others in the non-farm sector. They gave loans for building many artisan complexes which generated the employment potential and also increased the productivity in rural areas. These complexes were serving a variety of purposes like shoe-making, basket-making, beedi-making, rope-making, wig-making, mat-weaving and so on. Petty businessmen including vendors engaged in selling vegetables, fish, meat, eggs, groceries, cloths, utensils, stationary, etc., were also benefiting from these banks. Transport operators like auto-drivers and rickshaw pullers, cobblers, tailors, handloom weavers were also receiving financial support from the RRBs. Special efforts were made by the banks to develop the small scale, village and cottage industries such as rice husking, saw mill. bakery, oil ghani, carpentry, printing press, brick making, iron grill manufacturing, soap making, bamboo and cane products, umbrella making, cycle repairing, etc.

Moreover, the three RRBs are participating enthusiastically in Government's developmental programmes such as IRDP. Twenty Point Programme, Massive Central Assistance Programme, etc. The weakest of the society i.e., Scheduled Castes, Scheduled Tribes and Physically Handicapped borrowers are covered under the Differential Interest Rate Scheme. The RRBs also reserved 20 per cent of their total advances to Scheduled Castes, 10 per cent to Scheduled Tribes and 40 per cent to Backward Classes. As for the needs and necessities of each bank, the weightages might have changed, but it was obviously in accordance with their aims and objectives. Apart from all this, the banks are also lending a small portion of their advances for consumption purposes including loans on jewels and on deposits.

Thus the upshot of above analysis reveals that in the field of advances the three RRBs have done an excellent job of covering the poorer sections of rural society through their credit assistance. True to their image of a small-mans bank, they disbursed credit to only the needy, neglected and downtrodden sections of society. Though young and still on experimental level, they have been bravely participating in the welfare programmes of the Government. Individually each bank has been performing extremely well and achieved highly significant growth rates. Comparatively, however, Sree Anantha and Shri Venkateswara appeared more impressive than Rayalaseema. The reasons for the low lendings of Rayalaseema in its first 5 years were, perhaps the reconsiderations and rethinking on RRBs survival in the country. This thought was well supported by the Bank's performance in the last 5 years in which its landings were more than doubled.

On the whole, it can be said that the three RRBs were successful in their lending programmes. However, there is a large credit gap in Rayalaseema which needs immediately to be filled. The successive droughts in recent years enervated the agricultural economy of the region and the untimely rains weakened the poor farmers in many ways. So to meet the situation the RRBs should enhance their lendings and provide timely help to the needed sections. They should try to improve the irrigation facilities of the region by granting more and more loans and thereby meeting the drought situation. They should also provide drought relief measures such as cancellation of debts, postponement of debts, etc. The RRBs should, thus, try to work for the all-round development of the villages of the area, so that the region as a whole would prosper.

Credit-Deposit Ratio

Increasing the level of local deployment of deposits mobilised locally and also deployment of outside resources within the local areas was another marked feature of the scheme of Regional Rural Banks. In view of this, analysis of credit-deposit ratio attained by the RRBs selected would be an important indicator of their contribution to deployment for the concerned region. Table-15 provides the credit-deposit ratios of RRBs.

The credit-deposit ratio for all RRBs together in Rayalaseema increased considerably during the decade 1976-85, even much higher against the corresponding average figures for Andhra Pradesh. Thus the C-D ratio for Rayalaseema which was 55.4 per cent in 1976 slowly went up to 132.5 per cent in 1978 as against the State figures of 93 per cent and 286 per cent. Again in 1980, the C-D of Rayalaseema exceeded to 180.9 per cent as against 180.0 of State and in 1983 it slightly went down to 141.9 per cent as against 140.0 per cent of State and against in 1985, it stood at 164.8 per cent as against 160.0 per cent of State.

Table-15
Credit-Deposit Ratios of RRBs Selected

As at the End of Year	*Rayala-seema*	*Sree Anantha*	*Shri Venkate-swara*	*Rayala-seema Region*	*Andhra Pradesh*
1976	55.4	-	-	55.4	93
1977	80.4	-	-	80.4	177
1978	132.5	-	-	132.5	286
1979	187.9	20.8	-	187.5	235
1980	187.2	62.0	-	180.9	180
1981	211.2	115.5	45.7	188.6	190
1982	174.3	139.8	44.8	155.5	149
1983	152.0	139.8	96.5	141.9	140
1984	142.3	163.5	173.1	152.3	147
1985	152.7	211.7	153.0	164.8	160

Source: "Annual Reports".

All RRBs have had similar kind of improvements in their ratios. The C-D ratio of Rayalaseema increased from 55.4 per cent in 1976 to 132.5 per cent in 1978. which again went up 'to 211.2 per cent in 1981. But later on in 1983 it went down to 152.0 per cent and in 1985 it stood at 152.7 per cent. For Bree Anantha. the C-D had been increased progressively from 62.0 per cent in 1980 to 139.8 per cent in 1982, which again went up to 163.5 per cent and 211.7 per cent in the years 1984 and 1985. For Shri Venkateswara on the other hand" the C-D ratios had improved from 45.7 per cent in 1981 to 96.5 per cent in 1983 and to 153.0 per cent in 1985. As per the latest year, Sree

Anantha (211.7 per cent) stood ahead of other two (153.0 per cent) RRBs in having higher C-D ratio.

This analysis clearly points out that each of the RRB has deployed more of its resources within the local areas than locally raised. The RRBs, Thus, fulfilled the criterion of a sound credit system.

Recovery Performance

The recovery of loans continues to be the acid test of efficiency.

The three RRBs reported to have a satisfactory position for recovery of demand for loans. The available data on the recovery performance of the banks is shown in the following Table 16.

In the initial two to three years, the banks have had good recoveries as against the demand. Particularly, the Big Bank Rayalaseema had recorded good recoveries above 60 per cent during the 5 years starting from 1978 to 1982.

Table 16
Recovery Position of RRBs Selected

As at the End of Year	*Rayalaseema %*	*Sree Anantha %*	*Shri Venkateswara %*
1978	76	-	-
1979	68	-	-
1980	61	-	-
1981	60	65	-
1982	71	55	-
1983	46	42	69
1984	49	41	71
1985	43	42	58

Source: "Annual Reports"

It has thus recovered 76 per cent of total advances in 1978, 68 per cent in 1979, 61 per cent in 1980, 60 per cent in 1981 and 71 per cent in 1982. But during the next 3 years 1983, 1984 and 1985, being the severe drought years of the region, the recoveries dropped down to 46 per cent, 49 per cent and 43 per cent, thus giving rise to over dues. Similarly, Sree Anantha had good recoveries of 61 per cent and 55 per cent in the years 1981 and 1982. But during the next years 1983, 1984 and 1985, like for Rayalaseema, the recoveries came down to 42 per cent, 41 per cent and 42 per cent. In contrast, Shri Venkateswara had recorded good recoveries of 69 per cent, 71 per cent and 58 per cent, even under the drought years of 1983, 1984 and 1985.

The reason for the superior performance of Shri Venkateswara in comparison to that of Sree Anantha and Rayalaseema even in the drought years is due to its differential impact. The effect of drought which had occurred during 1983, 1984 and 1985 was very severe and hard in the districts of Anantapur, Cuddapah and Kurnool in comparison to Chittoor district, which had slightly better economic conditions in its area. The severity of drought in the former mentioned districts was such that even fodder was imported from other districts. Dearth of rains ruined the crops and the poor farmers repaying capacity was lost.

Therefore it is necessary to take steps by these banks to improve their performance in future in this field. For this purpose, they have to adopt means as follows:

- Reminding the borrowers through personal contacts
- Sending of demand notices in time, and
- Tie-up arrangements with marketing agencies

Financial Viability

The growth of any banking industry and its policy to handle the challenges of future largely depends on is financial strength and its Viability. A bank is said to be viable[6] if it attains a level of loan business giving it an income level which would enable it to meet not only all the expenses but also help it to build a minimum reserve over a period of time. Here, the viable level of loan business could be a range but not a fixed figure. Thus a RRB which is found to be viable with 10 branches covering a smaller area may become non-viable, if it has to open 70-100 branches with larger jurisdiction as it takes time to build up adequate business commensurate with the needs of increased number of branches. So in judging the viability of RRBs, the spread they have to achieve plays a significant role.

The Review Committee on Rural Banks (the Dantwala Committee) in 1977 had suggested that a RRB would linked to a margin of 4 per cent and a network of 50 branches, which could be expected to achieve in about 3 to 4 years time.

The working group on Rural Banks (1975), on the other hand, provided four dimensions for judging the viability of RRBs. They are[7] :

Area Dimension: Since the regional banks were to set up in areas which are under provided in the matter of credit facil1ties, the viability of these institutions depends on the type of area in which they are located and their future development prospects.

Financial Dimension: The Viability of a RRB; like every other bank, is a function of two variables namely, the expenditure ratio and the level of income earned by it. But it is fundamental for a RRB to work on a low level budget in respect of staffing patterns, salary scales and other establishment expenses. As regards income, it was stressed that RRBs has to increase the level of local deployment of funds, even as an aspect of viable operation. Instead of transferring their locally obtained funds to the central money markets, RRBs were to use them for effective and efficient disbursement of rural finance, so that they would not only serve the larger social purpose, but also make progress towards their own viability, as their own income would thus be higher.

Time Dimention: RRBs were prepared to operate even at a loss in the initial years, so that they would become viable over a few years after having good experience in rural areas. Unlike the commercial banks, which have the advantage of counter-balancing their losses in rural branches with that of profits earned in urban centres, the RRBs have to bear all their losses without counter-balances, as they work in only rural areas. So any loss in the initial years of RRBs will be reflected in their total operations, which would need to be subsided.

Task Dimension: The success of RRBs could also be judged by their efforts at expanding and extending the area of rural credit as by the conventional yardstick of profitability.

Summing up, the Working Group said, "It is equally necessary to ensure that the social objective does not provide an umbrella to inefficiency and the appraisal of the banks working should be based both on the fulfillment of objectives and control of cost-in short in achieving a favourable cost-benefit ratio."[8]

It could be verified from Chapter IV that RRBs allover India were incurring losses continuously for years and hence it was called a sick industry. Many researchers and policy-makers are presently wondering about the future of these banks on account of their in-efficiency in building a reserve required to maintain their survival. The three RRBs in Rayalaseema are no exception in this matter. All of them were incurring heavy losses for years and thereby proving non-viable. Even though they were in existence for several years as for the norms of Review Committee, and reached a level of loan business of Rs.3 crores in 3-4 years time, they failed to achieve the margins required for their survival. The reasons for their non-viability could also be judged from the above said four dimensions, particularly from the financial dimension.

Firstly, according to the area dimension, viability of RRBs depends on the development prospects of the area they serve. It is well known that the region of Rayalaseema was a backward and chronically drought affected area for decades. There is scope for agricultural development, but nature was completely against it. Lack of irrigation facilities, low and unpredictable rainfall, poor soils and successive droughts are affecting the deposit growth, lending policies and recoveries of RRBs in many ways. The restrained lending operations thus infected the overall income of banks, thereby leading to heavy net losses. Thus the backwardness of the area serving to the cause of non-viability of RRBs in Rayalaseema.

Secondly, as for the time dimension, all the three RRBs had completed 5 years of existence and one RRB viz., Rayalaseema was nearing its first decade of survival.

The RRBs has thus time enough to achieve viability. Yet, they are still non-viable. The institution of RRBs was set up not as a profit earning organisation but as a service-orienting one. As such the viability of these banks could not primarily be judged by their time of existence but by the benefit they achieved.

Thirdly, task dimension relates to the efforts made by the RRBs at. expanding and extending the area of rural credit. It is evident from the foregoing analysis of branch expansion programme, deposit mobilisation and advances given of the banks, that they have done their best to live up to their expectations. They served only the poor and downtrodden. They consciously cultivated saving habit among the rural poor. Thus the RRBs contributed much to the viability from the task dimension.

Lastly, financial dimension, which has of greater significance in determining viability, defines viability as a function of two variables viz. the expenditure ratio and the level of income.

Position Regarding Income

The details of incomes earned by the three RRBs and their respective growth rates are shown in Table-17 and Table-18.

The total income of each of the RRB was rising during the years from 1979 to 1985. For Rayalaseema the available data shows that the total income rose from again went up to Rs.249.98 lakhs in 1983 and to Rs.342.35 lakhs in 1985. Similarly, the total income of Sree Anantha increased from Rs.0.20 lakhs in 1979 to Rs.18.35 lakhs in 1981 which further has gone up to Rs.65.74 lakhs in 1983 and to Rs.155.83 lakhs 1n 1985. On the other hand, for Shri Venkateswara, it increased from Rs.3.72 lakhs in 1981 to Rs.31.62 lakhs in 1983 which again went up to Rs.138.38 lakhs in 1985.

The main source of income for the RRBs was interest earned on loans and advances and discounts. They constituted above 95 per cent of total income of all RRBs for almost all the years income from commission, exchange and brokerage was insignificant. As each bank's jurisdiction was confined to 1 or 2 districts, and were not permitted to undertake the banking services on a regular basis, there does not seem to have enough scope for the RRBs to increase their income from this category.

Table 17
Pattern of Income Earned by Selected RRBs

(Amount Rs. in lakhs)

Source of Income	*As at the End of Year*						
	1979	1980	1981	1982	1983	1984	1985
Interest and Discount							
Rayalaseema	51.56(82)	100.56(95)	166.33(97)	226.22(98)	243.85(98)	265.04(98)	336.01(98)
Sree Anantha	0.20(100)	3.10(75)	16.55(90)	40.92(94)	63.04(96)	95.06(96)	151.65(97)
Shri Venkateswara	-	-	2.12(57)	7.74(57)	25.31(80)	64.34(95)	131.98(95)
Commission, Exchange and BrokerAge							
Rayalaseema	0.21	0.27	0.46	0.67	0.85	1.02	1.83
Sree Anantha	-	-	0.13(1)	0.70(2)	0.25(-)	0.46(-)	0.46(-)
Shri Venkateswara	-	-	0.01(-)	0.10(-)	0.33(1)	0.31(-)	0.39(-)
Other Receipts							
Rayalaseema	11.13(18)	5.46(5)	4.34(3)	4.01(2)	5.28(2)	4.27(2)	4.51(1)
Sree Anantha	-	1.06(25)	1.67(9)	2.08(5)	2.45(4)	3.42(4)	3.72(3)
Shri Venkateswara	-	-	1.59(43)	4.69(42)	5.98(19)	3.21(5)	6.11(4)
Total							
Rayalaseema	62.90(100)	106.29(100)	171.13(100)	230.90(100)	249.98(100)	270.33(100)	342.35(100)
Sree Anantha	0.20(100)	4.16(100)	18.35(100)	43.70(100)	65.74(100)	98.94(100)	155.83(100)
Shri Venkateswara	-	-	13.54(100)	31.62(100)	13.62(100)	67.86(100)	138.38(100)

Note: Figures in parentheses are percentages to total,
Source: "Annual Reports"

Table 18

Distribution of Growth Rates of Income Earned in RRBs in Rayalaseema : Type-wise

Source of Income	Years	Linear Growth Rate			Compound Growth Rate		
		Raya-laseema	*Sree Anantha*	*Shri Venka-teswara*	*Raya-laseema*	*Sree Anantha*	*Shri Venka-teswara*
Interest on discount	Last 5 years	15.27**	44.12**	68.28**	10.52 ^{NS}	64.87*	171.83*
	All years	22.65**	46.15**	68.28**	28.40*	171.83**	171.83*
Commission, Exchange & Brokerage	Last 5 years	31.06*	-	-	34.99**	22.14 ^{NS}	122.55 ^{NS}
	All years	28.25*	-	-	37.91**	22.14 ^{NS}	122.55 ^{NS}
Other receipts	Last 5 years	-	18.74**	13.29 ^{NS}	-	22.14*	22.14 ^{NS}
	All years	-13.46 ^{NS}	21.43**	13.29 ^{NS}	-10.16 ^{NS}	25.68**	22.14 ^{NS}
Total	Last 5 years	15.06**	43.13**	63.30*	10.52 ^{NS}	64.87**	122.55*
	All years	26.52**	45.42**	63.30*	54.24**	162.29**	122.55*

Note:

1. * : Significant at 5 per cent level
   ** : Significant at 1 per cent level

NS : Not Significant

Other receipts including subsidy from sponsor banks constituted very high in the initial years. But, in the latest years, the income from this category was considerably reduced.

Table-18 provides the comparative growth rates for the incomes earned by the RRBs. Sree Anantha leads ahead of Rayalaseema and Shri Venkateswara in achieving highly significant linear and compound growth rates at 1 per cent level in its income. Between Rayalaseema and Shri Venkateswara, the former proved superior with higher growth, whereas Shri Venkateswara, on account of its young age, just manages to have significant level of growth rates at 5 per cent level. The source of income from commission, exchange and brokerage had grown significantly in Rayalaseema on account of its longer existence, while it grew insignificantly in the other two.

Position Regarding Expenditure

The details of different types of expenditures incurred by the RRBs and their respective growth rates are given in Table-19 and Table-20.

Table-19 depicts that the total expenses of the RRBs had been increasing during the period 1979-85. Accordingly, for Rayalaseema the total expenditure increased from Rs.64.07 lakhs in 1979 to Rs.161.29 lakhs in 1981, which further had gone up to Rs. 245.23 lakhs in 1983 and to Rs.376.56 lakhs in 1985. In the same way, for Sree Anantha, the total expenditure had mounted up from Rs. 0.18 lakhs in 1979 to Rs. 25.40 lakhs in 1981, which further rose up to Rs.79.25 lakhs in 1983 and to Rs. 173.36 lakhs in 1985. In contrast, for Shri Venkateswara, it increased from Rs. 3.58 lakhs in 1981 to Rs.40.47 lakhs in 1983 and to Rs.153.32 lakhs in 1985.

The main head of expenditure for RRBs was interest paid on deposits and borrowings. It accounted for almost 60 per cent of total expenditure for Rayalaseema on all years as for the available data. In the case of Sree Anantha and Shri Venkateswara, though the percentage of expenditure spent on this item remained at 13 per cent and 15 per cent in the initial years, it slowly rose up to almost 60 per cent for both the banks as the business expanded and the resources were mobilized

Table 19

Pattern of Expenditure Incurred by Selected RRBs

(*Amount Rs. in lakhs*)

Item of Expenditure	*As at the End of Year* 1979	1980	1981	1982	1983	1984	1985
Interest paid on Deposits and Borrowings etc.							
Rayalaseema	27.67(43)	56.09(59)	97.44(60)	139.50(62)	152.39(62)	162.97(59)	218.52(58)
Sree Anantha	-	0.60(13)	7.36(29)	23.39(45)	38.95(49)	58.63(54)	100.90(58)
Shri Venkateswara	-	-	0.54(15)	3.41(23)	14.34(35)	42.10(43)	95.15(62)
Salaries, Allowances, Provident Fund & Gratuity Contributions							
Rayalaseema	25.21(39)	26.66(28)	41.06(25)	56.46(25)	60.85(25)	71.73(26)	99.30(26)
Sree Anantha	0.05(28)	2.68(58)	12.00(47)	19.25(37)	27.50(35)	34.66(32)	49.72(29)
Shri Venkateswara	-	-	1.67(47)	6.76(46)	17.33(43)	24.40(31)	38.46(25)
Rents, Taxes, Insurances, Lighting etc.							
Rayalaseema	1.90(3)	1.55(2)	2.23(1)	2.85(1)	3.29(1)	3.55(1)	4.93(1)
Sree Anantha	0.03(17)	0.39(9)	1.98(8)	3.26(6)	5.33(7)	6.13(6)	10.27(6)
Shri Venkateswara	-	-	0.30(8)	0.74(5)	1.60(4)	2.17(3)	3.05(2)
Depreciation, Stationary, Printing, Advertisement, Postage, Telegrams, etc.							
Rayalaseema	3.51(6)	4.56(5)	6.90(4)	7.74(4)	7.48(3)	8.82(3)	11.33(3)
Sree Anantha	0.06(33)	0.06(13)	2.54(10)	3.32(6)	4.18(5)	3.81(3)	5.77(3)
Shri Venkateswara	-	-	0.70(20)	1.91(13)	3.79(9)	5.14(6)	6.19(4)
Other Expenses							
Rayalaseema	5.78(9)	6.62(7)	13.66(9)	17.86(8)	21.22(9)	30.23(11)	42.48(11)
Sree Anantha	0.04(22)	0.33(7)	1.52(6)	2.67(5)	3.29(4)	5.15(5)	6.70(4)
Shri Venkateswara	-	-	0.37(10)	1.92(13)	3.41(8)	5.35(7)	10.47(77)

Contd.

Item of Expenditure	As at the End of Year						
	1979	1980	1981	1982	1983	1984	1985
Total							
Rayalaseema	64.07(100)	95.47(100)	161.29(100)	224.43(100)	245.23(100)	277.30(100)	376.56(100)
Sree Anantha	0.18(100)	4.60(100)	25.40(100)	51.88(100)	79.25(100)	108.39(100)	173.36(100)
Shri Venkateswara	-	-	3.58(100)	14.74(100)	40.47(100)	79.16(100)	153.32(100)

Note: Figures in parentheses are percentages to total.
Source: "Annual Reports"

Table 20
Distribution of Growth Rates of Expenditure Incurred by RRBs in Rayalaseema : Item-Wise

Item of Expenditure	Years	Linear Growth Rate			Compound Growth Rate		
		Raya-laseema	Sree Anantha	Shri Venka-teswara	Raya-laseema	Sree Anantha	Shri Venka-teswara
Interest paid on Deposits and Borrowings, etc.	Last 5 years	17.19*	48.42**	72.97*	10.52 NS	82.21 NS	132.01*
	All years	24.60**	48.42**	72.97*	33.07*	149.50*	132.01*
Salaries, Allowance, Provident Fund & Gratuity Contribution	Last 5 years	19.88*	31.44**	51.34**	22.14**	34.99**	101.38*
	All years	21.77**	39.08**	51.34**	23.90**	153.09**	101.38*
Rents, Taxes, Insurance, Lighting, etc.	Last 5 years	17.78*	35.22*	38.17 NS	10.52 NS	34.99 NS	64.87 NS
	All years	17.22**	41.07**	38.17 NS	15.36·	135.64*	64.87 NS
Depreciation, Stationery, Advertisement, Postage, Telegrams, etc.	Last 5 years	10.65 NS	15.29 NS	39.48**	10.52 NS	10.52 NS	64.87*
	All years	15.89**	30.82**	39.48**	15.36*	83.52*	64.87*
Other Expenses	Last 5 years	27.90**	31.04*	53.44*	22.14 NS	34.99 NS	101.38 NS
	All years	29.74**	39.34**	53.44*	37.91**	111.70**	101.38 NS
Total	Last 5 years	18.80**	40.16**	62.31*	10.52 NS	49.18 NS	145.96**
	All years	27.32**	44.01**	62.31*	49.18**	171.83*	145.96**

Note:

1. * : Significant at 5 per cent level

** : Significant at 1 per cent level

NS : Not Significant

on an increasing scale. Next to this, the expenditure spent on category related to salaries, allowances, provident fund and gratuity contribution account for greater importance. The percentage share of this kind in the total expenditure was high during their initial years. But it was considerably reduced to 25-29 per cent in the latest years. The expenses relating to payment of rents, taxes, insurances, lighting, etc. was high for Sree Anantha in comparison to other two. The percentage share of this type was however reduced from 9 per cent to 6 per cent for the bank during 1979-85 period, while for Rayalaseema it went down from 3 per cent to 1 per cent for the same period and for Shri Venkateswara from 8 per cent to 2 per cent during 1981-85 period. Expenditure relating to depreciation, stationary, printing, advertisement, postage and telegrams also decreased from 6 per cent to 3 per cent for Rayalaseema, from 13 per cent to 3 per cent for Sree Anantha and from 20 per cent to 4 per cent for Shri Venkateswara. A considerable amount of expenditure was incurred on other items.

Thus it could be said from the above analysis that in the initial years of RRBs, the establishment costs were higher than the operating costs, but in latest years the operating costs have grown higher than the establishment costs.

Table-20 illustrates the growth rates for various items of expenditure incurred by the RRBs. Sree Anantha tops ahead of Rayalaseema and Shri Venkateswara in having highly singnificant linear growth in all items and Shri Venkateswara had highly significant compound growth in total expenses over the other two.

Position Regarding Profits/Losses

An analysis of income and expenditure of the RRBs thus reveals that both items were increasing significantly during the years. But the increase in expenditure was overweighing the increase in income, thus resulting in heavy losses. Table-21 gives the details.

Accordingly, both Shri Venkateswara and Sree Anantha were incurred losses on all their years of existence except in their starting years. As for the big bank Rayalaseema, the

Table 21
Profit/Loss Position of Selected RRBs

(Amount in lakhs of Rupees)

As at the End of Year	*Rayalaseema*	*Sree Anantha*	*Shri Venkateswara*
1977	-3.38	-	-
1978	-6.99	-	-
1979	-1.17	+0.02	-
1980	+10.82	-0.44	-
1981	+9.84	-7.05	+0.14
1982	+6.47	-8.17	-1.20
1983	+4.75	-13.51	-10.05
1984	-6.97	-9.44	-21.35
1985	-34.21	-17.52	-36.29

Source: "Annual Reports".

earning of profits and the incurring of losses were balanced half the years of its 9 years duration. Thus for the year ending 1985, the total losses were largest in Shri Venkateswara at Rs.36.29 lakhs in comparison to Rs.34.21 lakhs of Rayalaseema and Rs.17.52 lakhs of Sree Anantha. In order to verify whether the characteristic of getting losses was peculiar to RRBs in Rayalaseema alone or not, the data for the working results of 14 RRBs which were working in Andhra Pradesh during 1985 is provided in Table-22.

Except for Manjira Grammena Bank and the newly started Golkonda Grameena Bank and Sri Rama Grameena Bank, all the 11 RRBs in Andhra Pradesh were incurring heavy losses, their expenditure amount being higher than the income level. Even if we refer to Chapter IV, we get the information that, out of 188 RRBs which were in existence in 1985, only 34 were earning profits and the other 154 were incurring losses.

The reasons for this vulnerable position of RRBs and their consistent losses are as follows[9]:

- The income in advances, which was the major source to boost up the income of the RRBs selected, was not increasing upto the expectations. The expected income by way of interest on advances was often falling behind the target levels.

Table 22

Working Results of Regional Rural Banks in Andhra Pradesh (For the Year Ended December 1985)

(Amount in lakhs of Rupees)

Name of the Regional Rural Bank	*Date of Establishment*	*Income Amount*	*ExpenditureAmount*	*Profit/LossAmount*
Nagarjuna Grameena Bank	30.04.76	376.34	458.94	-82.60
Rayalaseema Grameena Bank	06.08.76	342.35	376.56	-34.21
Sri Visakha Grameena Bank	30.09.76	527.29	562.62	-35.33
Shee Anantha Grameena Bank	01.11.79	155.84	173.36	-17.52
Shri Venkateswara Grameena Bank	22.03.81	138.38	153.32	-14.94
Sri Saraswathi Grameena Bank	27.01.82	71.30	88.44	-17.14
Sangameshwara Grameena Bank	31.03.82	75.90	82.65	-6.75
Manjira Grameena Bank	31.03.82	109.69	109.52	+0.17
Pinakini Grameena Bank	11.06.82	84.29	105.68	-21.39
Kakatiya Grameena Bank	28.06.82	58.42	78.59	-20.17
Chaitanya Grameena Bank	25.03.83	35.49	50.41	-14.92
Sri Sathavahana Grameena Bank	28.03.83	31.82	43.91	-12.09
Golkonda Grameena Bank	15.02.85	5.37	4.22	+1.15
Sri Rama Grameena Bank	21.02.85	5.09	4.59	+0.50

Source:NABARD : "Statistics on Regional Rural Banks", 1985.

- The anticipated level of outstanding advances could not be maintained due to various factors like more recovery than expected, internal disturbances in the organisation, etc.
- The peak lending season for the region was May-September. During this period, the banks had to impose several restrictions on credit disbursements for want of adequate lendable resources. Thus they could not earn income by way of interest on loans as planned.
- There has been considerable increase in the cost of resources utilized for purveying credit. The margin left to the banks in lending the resources was very much reduced in view of increased dependence on refinance.
- The reduction of interest payment on the current account balances with the sponsor bank and other scheduled commercial banks from 9 per cent to 8 per cent, had its deterious impact on the RRBs.
- As there was recurring incidence of drought in the region from 1981 to 1985, the RRBs were forced to show much restraint in lending for crop loans as well as other activities connected to agriculture.
- There was not much increase in the short-term deposits, thus causing increase in the cost of funds used for lending.
- Lack of organized branch expansion and opening of new branches in the middle of years affected the substantial business of RRBs. For example, the Rayalaseema Grameena Bank earned profits during the years 1980, 1981, 1982 and 1983 in which it opened only 32 new branches with an average of 8 per years. Subdued branch expansion obviously reduced the establishment charges for the years, thus increased its income level higher than expenditure. While in the next 2 years, it opened as many as 39 branches and thus faced heavy losses.

- Since adequate number of staff had to be maintained to meet the needs of increased number of branches, the costs on establishment could not, but be incurred which had naturally reflected in working results. The hike in D.A. of staff members and rents and fresh appointments of sweepers/ messengers, etc., also contributed to losses.
- Non-accomplishment of per employee productivity/ business.
- Prevalence of undesirable intenal/industrial relations in the banks, and
- Due to non-adherence of the time schedules, the action plans failed in achieving their ultimate goal of reaching the break-even point.

In the light of the above findings, the following suggestions can be made to steer the RRBs on the path of profitability:

- RRBs can control losses only by increasing their income and reducing their expenditure. As the income of RRBs was mainly the margin between the average borrowing and the average lending rates, they should try to enhance it by expanding their loan portfolio. Quarter-wise disbursement of credit as per action plans would help to get more interest on advances and careful planning of remittance to get more interest from sponsor banks.
- In the loaning operations, due emphasis should be given on quality of lendings, rather than their quantity. In other words, the creation of productive assets through economically viable and technically feasible projects should be the main criteria for RRBs loaning. As the funds made available by Banks came out of scarce national resources, they cannot be treated as ameliorative finance but must be utilised to generate incremental income for the target groups.[10] As such only production-oriented and development oriented schemes should be undertaken which would not only

create a self-security for the loans advanced but would also facilitate repayment of loans. For this purpose, the investment capabilities of each borrower, both before and after the advancement of loan, must be assessed so as to arrive at the incremental income generated by the loan.

- The loan operations of RRBs should be planned in a diversified manner so that they would get income in an intensified way. For instance, crop loans should be largely given as it earns greater interest. The RRBs may also adopt an integrated system of rural credit, linking credit with marketing and involving State participation. Distress selling of products was common amongst the small farmers of rural areas due to their meagre resources and lack of waiting capacities for a favourable market price. The RRBs can extend marketing credit to such needy persons by pursuading them to become a member of nearest cooperative society. State participation, on the other hand, involves not only its contribution to share capital but its sincere and honest efforts in identification of beneficiaries and planning worthwhile projects.
- RRBs should be allowed to grant loans to richer sections in selected Villages in certain proportions (20-25 per cent) and under-maximised limits for individuals. This would help in attracting more local resources and ensure support of the rural rich to the activities of Grameena Banks.
- The performance of RRBs in the field of rural industrialisation particularly the small scale/cottage/ village industries has been limited. And they provide least amount for consumption purposes. The denial of adequate credit for consumption purposes, which was very pressing for poor people, inevitably compels to turn to moneylenders. Therefore, the ease for extending consumption loans may be examined while finance should be increasingly made available to small

scale and cottage industries after making a thorough survey of the potentiality of the area and availability of raw materials. They should establish close link with Khadi and Village Industries Commission, District Industries Centres, different government authorities and panchayats. In addition, RRBs must introduce a system of group loaning, in which it can serve more than one borrower under a single loan. For example, a single farmer who cannot afford to buy a pump-set or tube-well, himself, can jointly buy with farmers of contiguous lands and thus can enhance his income.

- Prompt and effective recovery of loans is as much important as increasing deployment of credit as recycling of funds is adversely affected by mounting overdues. Generally, loans may not be recovered from 'the ryot in time due to reasons such as natural calamities, under-monsoons, etc. and often extraneous factors tend to influence willful defaulters with very adverse impact on the whole credit system. The increasing overdues of Banks would thus make difficult the reissue of loans to the needy. So, in order to have better recoveries, apart from the efforts of the Banks' staff, the concerned local Government and the block level extension agency which were connected with the advancement of loan must be associated and held responsible for the collection of bad debts.
- RRBs should try to expand their resource base and plan to invest their funds in such a way that they will get more revenue. The areas for such investment are as follows[11]:
  - The SLR of RRBs, which they supposed to maintain at 25 per cent, should be enhanced to 30 per cent so that they would earn 10-11 per cent of interest by investing in Call Money/Notice Deposits as against currently earning 8 per cent interest from Current Account of commercial banks.

- Cash in hand Should be kept minimum. It shouid not exceed 2 per cent to 2.5 per cent of the deposits.
- Try to maintain 4 to 5 per cent of deposits with RBI towards CRR. Huge amounts need net be kept with RBI as there is no interest on the excess amount.
- Loans and advances should be planned in such a way that average interest earning on advances should be 1 per cent per annum.
- Filing of CGC claims where ever necessary without delay.
- Borrowing from sponsor bank should be kept minimum while refinance from NABARD and IDBI should be stepped up as it is more economical.
- Minimum funds should be kept in Current Account with sponsor bank and bare minimum amount in transit from Head Office to Branch and vice versa.
- Appropriate subsidies without delay, should be provided by the Government of India and State Government to RRBs for the successful implementation of welfare programmes such as IRDP and Twenty-Point Economic Programme. As these programmes are not remunerative business, the RRBs are making huge losses.
- RBI can examine[12] the facility of giving interest on excess balance over CRR (3 per cent) to RRBs and the sponsor bank can consider to pay interest at 9 per cent on Current Account and charge interest on lending at 9¼ per cent, and
- Efforts should be made to attract institutional deposits and government deposits. Ambitious plans are also to be drawn to mobilise public deposits.

• The Banks have to make efforts to identify areas where expenditure can be reduced and to play the loopholes in revenue income. Some of the ways to curtail recurring expenses are as follows :

- Avoiding advance payment to suppliers of furniture, stationery, printers, etc.
- Acquiring quality in durable assets like furniture, etc., so that there will not be frequent purchases.
- Ensuring proper utilisation of stationery.
- Proper planning of remittances.
- Proper planning of advance tour programmes.
- Observing strict economy in electricity, postal, telephone and telegram expenditure.

It is quite possible to achieve strict austerity in expenses of above said things, if elements of honesty and high degree of integrity s inculcated amongst the staff.

Further, a thorough study of the real needs of RRBs and their branches in the matter of staff is needed to be conducted. If it is found that the Banks are overmanned, they should reduce their bulk. Only those persons who are specially trained and attuned to the rural culture should be sent to these Banks.

- A phased and systematic method of branch expansion should be followed, so that the management would get time to concentrate to develop the business of new branches. If adequate time is provided in opening between 10 branches to another 10 branches, the losses made by new branches would be counter-balanced by old branches. For this, the RRBs should prepare clear-cut long-term perspective plans for 10 years in the area of branch expansion, deposit mobilisation, advances, etc. Performance budget should also be prepared to envisage the anticipated income and expenditure and the margin to be achieved. A case for setting up of mobile offices has also to be considered which would help in attracting deposits.
- It is advisable to the RRBs to encourage urban oriented branches to launch massive credit operations to the eligible borrowers in their areas to make up their losses and earn profits.

- There is a widespread criticism that mal-distribution of funds with misinterpretation of economic status, bogus transactions political influences, etc., are playing havoc with credit disbursal of RRBs in rural areas. Being illiterate, the rural poor are always forced to see the middlemen to understand the regulations and the lengthy procedures of the Banks. Sometimes" the Banks themselves delayed granting loans to get approval from Head Office. All this will add to increase the burden of ryot in the form of cost of credit and thus affects his repaying capacity. For this, careful identification and selection of projects relating to the poor are necessary. Simplification of procedures in lending would also help in reducing the cost of credit to be borne by the customer.
- Setting up of proper controls and vigilance squads will reduce the mal-distribution of funds. In his article entitled "Internal Controls and Checks and Branch Control in RRBs" the General Manager of Union Bank of India, R. Nigam has suggested[13] that the Head Office of a RRB should exercise strict control and continuous vigilance in the following areas :
  - Cash management;
  - Overheads,
  - Sanction, disbursement, supervision and recoveries of advances;
  - Balancing of books;
  - Inter-office reconciliation of transactions,
  - Scrutiny and adjustment of entries in sundry deposit and suspense accounts and
  - Security arrangements.

These areas of control are also applicable to three RRB in Rayalaseema. The instruments of control to implement them are as follows :

- Issue of circulars;

- Submission of periodical returns by branches
- Visits/Inspection of branches and internal audit.

Firstly, by issue of circulars the Head Office of a RRB can control its various branches by prescribing the procedures to be followed in accounting and reporting and the formalities to be observed while accepting deposits, granting loans, etc. It can also communicate the instructions received from Government and RBI in regard to various aspects of their functioning. Thus issue of circulars would ensure uniformity in conduct of business and accounting procedures.

Secondly, the Head Office can control its branches by asking to submit information about all important aspects of their transactions within prescribed time and in organised manner. It may call for periodical information and data required for compiling and submitting various returns prescribed by RBI and Government. Such returns received from branches should be scrutinized and compiled and irregularities/violations of instructions and undesirable tendencies should be recorded and placed before concerned higher officials for further verification and rectification.

Thirdly, periodical visits by senior officials of Head Office including chairmen to the branches would ac a most important check over their functioning. Setting up of an internal audit and inspection system would control the frauds and misappropriations to a large extent. At present RRBs are subject to external audit in addition to inspection by RBI. Educating the beneficiaries and offering them proper counseling is another important measure for preventing frauds in rural areas. Matters pertaining to disciplinary proceedings should be expeditiously attended to and wherever warranted, deterrent punishment imposed.

- The implementation of all above suggestions heavily depends on the efficient functioning of staff in position of RRBs who should work with a sense of devotion, commitment and belonging to organisation. Further, maintaining and improving good relations between the banks and customers, with public and with

Government is very important for a service institution like RRBs. Experience in the field of rural areas, however, shows that quite a large number of staff recruited by RRBs are urban-oriented and does not feel at home while working in interiors. Eminent and skilful employees are not willing to serve in villages owing to improper infrastructural facilities like education to their children, hospitals and recreation facilities. Employee turnover is another ticklish problem in RRBs. The employees of banks treat their position as stop gap in order to join in some other organisation like commercial banks or Government service.

Rural orientation of the staff can be possible only when the recruitment policy and procedures of RRBs are streamlined to ensure and infuse psychologically attuned personnel having a rural bias. Technically qualified persons with experience in rural credit and rural problems, preferably graduates in agricultural sciences, engineering, rural economics, etc., should be posted as managers of these banks. Important advantages of appointment of such persons are, they would work in rural areas at lower wages and they can understand farm problems easily. Further, appropriate training must be given to staff members of all cadres at various centres. Conferences and meetings should be held at frequent intervals and workshops in certain important places. It. has to be planned to associate management experts / consultants in drawing up training programmes and also to take up subjects relating to behavioural sciences. Certain other activities may also be planned for the self-development of staff members. In order to avoid the employee turnover", the employees of RRBs must be motivated by announcing suitable incentives like rural work allowance, promotions and providing loans. Almost all urban infrastructure facilities should be extended to the rural areas. These facilities not only help the bank personnel for their comfortable stay but also strengthen the working conditions of banks. A system of transfer of staff from one RRB to another RRB within the same State may be introduced to eliminate chances of vested interests amongst the staff. There must be uniform rules, regulations and emoluments applicable to all RRBs and steps should be taken to mitigate elements of employee dissatisfaction.

- The present working hours of RRBs i.e., from 11.00 A.M. to 5.00 P.M. need to be changed or partially modified. Most of the rural families during these hours were not free and busy in their farm operations. As such the working hours may be changed between 7.30 A.M. to 10.30 A.M. in the morning and 6.00 P.M. to 9.00 P.M. in the evening. This would help not only in improving loan advancement but also attracting more deposits.
- All literature of RRBs regarding deposit and saving schemes; interest rates, loaning policies, etc., should be published in simple language with illustrations and provided freely to customers. Local language should be liberally used in Bank passbooks, loan application forms, deposit forms, cheques, etc. This would make bank transactions easy.
- The geographical area and specific target group of people should be clearly demarcated for each RRB to avoid overlapping of the operations with cooperative and commercial banks.
- It is high time that RRBs should prescribe some definite norms of viability and adopt performance-oriented techniques of rural banking. It is to be seen that a branch of RRB must be able to have a loan business of Rs.20 lakhs each year and recover the same when due before it can become viable.[14] However, in future, before expansion of branches, care should be taken to estimate the potentiality of their areas in

contributing to estimate the potentiality of their areas in contributing to viability.

- In order to get a deep picture on the viability of RRBs, exercise on profit-loss should be done assessing the following aspects at micro level :
  - Interest on Deposits
  - Interest on Bank Borrowings
  - Establishment Charges
  - Interest on Advances
  - Interest on Bank Balances

Conclusion

The three RRBs in Rayalaseema viz., Rayalaseema Grameena Bank, Sree Anantha Grameena Bank and Shri Venkateswara Grameena Bank have successfully covered all the rural and un-banked centres of the region with their wide-spread branch network. They have been adequately staffed who were appreciably trained. All the three banks have achieved significant progress in the field of deposit mobilisation and advances. The Credit-Deposit ratio was higher for all the banks indicating increasing local deployment of funds. Their recovery performance was good.

However, a comparative appraisal of the Banks performance in the field of deposits mobilised and advances given during their first 5 years puts the working of Shri Venkateswara and Sree Anantha on a superior level over the Rayalaseema. In the last 5 years, the performance of Rayalaseema bank is better" partly because of longer years of working. Besides the performance in absolute terms, the assessed comparative linear and compound growth rates put the execution of Shri Venkateswara on the top in all the parameters over the other two banks on both first 5 and last 5 years. The reason for this better performance of Shri Venkateswara was the result of efficient and devoted work done by its personnel including the two chairmen that the bank had so far. Secondly, Chittoor district where the Bank was situated had slightly better economic conditions in comparison to severely drought-ridden

Anantapur, Cuddapah and Kurnool districts where the other two are operating. While the setback in Sree Anantha's performance in recent years can be forgiven for its drought-hit conditions, the inferior performance of Rayalaseema, even after about a decade's existence deserves immediate attention. So, there is a need for these two banks, particularly Rayalaseema, to rectify their methods and improve their performance, comparatively.

In the field of viability, the three banks have been suffering from same disease i.e., getting recurring losses. In fact, this is a common disease to RRBs all over India. Higher expenditures were overtaking lower incomes for recurring years. And the banks were failing to build up a loan business which gives them the viable status. So, it is the urgent duty of these banks to search for the means and methods to augment their revenues and reduce expenses. They should also try to build a level of loan business which ensures viable status. A service institution like RRBs should live for a long time to bring up the down-trodden and to achieve a better standard of living for the poor. So, they should not be allowed to perish for want of viability. Here, a lot depends on the staff performance which should be honest and devoted. Meanwhile, the losses of RRBs need to be subsidised.

Footnotes

1. Report of the Committee (Working Group) on Rural Banks, *Op.cit.*, p.124.
2. In Statistics, the tendency of growth, whether it is positive or negative is called secular trend or secular movement. The secular movement is that irreversible movement which continues in general in the same direction for a considerable period of time.
3. The Rayalaseema had also organized 8 Farmers' Service Societies, 4 each in Cuddapah and Kurnool. This is a favourable point for Rayalaseema in comparison to Sree Anantha and Shri Venkateswara who were so far unable to organize any such society.
4. Report of the Review Committee on Rural Banks, *Op.cit.*, p.114.
5. The working hours of a typical branch are from 10 a.m. to 5 p.m. on week-days and 10 a.m. to 2 p.m. on Saturdays. The working hours have not been adjusted to any time which might be more suitable to the prospective and actual clients.
6. Reserve Bank of India Bulletin : "Viability of Regional Rural Banks: A Study", *Op.cit.*

7. Government of India : "Report of the Committee (Working Group) on Rural Banks", *Op.cit.*, Paras 3.7 to 3.10.
8. *Ibid.*, para 3.11.
9. "Annual Reports of Rayalaseema, Sree Anantha and Srhi Venkateswara Grameena Banks".
10. Sahaya, R & Muninath Sharma : "Functioning of Regional Rural Banks of India", Agricultural Banker, Vol.9, No.2, April-June 1986, pp.14-18.
11. Phadtare, P.R : "Profitability of Regional Rural Banks-Suggestions", Agricultural Banker, Vol.9, No.3, July-September 1986, pp.18-22.
12. *Ibid.*
13. Nigam, R: "Internal Controls and Checks and Branch Control in RRBs", Agricultural Banker, Vol.10, No.3, July-September 1987, pp.1-7.
14. Sahaya, R & Muninath Sharma : *Op.cit.*

7

Conclusions

Rural development is an imperative of under developed countries to tackle the core problems of wide-spread poverty, increasing economic inequality, rapidly rising unemployment and under-employment and the retrogression of economic life in villages, with increasing burden of rural indebtedness, which is more or less a catastrophe.

Development of rural banking is a pre-requisite for accelerating rural development in the developing economies. The evil finance of the exploiting autonomous professional money lenders necessitates the development of institutional finance to discipline them and stimulate rural growth. The financial repression hypothesis postulates the integration of the dual money markets in the under-developed countries, so that financial development becomes a vehicle of economic development. Therefore, banking has a crucial role to play in economic development in mobilising savings, allocation of resources to more productive sectors and stimulation of entrepreneurship by bank financing. The German mixed banking system and the Japanese banking system are outstanding models that have fostered economic development.

In the developing economies innovative banking has a wider role to play in fulfilling the objectives of State policy. The innovative banking techniques have to facilitate the emergence of mass banking to advance rural development and economic development by giving an opportunity to people to participate in development efforts. Banks cannot be mere repositories of financial resources in planned economic development. They have to play a catalytic role in advancing rural development, spreading industrialization and the development of social services required for reaching the goal of welfare State. Banking thus becomes a tool of economic and social development.

India has emerged as a leading innovator in banking techniques in the course of the implementation of five year plans. Along with various plan projects, different types of development financing agencies were instituted. In particular, the banking industry has traversed long way specially during the last two decades as one of the accredited agencies of rural development. The multi-agency system comprising the three pillars of cooperative societies, commercial banks and regional rural banks for financing the agricultural and rural development sector has emerged as a significant institutional set up.

Although the cooperative movement had its beginning during the first decade of the century, its working over the decades revealed its failure to cope up with the credit requirements of rural population to the desired levels. The benefits of cooperative finance accrued mainly to big farmers and the distribution was uneven - not much of it has gone to the backward States. Shortage of funds and accumulation of overdues have been important drawbacks of the Co-operative finance as a consequence of which cooperatives were unable to shoulder further responsibilities for accelerating rural development.

Commercial banks entered the field of rural finance after the nationalization of the major commercial banks in 1969. With missionary zeal they pursued their efforts in rural lending. Massive branch expansion was launched with a thrust in rural areas and the share of rural offices in total offices have more than doubled. Credit to priority sectors has also gone up, significantly to agriculture. The introduction of schemes - Lead Bank, Village Adoption, Differential Interest Rates and financing of cooperatives have enhanced their role in rural finance. In spite of remarkable success achieved in rural finance, the commercial banks functioning involved high cost structure and absence of rural bias and knowledge in the implementation of the programmes. Moreover, the commercial banks used rural branches as deposit centres and neglected the rural interiors and their population. With their urban-oriented staff, they failed to develop an effective linkage with the rural communities.

At the end of 1975, the cooperative agencies and commercial banks have met about 40 per cent of the total farm credit and there was a wide institutional credit gap of 60 per cent which has a tendency of increasing on account of increasing demand of the rural economy. Moreover, the existing financial structure neglected the credit needs of the weaker sections in the rural society. Therefore the Government of India decided to establish "rural banks" as a new institution devised, to combine the features of co-operative and commercial banks without their weaknesses with the technical objective of lowering the cost of rural banking through the operation of such banks with local staff in rural environment which the rural poor would find most homely. Accordingly, the first five Regional Rural Banks were set up in the country on October 2, 1975.

The Regional Rural Banks were established in India with the sole objective of developing the rural economy by providing cheaper credit to weaker sections of rural people such as the small farmers, marginal farmers, agricultural labourers, rural artisans and other small entrepreneurs. The Regional Rural Banks Act of 1976 provided for the incorporation, regulation and working of the RRBs. With the favourable recommendations of the High Power "Dantwala Committee on Regional Rural Banks", RRBs have emerged as an integral part of the rural credit structure.

The regional rural banking witnessed phenomenal progress during the first decade of its operation in the country in several respects.

- The number of Regional Rural Banks increased from 5 in 1975 to 188 in 1985 over a decade covering 333 districts out of 433 districts in India accounting for a coverage of 77 per cent of the districts and accordingly the population. But there is a greater concentration of Regional Rural Banks and their branches in the States of the Western and Northern regions of the country. The State Bank of India along with its subsidiaries sponsored a good proportion of the RRBS accounting for 22.3 per cent.

- The branch expansion of the Regional Rural Banks has been steady and continuous despite their uneven geographical dispersion and slow progress during some periods. But, tremendous progress has been achieved in opening a large number of branches covering hitherto un-banked centres and remote villages in spite of numerous odds and difficulties experienced in opening branches in un-economic areas like rural, semi-urban, un banked and backward areas. Regional Rural Banks appeared in remote villages and unbanked areas of India. Thus, of the total 10,393 RRB offices that were established from October 1975 to February 1985, as many as 9,591 or 92.3 per cent have been located in unbanked areas.
- The RRBS achieved significant success in promoting banking habit among farmers, small entrepreneurs and artisans of the rural areas hitherto isolated from banking environment. The first decade of regional rural banking witnessed significant uptrend in the mobilization of rural savings as well as deposits in terms of aggregate increase for all the RRBS and also per RRB and per branch of RRB. For instance, deposit per RRB increased from Rs.3.33 lakhs to Rs.235.09 lakhs during 1975-80 period and from Rs.235.09 lakhs to Rs.683.95 lakhs during 1980-85 period, whereas deposit per branch rose Rs.1.18 lakhs to Rs.6.09 lakhs to Rs.10.20 lakhs during 1980-85 period.
- The business turnover of RRBS during the first decade increased substantially, it has grown faster and stronger day by day. Concurrently, the number of

beneficiaries served also increased. A comparison of the year-wise achievements in deposits and outstanding loans reveals that the growth in advances has been much faster than that in deposits. If the RRBS have to serve the weaker sections in a much better manner, they have to develop a sound deposit base and the management has to recognize this imperative need.

- The bulk of assistance of RRBS, both direct and indirect, had gone to small farmers, marginal farmers, agricultural labourers rural artisans and other small entrepreneurs in conformity with the objectives of their establishment. They promoted employment opportunities and income expansion in the remote areas facilitating the development of agriculture and rural welfare. Development of neglected areas and villages has a salubrious impact on the reduction of disparities. Thus, the RRBS have successfully maintained their image as a "small man's bank" by carrying the banking services to the door-steps of rural masses. They promoted mass banking in rural areas.
- The RRBS have rendered good service in achieving the target levels of integrated rural development. Accordingly, they facilitated the promotion of sound agricultural credit system, namely efficient and equitable deployment of credit.
- The higher levels of credit-deposit ratio of RRBS as compared to commercial banks is a favourable index of more resource development within the local areas as compared to mobilisation over wider areas of the commercial banks.
- The RRBS generated good employment opportunities for banking personnel.

It is quite clear from the above achievements in terms of the growth of regional rural banking, wide and remote areas covered and business turnover built up, RRBs have come to stay as a significant institution of rural development in India.

But the financial viability of the institution is not well-established. A large proportion of RRBs are incurring losses regularly, adversely influencing the profitability of rural banking. Instead of generating additional financial resources in the economy, a majority of RRBs were in red and any sick institution cannot survive for long with heavy losses, much less serve any social purpose. RRBS have not emerged as self-reliant financial institutions. Like the public enterprises in India, they are still a liability for the financial system of the country. Another criticism of RRBs is that the cost of supplying credit is quite high. It is also contended in certain quarters that credit deployment objectives of RRBS are such that they can never become viable. Moreover, the RRBS are also suffering from mounting over dues and they are not free from politicisation. There is also a demand for merger of RRBs with their respective sponsor banks.

The story of the working of the Regional Rural Banks in Rayalaseema which is a famine spot of India and the most drought-ridden region of Andhra Pradesh is more or less similar to the picture of the RRBs in India as reviewed earlier. The fifth chapter dealt with the growth of regional rural banking in Rayalaseema, while the sixth chapter reviewed the working of the RRBs on comparative levels.

The three RRBS of Rayalaseema region are the Rayalaseema Grameena Bank, Sree Anantha Grameena Bank and Shri Venkateswara Grameena Bank. They have successfully covered all the rural and unbanked centres of the region with their widespread network. They have been adequately staffed with trained personnel. Their recovery performance was deemed as quite satisfactory. The credit-deposit ratio was higher for all the banks reflecting increasing local deployment of funds. All the three banks have achieved significant progress in the field of deposit mobilisation and advances. Thus, in the sphere of deposit mobilisation, among the 188 RRBs functioning at the end of 1985, the Rayalaseema got 13th place Sree Anantha got 50th place and Shri Venkateswara got 56th place. In contrast, in the field of credit deployment they acquired 7th place, 26th place and 39th place respectively.

However, a comparative appraisal of the performance of the three banks in the field of deposits mobilised and advances given during their first five years puts the working of Shri Venkateswara Grameena Bank and Sree Anantha Grameena Bank on a superior level over the Rayalaseema Grameena Bank. During the last five years, the performance of Rayalaseema Bank is better partly because of longer years of working. Besides the performance in absolute terms, the assessed comparative linear and compound growth rates put the execution of Shri Venkateswara Grameena Bank on the top in all the parameters over the other two during the first five and the last five years and also all the years. The prime reason for the better performance of Shri Venkateswara Grameena Bank is to be traced to the efficient and devoted work done by its personnel including the two chairmen that the bank had so far. Secondly, Chittoor district where the bank was situated had slightly better economic conditions in comparison to more severely drought ridden Anantapur, Cuddapah and Kurnool districts where the other two banks are operating. While the setback in Sree Anantha's performance in recent years can be forgiven for its drought-hit conditions, the inferior performance of Rayalaseema, even after about a decade's existence deserves immediate attention. So there is a need for these two banks particularly, Rayalaseema, to rectify their methods and improve their performance comparatively.

In the filed of financial viability, the three banks have been suffering from the same economic disease of incurring, recurring losses like the RRBs allover India. Higher expenditures were overtaking lower incomes for recurring years. The banks were not successful in building up loan business which gives them the viable status. So it is the urgent duty of these banks to search for the means and methods to augment their resources and reduce expenses. They should try to build a level of loan business which secures viable status. A service institution like RRBs should live for a long time to bring up the downtrodden and to achieve a better standard of living for the poor. So they should not be allowed to perish for want of viability. Here, a lot depends on the staff performance which should be honest and devoted. Meanwhile, the losses of RRBS need to be subsidized.

The review of the working of the RRBs in India in general and Rayalaseema in particular over a decade reveals the naked fact that they have not emerged s self-reliant financial institutions. It is also argued that credit deployment objectives of RRBs is such that they can never become viable. The successful operation of certain RRBs shows that they have become viable only after longer existence and when their branch expansion was phased. It is also postulated that a branch of a RRB can attain viability when it builds up an optimum level of about 20 lakhs per year. The number of profit-earning RRBs which were 26 in 1976" increased to 56 in 1980, but decreased to 34 in 1985. Thus, it may not be possible for most of the banks to build up the optimum level of business in spite of best efforts in view of the backward economic environment surrounding the RRBs. Further the ongoing agitation by the employees of the hanks for revision of salaries and emoluments is intensifying the viability problems of RRBs.

If there is favourable upward revision of the salaries and emoluments, the profitability of the RRBs may decline further and involve in greater losses. Under such circumstances, RRBs become a linkage in the working of the financial system of the country.

Nevertheless, there is a need for an in depth study of the causes of the problems of RRBs and also the analysis of measures to improve their viability with a clear cut policy on wages, structure, ownership, control and more viable-resource development policy, so that RRBs can become a potent instrument of rural development in the long-run after the administration of remedial measures. The author has reviewed comprehensively the different steps that are to be taken to improve the performance of RRBs in the sixth chapter which need not be repeated here. The package of measures are to be viewed from the point of feasibility also, in so far, what is ideal is not practiced and what is practiced is not ideal under our social back-ground. But constant constructive effort may yield favourable results in course of time.

Bibliography

Books

Adbdi, Ali Issa, *"Commercial Banks and Economic Development: The Experience of Eastern Africa"*, Praeger Publishers, New York, 1977.

Agrawal, A.N., *"Indian Agriculture (Problems, Progress & Prospects)"*, Vikas Publishing House Pvt. Ltd., U.P., 1980.

Bedi, R.D., Theory, *"History and Practice of Cooperation"*, International Publishing House, Meerat (U.P.), 1983.

Belshaw, Horace, *"Agricultural Credit in Economically Underdeveloped Countries"*, FAO, Rome, 1965.

Bhattacharya, Sibnath, *"Role of Indian Rural Institutions in Economic Growth - A Critical Survey"*, Metropolitan Book Co. Pvt. Ltd. New Delhi, 1985.

Brahmananda, P.R., Nanjundappah, D. and Narayana. B.K. (ed). *"Indian Economic Development and Policy, Essays in Honour of Prof. De 'Souza"*, Vikas Publishing House Pvt. Ltd., New Delhi, 1979.

Chandrasekharam and Kathuria, G., *"Elements of Agricultural Finance"*, Progressive Corporation Pvt. Ltd., Bombay, 1973.

Chatterjee Rabindranath, *"Indian Economics"*, H. Chatterjee and Co. Ltd., Calcutta. 1951.

Choubey, S.N., *"Institutional Finance for Agricultural Development"*, Shubhada Saraswat, Pune, 1977.

Choubey, 'S.N., *"Principles and Practices of Cooperative Banking in India"*, Asia Publishing House, Bombay, 1968.

Darling, M.L., *"The Punjab Peasant in Prosperity and Debt"*, Oxford University Press, Bombay, 1932.

Desai, S.S.M., *"Rural Banking in India"*, Himalaya Publishing House, Bombay, 1979.

Desai, Vasant, *"A Study of Rural Economics : A Systems Approach"*, Himalaya Publishing House, Bombay, 1983.

Ghatak, Subrata, *"Rural Money Markets in India"*, Macmillan Company of India Ltd., Delhi, 1976.

Ghosh, D.N., *"Banking Policy in India - An Evaluation"*, Allied Publishers Pvt. Ltd., Bombay, 1979.

Ghosh, Alak, *"Indian Economy - Its Nature and Problems"*, The World Press Pvt. Ltd., Calcutta, 1980.

Goldsmith, R.W., *"Financial Structure and Development"*, Yale University Press, New Haven, 1969.

Goyal, O.P., *"Financial Institutions and Economic Growth in India"*, Life and Light Publishers, New Delhi, 1977.

Hanif, M.W., *"25-Point Socio-Economic Programme"*, S. Chand and Co. Ltd., Delhi, 1977.

Hough, M. Eleanor, *"The Cooperative Movement in India"*, Oxford University Press, Bombay, 1966.

Jain, L.R., *"Banking Law and Practice"*, Kalyani Publishers, New Delhi, 1978.

Lewis, Arthur, *"The Theory of Economic Growth"*, Harper and Row, New York, 1970.

Mohanan, N., *"Development Finance for small Farmers"*, Rainbow Publications, Coimbatore, 1983.

Memoria, C.B., *"Rural Credit and Agricultural Cooperation in India"*, Kitab Mahal, Delhi, 1983.

Nakkiran, S *"Agricultural Financing and Rural Banking in India - An Evaluation"*, Rainbow Publications, Coimbatore, 1980.

Sadhu, A.N. and Amarjit Singh, *"Fundamentals of Agricultural Economics"*, Himalaya Publishing House, Bombay, 1983.

Sanknran, S., *"Agricultural Economy of India"*, Progressive Corporation Pvt. Ltd., Bombay, 1980.

Sharma, B.P., *"The Role of Commercial Banks in India's Developing Economy"*, S. Chand & Co. Pvt. Ltd., New Delhi, 1974.

Shaw, Edward, *"Financial Deepening in Economic Development"*, Oxford University Press, London, 1973.

Shekar, K.C., *"Banking Theory and Practice, (Law & Foreign Exchange)"*, Vikas Publishing House Pvt. Ltd., Delhi, 1980.

Shetty, K. Shankar, *"Welfare State and Bank Nationalisation in India"*, Macmillan, Delhi, 1982.

Sinha, S.L.N. (Ed.), *"Reform of the Indian Banking System"*, Orient Longman Ltd., Madras, 1973.

Smith, Adam, *"Wealth of Nations"*, Modern Library, New York, 1937.

Subramanian, U.K., *"The Indian Financial System"*, Abhinav Publications, New Delhi, 1979.

Sundaram, I.S., *"Anti-poverty Rural Development in India"*, O.K. Publications, New Delhi, 1984.

Suneja, H.R., *"Bank Credit (Policy and Procedures)"*, Shakti Publications, New Delhi.

Tannan, M.L., *"Banking Law and Practice in India"*, Thaker and Co. Ltd., Bombay, 1979.

Toshi, M.R. and Sharma, D.P. (Ed.), *"Rural Banking in India"*, Oxford and ISH Publishing Co., New Delhi, 1983.

Wadhva, D. Charan, *"Rural Banks for Rural Development, An Analysis of the Working of Regional Rural Banks in India With Two Case Studies"*, The Macmillan Company of India Ltd., Delhi, 1980.

Wolf, W. Henry, *"Cooperation in India"*, W. Thaker and Co., London, 1927.

Government of India Publications, New Delhi

Fifth Five Year Plan 1974-79, Planning Commission, 1976. India - A Reference Annual, 1985.

Report of the Banking Commission (Saraiya Commission), 1972.

Report of the Committee on Cooperation in India, 1915. Report of the Committee (Working Group) on Rural Banks, 1975.

Report of the National Commission on Agriculture 1976 (Nathuram Mirdha Commission), Part I - Review and Progress, Part II - Policy and Strategy.

Report of the Royal 'Commission on Agriculture in India, 1925.

Report of the Rural Banking Enquiry Committee 1950 (Takurdas Committee), 1953.

Seventh Five year plan 1985-90, Planning Commission, 1986.

Sixth Five Year Plan 1980-85, Planning Commission, 1981.

Sixty second Report of the Estimates Committee.

Extension of Credit Facilities to Weaker Sections of Society and for Development of Backward Areas", Sixth Lok Sabha, 1977-78.

The Gazette of India, Extraordinary, Part II, Section I, The Regional Rural Banks Act, 9th February 1976.

The Indian Central Banking Enquiry Committee Majority Report (Mitra Committee), 1931.

Government of Andhra Pradesh Publications, Hyderabad

Andhra Pradesh Year Book, Various years.

Bureau of Economics and Statistics, Statistical Atlas, Various Years.

Perspective Plan for Rayalaseema Region, Andhra Pradesh, Vol. III, Methodology and Detailed Tables, 1972.

Planning and Development of Backward Regions, A Case Study of Rayalaseema, Vol.I, Resource Inventory, 1970.

Sixth Five Year Plan 1980-85, Andhra Pradesh, Vol.I, 1981.

Statistical Abstract of Andhra Pradesh, various years

Reserve Bank of India Publications, Bombay

All-India Rural Credit Survey (Gorwala Committee), Report of the Committee of Direction, Vol. II, The General Report, 1954.

All-India Debt and Investment Survey, 1971-72, Indebtedness of Rural Households and Availability of Institutional Finance, 1977.

Annual Report on Trend and Progress of Banking in India, Various years.

Functioning of Public Sector Banks - Report of the Committee (James Raj Committee), 1978.

Multi-agency Approach in Agricultural Finance, Report of the Working Group, 1978.

Regional Rural Banks: Report of the Review Committee, 1978

Report of the All-India Rural Credit Review Committee (Venkatappaiah Committee), 1969.

Report of the Committee on Integration of Cooperative credit Institutions, 1976.

Report of the Committee to Review Arrangements for Institutional Credit for Agricultural and Rural Development (CRAFICARD), (Sivaraman Committee), 1981.

Report of the Expert Group on the State Enactments Having a Bearing on Commercial Banks Lending to Agriculture (Talwar Committee). 1971.

Report on currency and finance, various years

Statistical Statements Relating to Banks in India, Various Years.

Statistical Statements Relating to Cooperative Movement in India, Various years.

Viability of Regional Rural Banks: A Study, Reserve Bank of India Bulletin, Vol.XXV, No.3, March 1981.

NABARD Publications, Bombay

Statistics on Regional Rural Banks, Various years.

The Annual Reports of National Bank for Agriculture and Rural Development.

Official Plan Reports and Records of Grameena Banks

Corporate Plan for 1981 to 1983, Sree Anantha Grameena Bank, Anantapur.

Corporate Plan 1983-85, Sree Anantha Grameena Bank, Anantapur.

District Credit Plan 1983-85 and Annual Action Plan 1983 for Chittoor District, Indian Bank, Chittoor.

Integrated Rural Development Programme - Cuddapah District (A.P.)- Annual Plan 1983-84, District Rural Development Agency, Cuddapah.

Lead Bank Scheme - Annual Action Plan 1985, Cuddapah District, Syndicate Bank, Cuddapah.

Lead Bank Scheme – Annual Action Plan 1986, Anantapur District, Syndicate Bank, Anantapur.

Performance Budget, Rayalaseema Grameena Bank, Cuddapah, Various years.

Performance Report 1980 and Performance Budget 1981, Rayalaseema Grameena Bank, Cuddappah.

Perspective Plan 1983-95 and Performance Plan 1983. Rayalaseema Grameena Bank, Cuddapah.

The Annual Reports of Rayalaseema Grameena Bank, Sree Anantha Grameena Bank, Shri Venkateswara Grameena Bank.

Other Publications

A Study of Regional Rural Banks, Agriculture Finance Corporation, Bombay, 1981.

Rural Development : Sector policy Paper. World Bank, 1975.

Techno-Economic Survey of Andhra Pradesh, National Council of Applied Economic Research, New Delhi, 1962.

List of Articles

"A Decade of Nationalised Banking in Andhra Pradesh: Data Andhra Pradesh, Vol.2, No.13, 1-15 July 1979.

Agitabh Krishna, Regional Rural Banks" Rural India, Vol.45, No.406, July 1982.

"Agricultural Conditions in Andhra Pradesh", Data Andhra Pradesh, Vol.3, No.5, 1-15 March, 1980.

"And Now Rural Banks". Editorial, Southern Economist. Vol.14. No.9, 1 September 1975.

Andhra Pradesh Impressive Growth, Commerce, Vol.149, No. 3820, 18 August 1984.

Appa Rao, B., "Regional Imbalances in Andhra Pradesh: Study of Trends Over Three Decades, Southern Economist, Vol.22, No.14, 1-15 November 1983.

Bagga, Autur Singh, "Role of Banking in National Economic Development, The Banker, Vol.XXIV, No.3, May 1977.

Balaji, K. Brijesh. "Rural Development: Some Constraints", Kurukshetra, Vol.XXX, No.23, 1 September 1982.

Bal, Bijor Kishore, "Role of Regional Rural Banks", Rural India, Vol.41, No.3, March 1978.

Balaji, N. and Lajapathi Rai, H., "Regional Rural Banks: An Evaluation", Indian Banking Today & Tomorrow, Vol.11, No.3, March 1986.

"Banking: Challenges on Rural Front", Bank of Baroda Weekly Review, Vol.23, No.24, 14 June 1985.

"Banking in Andhra Pradesh", Data Andhra Pradesh, Vol.1, No.12, 16-30 June 1978.

"Banking Trends in Andhra Pradesh", Data Andhra Pradesh, Vol. 3, No.9, 1-15 May 1980.

Batra, J.D., "Rural Banks for Rural Poor", Cooperator, Vol.509, No.10, May 1977.

Bhide, V.M., "Banking for Agricultural Development", The Banker, Vol.XXIV, No.I, March 1977.

Bottomley. A., Monopoly profit as a Determinant of Interest Rates in Underdeveloped Areas, Oxford Economic Papers, Vol.16, No.3, October 1964.

Chakravarthi, parimal, Our Rural Credit - Its Pros and Cons., The Economic Studies, Vol. 18, No.2, 1977-78.

"Changing Scenario of Rural Credit", Agricultural Banker, Vol.9, No.1, January-March 1986.

Chatterji, B.K., Exercise in Regional Rural Banking: Eastern Economist, Vol.71, No.3, 29 September 1978.

Chouhan, A.B. and Deobhankar, S.G., "Restructuring of Commercial Banks in India, Some Thoughts, Lok Udyog, Vol.XV, No.6, September 1981.

"Comparative Andhra Pradesh-2 (Regional Variations)", Data Andhra Pradesh, Vol.1, No.2, 15-31 January 1978.

Copp, H.James, "Rural Sociology and Rural Development", Rural Sociology, Vol.37, No.4, December 1972.

"Cuddapah, the Heart of Rayalaseema", Andhra Pradesh, Vol.XXII, No.10, August 1974.

Dantwala, M.L., "Regional Rural Banks, A clarification", Economic and Political weekly, Vol.XIII, No.42, 21 October, 1978.

Datar, M.K., "Banking and Rural Development", The Indian Economic Journal, Vol.26, No.2, October-December 1978.

"Development of Banking", Andhra Pradesh, Vol.XXII, No.6, April 1978.

Dhurjati Mukherjee, Banks and Rural Development", Khadi Gamodyog, Vol.XXIII, No.3, December, 1976.

Datta, Babatosh, "Regional Rural Banks", Economic and Political Weekly, Vol.XIII, No.36, 9 September, 1978.

Dongre, Yashvantha, "For Rural Growth", Yojana, Vol.29, No.24, 1-15 January 1986.

"Fifteen years of Bank Nationalisation", Bank of Baroda Weekly Review, Vol.22, No.29, 20 July 1984.

Ganguly, A.K., "Rural Banking: A Point of View", Margin, Vol.9, No10, January 1977.

Ghodke, Manju, "Poverty and Alleviation Programmes, The Economic Times, Vol.1, No.264, 26 June 1986.

Ghosh, B.K., "Some Reflections on Rural Banking and Agricultural Financing by Commercial Banks", Agricultural Banker, Vol.a, No.1, January-March, 1986.

Gupta, B.N., "The Changing Scene of Rural Development", Rural India, vol.41, No.3, March 1978.

Gurley, J., "Banking in the Early Stage of Industrialization", American Economic Review, vol.57, No.4, September, 1967.

Indra Yeshwanth, "Blossoms in the North-Eastern Region-Regional Rural Banks", Indian Cooperative Review, Vol.XXII, No.3, January 1985.

Inu Jain, "Rural Credit and Regional Rural Banks", Khadi Gramodyog, Vol.XXVIII, No.3, December, 1981.

"Issues Before Regional Rural Banks", Bank of Baroda Weekly Review, Vol.13, No.30, 25 July 1975.

Jha, Naresh, "Role of Banking in Rural Development, Southern Economist, Vol.20, No.24, 15 April, 1982.

Joseph, S.C., "A Strategy to Eradicate Poverty", Yojana, Vol.XXII, No.9, 16 October, 1977.

Joshi, Navin Chandra, "Rural Development Through Banks", Kurukshetra, Vol.XXX, No.7, 1 January, 1982.

Joshi, P.N. "Banking as a Lever for Rural Development", Pigmy Economic Review, Vol.229, No.6, January, 1984.

Kamleswara Rao, S. and Bhagavan Rao, C.H., "Organisational Superiority of RRBs over cooperatives", The Tamil Nadu Journal of Cooperation, Vol.75, No.7 & 8, January-February, 1985.

Kamat, G.S., "Are Regional Rural Banks Deviating from their Assigned Role?", Capital, Vol.CLXXIX-4479, 1 September, 1977.

Khan, F.H. "Regional Rural Banks in the Red – A Revamp on the Cards", Indian Cooperative Review, Vol.XXIII, No.1, July, 1985.

Krishnaji, P., "Rationale of Rural Banks", Easters Economist, Vol.104, No.6, 16 Jaunary 1976.

Malyadri, V., "Coordination Between Regional Rural Banks and Cooperatives", The Banker, Vol.XXIII, No.10, December, 1977.

Mehta, R.R.S., "What is Rural Banking", Indian Banking Today & Tomorrow, Vol.10, NO.3, March 1985.

Melhotra, H.C. and Kulshretha, D.K., "Development of Banking in Rural Areas", Economic Affairs, vol.22, No.11, November 1977.

Mishra, S.N., and Sharma, Kushal, "Evolution of Rural Development of Strategies". Kurukshetra, 16 June 1983.

Modak, Pradip Kumar, "Role of Rural Banking in India's Agrarian Society", Khadi Gramodyog, Vol.XXX, No.5, February, 1985.

Munidoraswami Naidu, K., Arundati Suvarchala, G. and Naga Obulu, D., "Regional Rural Banks in Andhra Pradesh : A Review", Khadi Gramodyog, vol.XXXI, No.12, September, 1984.

Nambiar, P.C.D. "Bank Finance for Agriculture", State Bank of India Monthly Review, Vol.XVII, No.9, September 1978.

Narasimham, M., "Rural Credit and Regional Rural Banks", Southern Economist, Vol.14, No.11, October 1975.

Narasimham, M., "Some Reflections on the Indian Banking Scene", Pigmy Economic Review, Vol.29, No.7, February 1984.

Natarajan, B., "Agricultural Credit and Banking", The Banker, Vol.XXV, No.1, March 1978.

Natarajan, B., "Banking and Rural Debt Redemption", The Banker, Vol.XXIII, No.9, November 1976.

Narayana, D.L., "Rayalaseema : A Famine Spot of South India, "The Asian Economic Review, Vol.IV, NO.3, May, 1962.

Naresh Kumar, "Rural banking as main plank of rural poor", Khadi Gramodyog, Vol.XXVIII, No.11, August 1982.

"Need for Integrating Rural Credit Institutions", Capital, Vol.10, No.3, July-September 1987.

Panda, Prabhakar, "Rural Development : Role of Banks", Rural India, Vol.44, No., August 1981.

Pande, P.N., "Reaching Benefits of Rural Development to all". Kurukshetra, Vol.XXX, No.9, 1 February 1981.

Patel, A.R., "Improving Viability of Regional Rural Banks", Southern Economist, Vol.16, No.7, 1 August 1977.

Patrick, Hugh, "Financial Development and Economic Growth in under developed Countries", Economic Development and Cultural Change, Vol.14, No.2, January 1966.

Phadtare, P.R., Profitability of RRBs - Suggestions", Agricultural Banker, Vol.9, No.3, July - September 1986.

Prabhu, S.N., "Role of Rural Banks in Helping Small Farmers", Southern Economist, Vol.44, No.8, August 1981.

Ramakrishnan, K.R., "Problems & Prospects of Regional Rural Banks", The Banker, Vol.35, No.1, March 1988.

Ramana Murthy, D.V., "Regional Rural Banks - An Assessment of Performance", Southern Economist, Vol.16, No.7, 1st August, 1977.

Rao, V.K.R.V., "Has Rural Poverty Increased in India?", Eastern Economist, Vol.72, No.12, 23rd March, 1979.

"Regional Rural Bank's Role in Rural Development", Bank of Baroda Weekly Review, Vol.20, No.8, 19 February, 1982.

"Report on Regional Rural Banks", Indian Finance, Vol.CII, No.5, July 1978.

Roy, T.S., "Banking as a Tool for Development", State Bank of India Monthly Review, Vol.XVIII, No.10, October, 1978.

"Rural Banks", Editorial, Statesman, Vol.4, No.2, 27th July, 1978.

"Rural Banks Have Come to Stay", Southern Economist, Vol.17, No.15, 1st August 1978.

Sahaya, R. and Muninath Sharma, "Functioning of Regional Rural Banks in India", Agricultural Banker, Vol.9, No.2, April-June 1986.

Saxena, D.N., "Rural Banking and Profitability", The Banker, Vol.XXXIII, No.2, April, 1976.

Sharma, K.S., "The Role of Financial Intermediation in Mobilisation and Allocation of Resources for Rural Development". The Indian Economic Journal, Vol.26, No.2, October-December 1978.

Singh, R.K.P., "Business Planning in Regional Rural Banks", Khadi Gramodyog, Vol.XXXIII, No.4, January, 1987.

Sivasankar, P.R., Dilip Kumar, I. and Gnana Prasuna, B., "An Anatomical Study of Regional Rural Banks in India", Southern Economist, Vol.25, No.6, 15th July, 1986.

Singh, T.N., "Institutional Credit for Rural Development", Agricultural Banker, Vol.VI, No.1, January-March 1983.

Srivastava, S.C. and Subramanian, B., "RRB Operation : An Evaluation", Eastern Economist, Vol.78, No.9, 5 March 1982.

Subrmanya, K.N., "Rural Indebtedness and the Role of Rural Banks", Southern Economist, Vol.15, No.22, 15 March 1977.

Sunil Kumar, "Regional Rural Banks and Agricultural credit - an evaluation", Economic Affairs, Vol.27, Nos.7-9, Qr.3, 1982.

Swaminathan, M.S., "Changing Rural Scene", Southern Economist, Vol.19, No.24, 15 April, 1981.

"The Dantwala Recommendations", Indian Finance, Vol.CII, No.9, August 1978.

"The Regional Rural Banks", Indian Finance, Vol.XCIX, No.8, February 1977.

"The Regional Rural Banks Ordinance, 1975", Indian Cooperative Review, Vol.XXVI, No.9, August 1975.

Thingalaya, N.K. "Banks and Rural Development : Some Crucial Issues", Pigmy Economic Review, Vol.7, No.3, October 1981.

Thingalaya, N.K., "Rural Credit: Structure and Flows", Indian Journal of Agricultural Economics, Vol.XXXIV, No.1, January-March 1979.

"Twenty Two Years of Economic Development of Andhra Pradesh, Facts and Figures", Andhra Pradesh, Vol.XXIII, No.2, December 1978.

Varshaneya, J.S., "Bank Nationalisation and After", Yojana, Vol.30, No.13, 16-31 July 1986.

Vyas, M.Mahendra, "Financing Agriculture - Multi - Agency Approach", The Banker, Vol.XXVI, No.9, November 1979.

List of Journals and Bulletins

Agricultural Banker, Quarterly, New Delhi.

Bank of Baroda Weekly Review, Bombay

Bank of India Bulletin, Monthly, Bombay

Data Andhra Pradesh, Fortnightly, Hyderabad.

Economic Affairs, Monthly, Calcutta.

Eastern Economist, Weekly, New Delhi.

Economic and Political Weekly, Bombay.

Economic Studies, Monthly, Calcutta.

Economic and Statistical Bulletin (Andhra Pradesh) Quarterly, Hyderabad.

Indian Cooperative Review, Quarterly, New Delhi.

Indian Banking Today & Tomorrow, Monthly, New Delhi.

Journal of Indian Institute of Bankers, Quarterly, Bombay.

Khadi Gramodyog, Monthly, Bombay.

Kurukshetra, Fortnightly, New Delhi.

Pigmy Economic Review, Monthly, Manipal.

Reserve Bank of India Bulletin, Monthly, Bombay.

Rural India, Monthly, Bombay.

State Bank of India Monthly Review, Bombay.

Southern Economist, Fortnightly, Bangalore.

The Journal of Banking Studies, Quarterly, New Delhi.

United Commercial Bank Review, Quarterly, New Delhi.

Yojana, Fortnightly, New Delhi.